INSIDE PADRAIG HARRINGTO

OBSESSED

INSIDE PADRAIG HARRINGTON'S HEAD

OBSESSED

Paul Keane

Irish Sports Publishing

Published by Irish Sports Publishing (ISP)
Unit 11, Tandy's Lane
Lucan, Co Dublin
Ireland
www.irishsportspublishing.com

First published 2012

A CIP record for this book is available from the British Library

ISBN 978-0-9573954-1-1

Printed in Ireland with Print Procedure Ltd
Typesetting: Paul McElheron
Cover Design: Jessica Maile
Photographs – Front Cover: Getty Images
Back Cover: Inpho Sports Agency

To
Lorna and James

Contents

ABOUT THE AUTHOR

Paul Keane is a freelance sports reporter with the *Irish Daily Mail*, *Metro-Herald* and *Irish Sunday Mirror* newspapers. This is his second book following the successful 'Gods Vs Mortals, Irish Clubs in Europe: A Front Row Seat at 10 of the Greatest Games', in 2010.

He graduated with a BA in Journalism from Dublin City University in 2002.

A lifelong member of Black Bush Golf Club in County Meath, he plays to a five handicap and lives nearby with his wife, Lorna, and son, James.

He can be contacted on Twitter handle: keanepaul11

Acknowledgments

It is 24 years since I first heard the name Padraig Harrington. He streaked to victory in the 1988 Leinster Boys' championship at Royal Tara Golf Club, a few miles down the road from my native Dunshaughlin. I was eight years old that summer, receiving lessons from Royal Tara club pro, Adam Whiston, and remember the buzz of excitement created around the club by Harrington's 11-stroke victory. He was just 17 but shot 67 in one of his four rounds on a demanding parkland layout. Gerard Sproule played in that event as did Gary Murphy, both of whom were interviewed for this book and describe how a star was born and subsequently rose high in the sky.

They are among Harrington's closest friends, allies and colleagues who gave freely of their time for interviews and to whom I owe a debt of gratitude.

Also interviewed were; Paul McGinley, Jean Van de Velde, Conor O'Shea, Bob Torrance, Des Smyth, Stuart Cage, John Philp, David Higgins, Howard Bennett, Michelle McGreevy, Micheal O Muircheartaigh, Dessie Farrell, Paul Caffrey, Jody Fanagan, Michael Kavanagh, Stephen Dundas, Niall Fitzgerald, Dr Liam Hennessy, Pat Ruddy, Clive Brown, John O'Leary, Chris Whittle and Colin Byrne.

The 1988 Leinster Boys' win was Harrington's first significant golfing success and is wonderfully recalled in Royal Tara Golf Club's centenary book of 2006. It is one of many books that I borrowed from, a little and a lot, to help piece together the story so far of an incredible career. Those books are:

'Bagman 2, Back Inside the Ropes with Golf's Leading Looper', by Colin Byrne (Red Rock Press). 'Stories, Observations, Suggestions 50 Years as a PGA Professional', by Howard Bennett. 'Ben Hogan, An American Life', by James Dodson (Doubleday). 'Don't Choke, a Champion's Guide to Winning Under Pressure', by Gary Player (Skyhorse Publishing). 'Fifty Years in a Bunker, The Creation of a World Top 100 Golf Links at the European Club', by Pat Ruddy (Ruddy Golf Library). 'Golf is a Game of Confidence', by Dr Bob Rotella with Bob Cullen (Pocket Books). 'Your 15th Club, The Inner Secret to Great Golf', by Dr Bob Rotella (Pocket Books). 'Golf is Not a Game of Perfect', by Dr Bob Rotella with Bob Cullen (Pocket Books). 'The Golfer's Mind, Play to Play Great', by Dr Bob Rotella with Bob Cullen (Pocket Books). 'Padraig Harrington's Journey to the Open', by various authors (Bantam Press). 'Room at the Top, Golf the Torrance Way', by Bob Torrance with Norman Mair (Pan Books). 'The Life of O'Reilly, The Amusing Adventures of a Professional Irish Caddie', by John O'Reilly and Ivan Morris (Clocktower Press). 'Into the Bear Pit', by Mark James with Martin Hardy (Virgin Books). 'Power Golf', by Ben Hogan (Gallery Books). 'Sam, The Autobiography of Sam Torrance' (BBC Books). 'Touching Greatness', by Dermot Gilleece (Transworld Ireland). 'The Big Miss', by Hank Haney (Crown Archetype).

I relied heavily on the archives of Ireland's national and regional newspapers and hope I have given due acknowledgement to individual papers and journalists where necessary. Many of Padraig's quotes are sourced from official press conference transcripts and, therefore, are not specifically credited. Those from golf magazines and TV interviews, I have acknowledged throughout.

To my wife Lorna, simply, thank you. To James, always keep your left arm straight. To Mam and Dad, thanks for always lending an ear.

Thanks to Gareth Makim at *Metro-Herald* and Joe Callaghan at the *Irish Daily Mail*. Likewise, to Pat Nolan, Micheal Clifford, Michael Scully, Brendan O'Brien, Kevin Garvey and Gavin Cummiskey for their encouraging words and help with contacts. Thanks finally to Liam, Kevin, Jenna and the team at ISP.

Prologue

A speeding white Titleist golf ball punctures the summer haze, nosedives into a sliver of semi-rough and bounds deep into the jungle at Royal St George's Golf Club. A thicket of spectators to the left of the long 14th hole speak in hushed, excited tones. They have been very fortunate indeed. For once, the blue roping that stretches along each hole into apparent infinity, separating golf fans from the action at the 2011 British Open, has been rendered useless. Soon, the thicket is a forest of twitching bodies, stooping and leaning in over a belligerent looking group of ragwort weeds that have sucked the ball down into their embrace. The crowd shuffles back a couple of steps through the shin-deep grass, form a more orderly semi-circle and wait patiently for the ball's owner to arrive.

Padraig Harrington and his caddie, Ronan Flood, crest the hill and bear left from a duo of players towards the area. Anticipation rises in the group as the triple major champion strides closer. Already, those piercing brown eyes that are as much Harrington's trademark as the sloping sailor's gait, are quantifying the extent of the error. The command centre between his ears is working at full speed now, and, as he lifts the rope up, slides his powerful frame underneath and marches over to the spot where his errant drive has crash-landed, he is a picture of studious concentration. There is no anger in those eyes. Acceptance of every shot, no matter how bad, is at the kernel of his sports psychologist Dr Bob Rotella's teachings.

Close up, Harrington is a formidable presence. A couple of months shy of his 40th birthday, he is lean and toned, a chiselled testament to the strength and conditioning work he has regimentally applied himself to under fitness advisor Dr Liam Hennessy. He feels fitter and stronger than ever. It is no surprise to hear former US President Bill Clinton remark after a practise round in Harrington's company that, even at 39, 'he looks like he could play professional football'. There are no compliments now though. As he comes to a halt and looks down at the end result of his wayward drive, profiling the scene like a criminologist, his tanned brow is furrowed and creased. The curious looking grey, flat cap he is wearing for a cancer charity, which covers his shock of dark hair, appears to invite a playful comment. But his mood is sombre and his body language unreceptive. He is in his office. "Wedge," he says calmly to Flood who pulls out a 54-degree Wilson Staff FG Tour club with Rifle Flighted shaft, and hands it over. Suddenly, Harrington is up on the balls of his feet again, pacing off towards a section of heavy rough behind the crowd that hasn't yet been trampled down. His eyes, trained on the ground, dart from one spot to another like a beggar searching for coins on a street before they eventually come to a halt. The crowd enjoys a silent moment of communal realisation as he launches into a series of practise swings on an identical group of weeds.

Harrington is in the mire but he is in complete control of his emotions. The focus etched on his face is almost hypnotic. Does he even know the crowd is there? He could be standing in front of the 18th green at Carnoustie in 2007 all over again, in the zone, spinning a 48-yard wedge shot in tight against the pin to rescue the greatest up and down of his career. Thrusting his wedge back and forth with surgical, slashing motions, he scatters undergrowth through the air in Sandwich. The resistance of the thick grass and weeds against the force of the clubface is the essential data that is being channelled through his wrists and processed by his brain.

He walks back towards his ball, looks out to the fairway and picks a spot in the distance he wishes to hit to. There is no guarantee he'll shift the ball even 10 yards. The words he has written about this hole in a brief guide to the course must play on his mind. "Expect to see many birdies as well as double bogeys," he predicted of the 547-yard hole that is flanked by out-of-bounds all the way up the right, "or worse." There is another conference with his caddie before he finally engages his pre-shot routine, the last act before striking the ball. Over on the fairway his partners wait, the American, Matt Kuchar, and new British Amateur champion, Bryden

Macpherson. Standing rigid, staring forward intently, Harrington begins to paint a mental picture of the perfect stroke he wishes to exact when an official shouts across to him, "Time, Padraig." He must take his shot or risk being put 'on the clock' for slow play.

He has been scolded by his peers over the years for pedantic play. The claim that he traversed the course like an accountant, the profession he holds a degree in, gained some currency, and it's a reputation he hasn't entirely shaken off. "If you're playing a two ball with Padraig Harrington," says Colin Byrne, a hugely experienced European Tour caddie, "and I've done this with a lot of players that wouldn't have played with him before, I've mentally prepared them before we go out, because you're going to be on the clock probably within about five holes. So you get your head around this. It's not a criticism, it's just the way he is. He's a detailed, detailed person. There isn't a molecule that is left unexamined before he pulls the trigger on a shot."

The interruption by the official barely breaks his concentration. It is obvious that he has learned how to handle such situations and he moves into position beside the ball, planting both feet down solidly. As he swings the club back on a slightly higher plane than normal, ensuring a descending blow upon the deeply embedded ball, there is a powerful coil of his black t-shirted torso against his lower body which remains rooted to the ground like oak. The enormous store of energy generated by a move perfected under the watchful eye of long-time swing coach Bob Torrance is released in a split second as the club face comes crashing down upon the ball. It is said of Torrance, the gnarled octogenarian whom Harrington has regularly described as a 'genius' teacher, that he once sat silent in his driving range on the west coast of Scotland while a young player with talent to burn crunched balls out into the yonder for half an hour. "Aren't you going to look up from your newspaper?" the player eventually asked, frustrated and miffed at how the whole tutor process was going to work. "I've got ears, don't I?" growled Torrance, a response that has gone down in coaching folklore.

The sound of Harrington's wedge making crisp contact with his ball and advancing it, miraculously, some 70 yards to safety is equally unmistakable to the trained ear. The tension that had brimmed in the crowd comes pouring out now in roars of approval. As he follows his ball back to the fairway those left in his wake savour a moment in time, a little piece of magic from a master of the majors.

That afternoon, on the first day of the 2011 British Open championship, the hordes of spectators filling the three grandstands around the 18th green gave rapturous applause as the threesome of Harrington, Kuchar and Macpherson approached. It was a gesture of appreciation towards Harrington in particular, who responded in statesman like fashion by striding clear from the group, removing his cap and beaming broadly. Three years earlier, he walked that same walk up the 18th hole at Royal Birkdale on the Sunday evening knowing he was about to be named the Champion Golfer for the second consecutive year.

In many ways he was one of them, one of the crowd. Never seemingly destined for greatness like a Tiger, a Rory or a Darren, he was an ordinary player that achieved great things, thanks to his unrivalled and often obsessive streak of determination, fuelled somewhat by an odd fear that he might wake up one morning and find his swing had mysteriously deserted him. He had surrounded himself with experts and worked harder than anyone could have possibly imagined to realise his dreams and, for a remarkable spell in his mid-30s, dominated the game with three major championship wins in just 13 months. He was a modern hero of the British Open with back-to-back victories at Carnoustie in 2007 and Royal Birkdale in 2008.

The strange thing was, as Harrington soaked up the adulation and the applause around the 18th green at Royal St George's, he was three over par, the same tally as a struggling Kuchar and two worse than the group's form player, Macpherson. It was in keeping with the new status quo of indifferent scoring that had dogged his career for the best part of three years. After his heroics at the 14th, he'd proceeded to double bogey the next, a long par 4. The following day he shot 71 and missed the cut for the second successive year. That weekend, the show simply moved on without him.

The reception he had received at the 18th hole, and the one replicated all around the course on Thursday afternoon, was in recognition of past deeds more than present performance. The genius moments had grown fleeting.

Five months later, Bob Torrance sits by a radiator in the kitchen-cum-storage area of his modest golf school in Largs, north Ayrshire. It is a remote coastal outpost, about 25 miles north of a famous stretch of links land that includes Royal Troon and Prestwick Golf Clubs and 40 miles west of Glasgow, an unlikely place for one of the world's most renowned golf coaches to work out of. But it is his home. A few hundred metres down the road from the driving range, where he can be found most weekdays in daylight hours, is the house he shares with his wife, June. It is hardly a 5-iron away from Largs Bay. Hit another couple of decent drives up the A78, turn a corner or two and you'll find yourself at the entrance to Routenburn Golf Club, the charming old James Braid track where he first 'pured' a hickory shafted cleek as a 16-year-old and fell instantly in love with the game. It is where, in 1963, he took on the role of greenkeeper/professional and, later, taught his famous son, Sam, the fundamentals of the game. As he settles in his chair, it is close to freezing outside on a cloudless Friday morning in December. He is insulated by a warm, green coat and tweed cap and begins to discuss the break-up of his coaching relationship with Harrington. The split was confirmed at the Irish Open in July, two weeks after the British Open setback. Disappointment is still there in his voice. "I was with Padraig for nearly 15 years," he says. "I like Padraig an awful lot, he's just like a son to me. I personally think, I'm 80 now, and I think in the back of his mind he's saying, 'Well, Bob's not going to be here forever so I need to do it myself'. I think that's what he's doing."

He refers to a disagreement they had about a part of Harrington's swing that the player wasn't happy with and wished to change, specifically the positioning of his right elbow. "But you see his right elbow never flew at all," contests Torrance, jumping straight into a stream of thought that has been bothering him for months. "I mean, there's a clip they show on the golf programme on TV, when they're introducing it, of him swinging and it's perfect."

Harrington's take on the break-up was that a beautiful friendship was sailing perilously close to the rocks. "Bob doesn't trust what I'm doing at the moment," he said in Killarney, and, partly to avoid reducing their relationship to rubble, the partnership was dissolved.

Gordon Sherry, the great Scottish hope of the early 1990s and the star attraction of the 1995 Walker Cup team that Harrington was part of, is out in one of the driving bays in Largs, giving lessons to a promising looking young female player. Elsewhere, a couple of twenty-somethings with swings as smooth as butter stand around chatting, randomly swishing clubs to pass the time until Torrance is available to inspect their progress. Their mentor is teaching golf for more than half a century and has seen it all from here. "That's where Lee Westwood used to land in the helicopter," he says, thrusting a finger out towards an area of the range.

His academy is part of the Inverclyde National Sports Training Centre. It is where another former pupil, European Tour professional, Marc Warren, turned up a fortnight after missing the cut in a tournament. By Torrance's reckoning, Warren should have been up in Largs the very next day, practising his backside off. "He's too interested in buying big flats and Aston Martins," he blasted at the time. Needless to say, that relationship was cut short. A strong work ethic is essential to Torrance and is what drew him and Harrington together. At first, it was Harrington's admiration of close friend Paul McGinley's ball-striking at the 1997 World Cup and the work his fellow Dubliner had done with Torrance that led him to the swing guru. But what bonded one of the most successful pupil/teacher relationships in the history of the game was their mutual love of hard graft. Off hand, Torrance can only recall two players whom he felt that to tweak their swings would be to offend the Gods of the game. One was his hero, Ben Hogan, the other Rory McIlroy. "McIlroy came to me and asked me about his swing," he recalls in a gravelled Scottish accent, roughened by an addiction to Silk Cut Purple cigarettes. "I said to him, 'You just leave your swing aloooone. Dunnay touch it for nobody'." But his overarching approach to teaching has always been that perfection is an acquired talent.

"You must always strive for it," he says. "You'll never get perfection but, as soon as you stop striving for it, you're finished. That's you finished."

In front of him upon a small table is an ashtray, the wrapping from a 20 pack of cigarettes, a mug, half-full with coffee, and an opened packet of biscuits. Sliding out a fresh cigarette from the box, he gestures this time in another direction. He is pointing out towards the far end of the range that sits at the top of a hill overlooking the pretty town of Largs, made famous by the last Viking invasion in the UK in the 13th century, and the island of Cumbrae. "Myself and Padraig were down there at the bottom of the range one night," he says. "It was dark, very dark and blowing a blizzard of snow and sleet right out of the hill there. Padraig says to me, 'You won't see many players practising in this, Bob'. I says, 'You'll nay see many coaches standing here either.' But if you're my pupil, and you're willing to do that, then I'm willing to stand there. No matter what the weather is like. If Padraig wanted to stand there for ten hours, and he did, then I would stand there for ten hours. You only get out of life what you put into it. The more you practise the better you get. If you're doing the right things with your practise you'll get better."

Harrington wasn't the first Irish golfer to seek his assistance. Torrance was working with John O'Leary when he won the Irish Open at Portmarnock in 1982. And he coached David Feherty, Darren Clarke, Philip Walton and McGinley. More recently, he has worked with Kilkenny man, Gary Murphy. But Harrington was different. That much was obvious from the start. "His father warned me about him, you know," says Torrance, smiling as he recalls their first official session in 1998. "His father was the nicest man I ever met, Paddy Harrington. He said, 'Padraig will shoot 68, 70 and then say to you, "The 70, I played great but the 68 I played rubbish".' Aye, his Dad warned me about that. He's got a funny mind, Padraig, but it's a good mind." Seven years after coaching Ian Woosnam to the US Masters title and number one spot in the world, Harrington was the blank canvas he craved. "I said to my wife one day, 'I would love to get hold of a young man with a bit of talent, that's willing to work'," he recalls. "I told her, 'That's what I would like to do with my life.' So Padraig came down here on the first day and we were up here until half past nine at night. We walked into the house for dinner and June says to me, 'You've got him!' I knew it myself because Padraig was willing to work. He was willing to listen. We were working as a team. Padraig was down here every week or every fortnight for years. He was a very good pupil to work with. He used to say to me, 'I don't care how I hit the ball here Bob. If you tell me it's right, I'm going to go back and work on it.'"

Practise has always been Harrington's poison. Over the years, those closest to him have pleaded with him to cut it back, to curb his instincts for self-flagellation. "A good worker is someone who does the right amount, the optimum – I do too much," he admitted, shortly before officially replacing his coach of 10 years, Howard Bennett, with Torrance. "I hit too many balls. I spend too much time on the range and tire myself out. Everybody around me tries to stop me practising." But he found a kindred spirit in his new coach, who shared the same thirst for perfection and would happily match his man, hour for hour, on the range. Torrance's eyes had been opened to the value of hard graft by the career of nine-time major winner, Ben Hogan, the taciturn Texan who, by the Scot's estimation, was by some way the greatest golfer of all time. "Outside of my family, it was the greatest thrill of my life to meet Hogan," he says, eyes lighting up as he tees up a story he loves to tell. "June said to me, 'You're always going on about Hogan, why don't you write him a letter?' I said, 'Well, I will,' and I wrote him a letter. I wrote in that letter, 'You're the only man I ever seen that I couldn't have suggested something that would make you better'. I think everything he did was perfection. I said, 'My life's ambition is to meet you'. He wrote back and said, 'I would like to meet you'. I was at a tournament when June phoned me. She said, 'A letter is here from Ben Hogan'. I went straight home and went out to his place the following week. I visited him at his house and at Shady Oaks. You couldn't meet a nicer guy. His reputation was all wrong. You see he got a bad time when he was young with the press. He wasn't good when he was young. His ball striking wasn't good. But he worked and he worked until he got it right."

There is much of Hogan in Harrington and it is a fitting coincidence that they both hail from towns called Dublin, either side of the Atlantic. As youngsters, both were told that they had brothers who were more talented.

In Hogan's case, it was suggested that, even as a 19-year-old pro he wasn't as good as older brother, Royal, while Harrington accepted that his elder sibling, Fintan, had the best swing of the five Harrington boys. The pair would surely have concurred too about the absolute necessity of a good short game. Hogan practised his wedge play so much that he labelled the club his 'equaliser'. As for Harrington, his precise short game was easily his most valuable asset throughout his career. "God gifts everybody in certain ways," says Paul McGinley, Harrington's golfing ally for the last 20 years. "Padraig was born not alone with a great short game, but the tenacity to go with it."

What really excited Torrance, though, as he got to work with Harrington was the prospect of overhauling his long game and turning a weak cutting motion into a powerful drawing action. "He would practise until he couldn't swing the club anymore," says Torrance, reminiscing on the same work ethic he had seen in Hogan who battled a vicious hook for years before making it in the game. "The work ethic, aye, Padraig's work ethic definitely reminded you of Hogan. I mean, I'd go to Padraig's house and we'd just hit balls all day, all day from his back door. He's a perfectionist, aye, he's got that in him."

In 1953, Torrance travelled the breadth of Scotland to the eastern coast of Angus to watch Hogan win the only British Open Championship he ever entered, at Carnoustie. More than 50 years later, in 2007, his shining light, Harrington, claimed the same title on the same stretch of punishing links. If ever there was a soldering experience in a relationship then this was it for teacher and pupil. "Oh aye, it was brilliant, brilliant it was," says Torrance. "And Padraig said that at the time. He said, 'I wanted to win here at Carnoustie. Because it's special for Bob. Because Hogan won here'."

Now, four and a half years on, Torrance is sitting in the room where it all started, talking about the end of the affair. He stresses that they are still friends, just not colleagues. "I mean I loved Padraig and he loved me," he says. "I think maybe I took the place of his father after he died (in 2005). I'm only guessing that. But I know I treated him like a son."

As is often the case with the most passionate and meaningful relationships, it was a steady breakdown rather than a specific burnout moment that preceded the split. "We always had a good argument," said Harrington by way of explanation for his decision in Killarney. "But at the moment there is less arguing, there is just frustration and tension rather than getting it out there." They'd disagreed about fundamental issues to do with Harrington's swing for a number of years with the Irishman, for his part, 100 per cent dedicated to continuing an overhaul that he'd begun before his major triumphs but which had stumped the golfing world. 'How could anyone win three majors and even contemplate taking a wrecking ball to their swing?' was the general reaction. Torrance expressed similar sentiments when news broke of their split and he was asked for his reaction. He'd been attending the Irish Open, not to work with Harrington, but with the experienced Scot, Stephen Gallacher, another pupil, who was also participating in the event.

"I think it's crazy," said an exasperated Torrance of Harrington's lust for change. "He is as high as he can go in golf, the only ones he never won were the Masters and the US Open. He won two (British) Opens in a row and then he won the PGA, and he has won tournaments all over the world." He warned of dire consequences should Harrington press on with his plans. "He has been going down one road that I think is wrong," he continued. "He is determined to go down that road, the wrong one. We've been together for 15 years and always discussed it. And then he just decides the right elbow is the problem. I said to him, 'You're going down the wrong road. If you go down too far, you won't come back'. He said he just wanted a few weeks break so the ball is in his court. It is not in my court. You cannot make changes at 40 in golf. You can make them when you are in your 20s but once you get to 40, it is too late. We discussed it and I said, 'I don't know what road you are taking, do you think it is the right road?' I said, 'Go ahead then'."

Throughout the process of interviewing subjects for this book, a recurring theme has been one of regret that the end of such a storied partnership was played out so unceremoniously in the media. Both men deserved better.

Asked if he saw the break-up coming, Torrance instinctively replies, 'no'. The word has barely tripped from his tongue when he retracts it and concedes that, yes, there were warning signs along the way, from as far out as 2009. He cites an incident during tests by biomechanics experts on Harrington's swing at the Titleist Performance Institute, in December 2009, an area of coaching Harrington has increasingly turned to, as perhaps the nadir of their relationship.

"Ach, I did see it coming in a way," he says. "He asked me to come out to the Tiger Woods tournament (Chevron World Challenge) and then we went down to San Diego to the Titleist academy. This guy was telling him things that I just didn't agree with. I told Padraig that. I said to the man, 'I've been with him 15 years and I've never seen him doing that, what you're telling me he does'. They strapped him up like an astronaut against a big white wall. They were videoing him and he was hitting wedges. They were hitting the roof! He said to Padraig after he put the film on, of the shadows against the white wall, 'That's perfect, and that's perfect and that's perfect'. I said, 'If those three swings were perfect, why's he hitting that bloody roof then? Why's he hitting the roof with a wedge? He shouldn't be doing that'. That upset Padraig because I was telling this guy that he was telling Padraig the wrong things. You see, in this game, they're trying to reinvent the wheel. It's impossible. You go back to Byron Nelson, Sam Snead, Ben Hogan, these guys were brilliant. There's nothing better than those three right now. This is the most difficult game man ever invented and the simpler you keep it the better."

From Harrington's perspective, three years of consistently poor results, save for a spike in form in the second-half of 2009, was about as much as he could take. Something had to give. The prevailing wind that had lifted him to three major titles in a 13-month spell between 2007 and 2008 had shifted. Now he found himself battling against the force of a hurricane, losing ground and slipping backwards. In early June, 2011, he woke one Monday morning to found himself outside the world's top 50. It was a position he hadn't been in since October 1999. By the start of 2012 he was perilously close to falling outside the top 100 and it frustrated him, deeply. Not because he viewed his game through the prism of the world rankings list but because he knew he was capable of so much more. He couldn't understand why the vast energy that he continued to invest in his mechanical swing was resulting in such flawed numbers, event after event. It's why he told everyone, week on week, that he was happy with his game and was just waiting for his luck to turn. And it's why everyone kept walking away from him so puzzled: 'If he's playing so good then why's he just missed another cut?'

Harrington acknowledges now that he didn't help himself. His openness with the media and willingness to answer any question as honestly as he could appeared to uncover a maverick player, hell bent on stripping back his swing at whatever cost.

Before his defence of the British Open title at Turnberry, in 2009, he likened himself to a Texan golfer, only this time it wasn't Hogan but Howard Hughes, the eccentric billionaire inventor who played to a low handicap in his day and, as a child, had a fondness for taking motor car engines apart and putting them back together again. "When Howard Hughes was a kid, he bought a Model-T Ford or a Mercedes and wanted to pull it apart – that's me with my golf game," offered Harrington, illuminating his thoughts in typical Technicolor. "I probably wouldn't be able to accept performing without knowing why. Even if I was performing, I don't think I would enjoy winning if I didn't know why I was winning. I think the ultimate satisfaction of winning is understanding how I got there. And I pay very little respect – unfortunately, while I admire it – I pay very little respect to somebody who wins without knowing why. I have very little time for wasted talent and very little time for the talent that has no understanding of what they do. If somebody was the best at something in the world and they couldn't tell me why they were there – and I mean the detail of why they were there – I wouldn't be interested."

Alongside his own comments, reports claimed that Padraig had been known to 'change hotels because the curtains in his room weren't heavy enough to chip (golf balls) into at night', that, 'his wedges must have razor-sharp grooves', and that 'his grips must always go on at a certain angle'. None of these is entirely outrageous but, added together, they all lent to a sense of Harrington being an eccentric in a race to the bottom of his golfing game.

Harrington got a feeling for the way he was being presented by the tone of journalists' questions at press conferences. He claims not to have read a newspaper article about himself since he was 18, when a comment bothered him so much that he lost his focus in a subsequent competition. But it didn't take a genius to figure out that he was being filleted in the sports pages for his decision to persist with the swing changes.

Those who knew him weren't shy about tossing in their tuppence-worth either. One morning at his palatial Rathmichael home in south Dublin he answered the door and found the postman waiting with a package. While he scrawled his signature down and signed for the parcel, the postman filled the silence by offering his opinion on the state of the golfer's play. "By Jaysus, Padraig, you're playing a lot of shite at the minute," he blurted, dead pan.

Around the same time, Harrington was among a group of adults and children when his son, Ciaran, sauntered off into some long grass. "Where's Ciaran gone?" asked a concerned member of the gathering. "He's like his Dad," came the pithy response from one woman, "he's in the rough."

If Harrington made one mistake, and he has acknowledged this, it is that he gave them all such fuel to throw on his fire. "I should have kept my mouth shut," he said in January of 2012. "I shouldn't have explained myself at any stage. That's the big mistake I made." He'd won at Carnoustie with a draw swing. But his blocked drive at the 72nd hole, which caused him so much distress and almost cost him the title, shocked him so much that, when he retained the Claret Jug 12 months later, he was playing to a controlled fade. Even in the most productive spell of his career he was pulling the hood back on his engine and stripping out the head gasket to make the whole thing run more efficiently. Nobody complained then. "My problem was that, after 2008, I was being asked more about it, because of my higher profile," he reflected. "And I gave honest answers. I would have given the same answers in 2006 but the questions weren't being asked."

By mid-2011, Harrington had had enough. Despite press coverage that continued to be damning, he'd felt comfortable with his swing for some time and believed the myriad of changes he'd made should have been yielding greater dividends. All too often he was leaving his best golf on the practice ground, something he'd been guilty of a decade earlier when he'd earned the reputation of a serial second-place finisher. Back then he would routinely pound balls into oblivion on the Saturday night of a big tournament and go out the following day lacking the sort of mental sharpness required to close out the event. He had been playing for the future, not the present and, while the circumstances were different in 2011, the end product was the same; a terrible sense of under-achievement.

The situation came to a head at that Irish Open in Killarney where, coming off the back of his British Open difficulties, he shot 73, 72 and missed the cut. They weren't bad scores, per se, but his play lacked that vital spark to pull him down below the 70 mark and into contention.

The media corp was just as frustrated to hear Harrington reiterate how he had played well again but failed to score. "I played great at the Irish Open," he stated, months later. "Just hit it great and missed the cut. I really hit the ball well in practise and I hit it well on the course. And the frustrating thing is then trying to explain yourself. You know, people ask the question, 'How come you're playing badly?' And you're saying, 'Well, actually, I'm not playing badly'." That evening, after admitting in the press room that 'something has to change', news broke of his split from Torrance. His head had been left spinning by back-to-back missed cuts at the two events he'd cherished most, the Irish Open and British Open. Yet it was no knee-jerk reaction to offload his beloved mentor. As much as they'd disagreed over fundamental issues to do with his swing, the decision was also related to the point in his life that Harrington had reached.

It is a safe bet that, as Torrance suggests, the break-up was coming for some time in the minds of both parties. In the brutal world of professional golf, everyone is expendable. Years earlier, Harrington had similarly offered no apologies for sacking his former caddies, John O'Reilly and Dave McNeilly. Both had provided something he needed at particular times, in the late 1990s, when he'd just came on Tour, and in the early 2000s. But they weren't going to take him to that next level he aspired to so they were jettisoned. Now, 69th in the world rankings, he would stand firm and cut Torrance loose too. And for the same reasons. Because what he needed in the past from Torrance, to coax and cajole him as he spent endless hours searching for his swing 'in the dirt', just like Hogan, wasn't what he needed now. What he believed he needed was to get back in tune with his mental game. To feel fresh again. The coach he once claimed he'd never split from, 'even if he was on a zimmer frame' had, to put it bluntly, become a distraction.

"I knew he was unhappy," said Torrance at the time. "One of the big things he said, and I believe this, was when I was standing behind him, he knew I was thinking, 'That's a terrible swing'. Padraig said he couldn't concentrate when I was standing there and he couldn't concentrate when I wasn't. So, where could you go from there? He still says he works on exactly what I told him, except this one thing (elbow). He knows it's wrong but he is determined to do it. There you go."

The one thing, it seems, they both agreed upon was that, when it came down it, the biggest problem of all was not a physical one but a mental one. "His game is in bad shape because of his mind, not because of his golf," added Torrance poignantly. "I've told him that and he agrees. That's why he wants away." Perhaps Torrance had finally come to appreciate the warning given by Padraig's father, Paddy, all those years earlier when they'd first met. A funny mind indeed, but a good one. "When I prepare for tournaments," said Harrington a couple of months later, shedding further light on his decision to leave Torrance, "I prepare by getting my head right. I do more of the mental stuff and just found myself maybe being undermined at that. I just felt we were arguing over different things."

The dust has settled now. Life goes on in Largs. Often in weather conditions that no 80-year-old should be subjecting himself to, Torrance can be found, imparting the basics of grip, posture and swing plane. and dropping nuggets of pure gold about a life lived through golf to anyone who turns up showing a little talent and a mind for application. "I think everyone who has been in contact with Bob would nearly love to see him go (die) in Largs, do you know what I mean?" says former European Tour player and one time Torrance pupil, Gary Murphy, whose association with Harrington stretches back to their amateur days. "I think they'll definitely spread his ashes across that plot of land up there because that's his shrine really."

Over in Dublin, Harrington is finally showing signs that he has found a spark to get it all going again. He has enlisted the help of Pete Cowen, a swing coach very much in vogue after guiding Darren Clarke, Louis Oosthuizen and Graeme McDowell to their major wins in recent seasons. Rotella is still classed as part of 'Team Harrington' though he has also been working with a new sports psychologist, Jim Murphy. His background is in baseball and he has helped Swedish golfer, Henrik Stenson, also a student of Cowen's. "I had read his book, Inner Excellence and agreed with everything in it," said Harrington, who has gorged himself on psychology tomes since he was a teenager. His most intriguing move, however, has been to seek out the services of Dave Alred, a renowned rugby kicking coach who broadened his client base to include athletes of all varieties. He focuses specifically on how to make them perform better under pressure.

Luke Donald began working with Alred in early 2010 and a year later was sitting at number one spot in the world. Golf being the ultimate game of mimicry, Harrington fancied that Alred might do for him what he had done for Donald, another mechanical player with an indefatigable work ethic. In fact, while Rome burned around him at the 2011 Irish Open, he wasn't found fiddling, driving for two and a half hours to set up a meeting with Alred. Like he said, he needed change and wasn't afraid to make it happen. "When I'm on the range, I try and hit every shot now like it means something," said Harrington in January, 2012, trumpeting Alred's importance before enjoying a thrilling return to form at the major championships.

In March, 2012, while the top 50 golfers in the world contested the WGC Cadillac championship at Doral, a troop of major winners – David Duval, Angel Cabrera, Shaun Micheel and Todd Hamilton – and a former WGC event winner – Stenson – went in search of their 'A' games at the Puerto Rico Open. For some, even finding their 'B' game would have made a nice change. Cabrera is just 23 months older than Harrington and achieved his major wins in the US Open and Masters tournaments at roughly the same time. But 'El Pato' travelled to Puerto Rico as the world's 165th-ranked player. The dispiriting tale of Duval, almost exactly the same age as Harrington and a Walker Cup opponent at Portmarnock in 1991, has been well documented. It took a further turn for the worse that week in Puerto Rico. The former world number one missed the cut and slipped another 10 places in the rankings to 599th. He has been as low as the 800s.

"I know the other side of it, I know what the awful golf is all about," said Duval when he came from nowhere to get a run going in the 2009 majors. So does Harrington. He was 96th in the world approaching the 2012 US Open. But, like Duval in '09, he found major form again out in San Francisco, backing up an excellent showing at the Masters.

At the age of 40, he contested all the way into Sunday evening at the first two majors in 2012, finishing tied for eighth and fourth at Augusta and The Olympic Club. His subsequent joint 39th and 18th place finishes at the British Open and US PGA championships made him one of the most consistent scorers in major competitions in 2012. He is competitive again in regular European and PGA Tour events, too, and gave a solid performance at his own Irish Open, finishing seventh and figuring strongly until Sunday afternoon. The turnaround, it appears, is virtually complete. Surrounded by new faces, he enters the autumn of his career believing that his game is better than ever.

PART I 2005 AND 2006

Chapter 1
2005

Christmas, 2005. Dublin, Ireland.

The phone buzzed and whirred in Padraig's pocket. Frustrated by the interruption, he laid his wedge down by the neatly trimmed practise green at the rear of his home and jabbed a finger at the answer button. It was his eldest brother, Tadhg.

"You're disturbing me," said Padraig.

"Why, what are you doing, pitching balls on a green?" asked Tadgh.

"Correct."

It was the response Tadhg had been hoping for. It had been a long five months since the passing of their father, Paddy. Everyone had taken it hard and Padraig was no exception. He'd missed the British Open at St Andrews for the funeral and though he returned the following week to play at the Deutsche Bank Players Championship of Europe, finding a brief release from his grief in competitive tournament play, his heart hadn't been in it.

"I don't think Padraig hit the ball out of his way for six months," admitted Tadhg.

Their father's death had been the low point of a tough few years. Paddy, a teetotaller known to occasionally smoke a pipe, was first diagnosed with oesophageal cancer in July, 2002. He underwent an operation that October and hoped he might have beaten the disease after a couple of clear years. But it returned with dark intent in early 2005, and this time the prognosis given by specialists wasn't good. He hadn't long left to live.

Padraig first learned that the cancer was back with vigour shortly after winning his maiden title on the US Tour, The Honda Classic, in March.

The following June, he backed up the victory on American soil with another incredible performance to take the Barclays Classic championship from Jim Furyk. They were summit achievements in his career but clouded somewhat by the brooding spectre of his father's terminal illness and his final days. From March until high summer in 2005, as Padraig's profile increased and, likewise, the public's awareness of his father's grave condition, so, too, did the level of media scrutiny on his situation. "So what's the latest update, Padraig? How's your dad doing? How are you coping?" The questions were incessant and draining. And yet there was clearly worse coming down the line. Padraig was asked again on the evening of the Barclays triumph at Westchester Country Club about Paddy's condition and spoke movingly, saying, "I'm sure he's glad he hung around this long." And, in what proved to be a poignant admission, he added that he was looking forward to getting home to celebrate with his old man and to seeing exactly how he was doing. "He was given a couple of weeks back in march, so he's doing ... look, it's good that he's managed one more win anyway."

Padraig flew back into Dublin to find a sick man, clinging on to life. Paddy died inside a fortnight and was laid to rest on July 14, the Thursday of the British Open that Padraig was meant to tee off in at 1.20pm alongside Chris di Marco and Nick Price. Golf didn't seem to matter much. "I said the week before my dad passed away that I would be happy enough to pack the clubs away and leave them for a year," he told reporters after shooting what was, in the circumstances, an impressive 70 on the opening day of the Deutsche Bank tournament in Germany. "I am not bad when I am on the golf course but it is hard to get motivated when I am off the golf course to get back on the golf course."

A fog of grief shrouded his thoughts and, in the coming weeks and months, he struggled with the media's constant craving for neatly packaged sound bites about how he was dealing with his loss. "I'm good at hitting a little white golf ball, very good at hitting a little white golf ball, I do quite nicely at it," he said in a 2009 interview with BBC TV. "(But) I don't know how to relate my experiences to death, my father's death, and yet people are asking me in the public arena to comment on it. When it comes to the death of my father I'm just like everyone else, I have no idea of putting it into words. I just felt totally inadequate in my ability to deal with it."

Step into the entrance hall at Stackstown Golf Club in the foothills of the Dublin mountains, turn to your right, and on the wall across from the 'Harrington Room', an impressive homage to Padraig's career achievements, hangs a giant frame. Within the frame are the photographs of each of the club's captains since its formation in 1976. Thumb just one place to the right of the first mug shot and you come upon Paddy Harrington's face, the 1977 captain. He was in his mid-40s when the picture was taken, only a few years older than Padraig is now. Save for a little greying around the temples, there is everything of one in the other. The avuncular pose is familiar, so too the powerful upper body, though it's the jutting Harrington jawline that is pure Padraig. It's true what they say; to understand the son, you must look to the father.

Paddy was a native of Castletownbere in west Cork and, early in life, developed a love for Gaelic football. He excelled at it and it was in this arena that the earliest sign of the acute work ethic that he would pass down to his five sons can be traced. As a boy, Paddy was predominantly right-footed, like the majority of his friends and team-mates. All he required to perform magic on the field of play was that right foot and a football. But when he suffered an injury to his instep, his progress was halted. The advice was to stop playing, for a few months. Immediately, the world of mucky fields and sweat and tears that he adored was shut off from him. He was crushed but, crucially, undeterred and, after a couple of days, concluded that there was indeed a way around the problem, through hard work. If he couldn't kick off his right foot then he would simply kick off his left.

At the outset, playing football off his weak left side was more a penance than a pleasure. But with the passion of a perfectionist he soon got there. It is said that, in just months, there was no discernible difference in the quality of his kicking from either foot. When the injury eventually healed, he continued to strike off both sides. As a defender, and sometimes a midfielder, the rare quality of kicking strongly from both feet saved him crucial milliseconds in the heat of battle and won him many personal duels down the years in big games.

A powerful, combative, half-back, he reached the very top of the amateur sport in the 1950s with Cork and is remembered for contesting two All-Ireland finals, in 1956 and 1957, the highest level at which a Gaelic footballer can compete. He must have smiled to himself at a tribute paid in the national media in 1959, describing him as "one of the most remarkable two-footed players the game has known". If only they knew. Proficiency through practise, it was to be his calling card through life, whatever he turned his hand to.

Like his father, Padraig grew to love Gaelic football too. Ask him about his memories of Ryder Cups or legendary British Opens from his early teens and he'll draw a blank. Until Jack Nicklaus piqued his attention with that stirring comeback to deny Greg Norman at the US Masters in 1986, he was more interested in the national pastime. He was a handy footballer too, playing for the local Ballyboden St Enda's club and captaining Colaiste Eanna to a Dublin Senior Colleges final at Croke Park as a 17-year-old. His position? Half-back of course, the same as his dad.

A funny thing happened during that Colleges final in May of 1989. Harrington was also the team's free-taker and kicked one beautiful long-range effort straight over the crossbar for a point. It's common for goalkeepers to make a routine leap in the air in such instances, as the ball flies overhead. But the opposing St Vincent's College keeper went a little further, leaping up, hanging out of the crossbar and bringing the entire structure crashing down. Thankfully, pride was all that was damaged and the game continued.

Harrington never recounted that incident publicly, not because his side took a heavy beating in the end, 2-9 to 0-5, but probably because the occasion turned out to be memorable for a different reason. He was marking rising star Dessie Farrell, the speedy young forward who would inspire an All-Ireland winning Dublin team six years later at the same venue. Harrington diplomatically recalls that Farrell, small and fast, "ran rings" around him, though the stats tell a different story – Farrell registered just a single score all afternoon.

Either way, the real damage suffered was not to Padraig's reputation but to his wrist as he attempted to get to grips with his elusive opponent. It was after a trademark Farrell swivel of the hips and dash, that Harrington turned to chase down his man but lost his footing, and came crashing down on his left wrist, spraining it badly. As bad luck would have it, he was scheduled to play for the Leinster Youths golf team the very next day, in the Interprovincial championship in Ulster. Michael McGinley, Paul's father, was Leinster manager and the last thing he'd told Padraig was not to get injured in the football game. Dessie Farrell takes up the tale: "So Padraig went on up to Ulster, obviously had hurt the wrist playing football, and never said anything about what had happened. I don't think he played particularly well in the golf. But it wasn't until years later that he told Michael McGinley the real story."

Harrington escaped an ear-bashing from the team manager by telling a white lie, that he'd slipped in the shower in the hotel before the golf. Nonetheless, the incident more than likely convinced him that it was time to make a choice and settle on one sport. Unsurprising, the scratch handicapper dropped Gaelic football, just like he'd had to do with soccer having played that game too for the local side, Broadford Rovers. Many years later, he stated that he just never quite felt the same compulsion to grind himself into the dirt as a Gaelic footballer like he did when practising golf. "I didn't work as hard at my Gaelic football," he admitted. "I look back at it and look at my training and say, 'Yeah, I took part but did I give it 100 per cent?' No. Maybe I didn't know better at 15, 14 years of age and maybe if I did I would have been a footballer. I loved golf and that must be why I'm obsessive about it. I liked playing football, and there's a massive difference between those two words. If you like playing it, and you'd like to be successful, then you'll probably go nowhere. If you love it, and you want to be successful, you'll kill yourself trying to get there."

At his old GAA club, Ballyboden St Enda's, they wonder how good Padraig could have been. As good as the auld fella maybe? "He was handy," recalls Farrell. "He kicked the frees as well. He was tall, athletic and obviously came from good stock in terms of his father's background. It's very difficult to say. I would have only seen him playing that one game. But he obviously had the motivation and definitely he had a level of talent. I'm sure if he applied himself to Gaelic football the way he does to golf, there's no reason to believe that he wouldn't have made the top grade." Another man well placed to answer that question is Niall Fitzgerald, a former Cork team-mate of Paddy Harrington's. He first teamed up with Rochestown College student, Paddy, as a midfield partner on a combined colleges team in 1950. "Padraig is big enough and he's strong enough," says Fitzgerald. "The only thing I'd have to ask of Padraig is, would he have had the same dash as his dad? Because Paddy was fast. He could go. A very forceful player."

Fitzgerald, a retired army man, plays a little golf himself these days and watches Padraig on TV when he can. At times, he says he could be staring at a mirror image of Paddy when the son of his old friend comes into frame. "They're very much alike," he says. "They both have a unique walk. Padraig's is maybe a bit more exaggerated with the toes turned out slightly. But Paddy definitely walked a bit like that. And his features, facially, he's quite like his dad that way too."

Paddy took a job with the Garda Siochana as an 18-year-old and moved to Dublin in 1952, eventually rearing a family of five boys with his wife, Breda. He continued on playing for Cork throughout the 1950s and displayed an admirable determination to answer his beloved county's call. He trained regularly on his own in Dublin and made the four-hour journey back home for big games and important training sessions. Again, it was a sign of the fierce commitment that he would pass on to Padraig that he didn't simply take the easier option and play for Dublin where he was living. "Generally speaking I think he trained on his own in Dublin," says Fitzgerald. "He joined us in Croke Park, we'll say, for games and then he was gone off quickly afterwards. We were good friends but he was a very independent fella. I admired that in him."

As a kid growing up, there was that same independence in Padraig. He, too, was a free thinker, never led by others and as friendly with the geeks in class and the straight 'A' students as he was with the 'hard lads'. It would appear that he is viewed in similar terms on Tour, even now, a friend to all but someone so intense of thought that he could never quite be nailed down or characterised in one particular box by his peers. At turns described as 'aloof' and 'serious' by commentators, Padraig's seeming distance is, perhaps, a consequence of his attitude to drink.

According to Padraig, his dad didn't drink for the last 30 years of his life. "I would suggest that drink probably wasn't the best thing for him," he said. That apple didn't fall far from the tree either because Padraig followed on the tradition of abstinence. As he has said himself, practise, not lager or liquor, has always been his poison. He has indulged only on very special occasions, most notably after Ryder Cup successes when he quaffed champagne and drank Jack Daniels with Coke. But, generally, he just doesn't like the taste. That's some statement for an Irishman to make and it perhaps partly explains why some might have come to the conclusion over the years that he wasn't 'one of the boys', in the boorish, 3.30am 'last orders, please' sense of the term. There was a serious side to it all, of course. There often is where alcohol consumption is concerned. He noticed quite early in his career that certain players stayed up drinking until all hours to give themselves an alibi or a get-out clause for expected poor play the following day. "Well, I had six pints last night," he would hear them saying. "They didn't care for the stress," Padraig surmised. "It was a way out, really. I see a little of that in the pro game, too."

For the last 20 or so years of his life, Paddy was effectively a free man having availed of early retirement from the Gardai. It is Padraig's belief that he never should have entered the police force in the first place. His dad much preferred building people up to breaking them down or sticking them in a cell for the night. As a result, tales abound of him giving taxi fares to drunks and avoiding serving summons papers like the plague. "One of our top Irish athletes," said Padraig in 2008, "pulled me aside recently to tell me that, when he was young, my dad could have arrested him but didn't. Instead, he kicked his backside and sent him home. Dad was too soft to be a policeman really."

Coaching was where Paddy Harrington's real talent lay and, after turning 50, he devoted much of his time to helping a teenage Padraig achieve his golfing potential. In doing so, he noticed a familiar, determined spirit in his son. He encouraged and channelled it. It helped, of course, that Paddy had a strong background in golf himself as one of the founding members at Stackstown, a then Garda-only club that he physically helped build. He played to a four handicap at one stage. Shortly before his death, he recounted a winter's afternoon when a teenage Padraig begged him to take him to Stackstown even though the course was covered in a blanket of snow. Just like Bob Torrance years later, Paddy was happy to match Padraig's commitment and the pair of them drove up to the empty course. "He (Padraig) cleared away snow from one of the tees and began hitting balls into a sea of white," recalled Paddy. "The thought of missing a day's practise would have killed him." Like father, like son.

Much further down the line in Padraig's professional career, in 2002, he prepared for the British Open by spending a day at a favourite haunt of his, the European Club links in Wicklow. The course was hosting the local section of a prestigious club competition but, having issued an open invitation for Padraig to come down whenever he wanted, owner Pat Ruddy saw to it that he was left in peace on the Saturday before he travelled over to Scotland. Padraig splashed balls out of the bunker at the par 3 second for a couple of hours. Then he moved down to the par 4 seventh. It is the hardest hole on the course that stretches out to 470 yards off the tips and demands a perfect drive and approach shot. He was practising for so long between the two holes that Ruddy had to turn away autograph hunters who'd got word of the star in their midst and attempted to approach him. All along, Paddy was by Padraig's side, cajoling and encouraging.

In the months before cancer returned to ravage Paddy's body in 2005, he and Padraig travelled over to Largs together for a practise session with Torrance. "He rang me one evening after it," says retired RTE Sport broadcaster, Micheal O Muircheartaigh, who first befriended Paddy when he was playing for Cork in the mid-1950s. "It was top-class coaching and he told me, 'I took in every word that he said. It might transfer to the two of us'. Now the chances of what Bob Torrance was telling Padraig having any relevance to us were slim but Paddy said to me, 'Will you meet me at the Spawell (driving range) and we'll try it out?' That was typical of the sort of man Paddy was. If he had something that he thought was of value, maybe of value to somebody else, then he'd think of those people. That's why he rang me that day."

Padraig would ring Paddy too, religiously, on the afternoon or evening after a competitive round. He would recount, blow by blow, where he'd made gains or let chances slip away. It was these calls that he missed most from July, 2005. "His father had a huge influence on him," says Stackstown's long-time head professional Michael Kavanagh, who knew both father and son well. "He was a lovely man, Lord have mercy on him, and he had a huge influence on Padraig's career. He shaped him, as a person. I would say he did that, very much so."

Paddy ultimately missed Padraig's greatest achievements in golf, his major triumphs in 2007 and 2008. He missed him playing at the Ryder Cup at The K Club in 2006 and becoming the third-ranked golfer in the world, behind Tiger Woods and Phil Mickelson. But, like all good coaches, he probably derived as much pleasure from the journey to success as he would have done from the actual arrival at greatness in Carnoustie and beyond. The very last piece of coaching he imparted to Padraig was done so inadvertently, in the way he bore his illness and his dying days, with composure and dignity. According to Padraig, he learned through this that there is a payback for effort. He was referring to Paddy's unyielding and comforting faith in God, developed through a lifetime of unbroken attendance at Mass as a practising Catholic, that allowed him to embrace his own mortality at the end. He even drew up the instructions for his own funeral. "He died a slow death, six months, and if you are going to die a slow death, you had better have faith," said Padraig. "He had faith. I can't remember a day when he didn't go to Mass, but he was paid back. He put so much effort into his religion and the payback was how comfortable he was."

Paddy's eternal resting place is a plot in Kilmashogue cemetery that looks out across a mature valley onto Rathfarnham Golf Course below. It is golfing country, a short distance from seven different courses. On a bench beside his headstone, the following words are etched, "Never get too high in victory or too low in defeat. In the heat of battle do the simple things simply." It would be trite to suggest that time healed all wounds or that life moved on easily for Padraig after his father's passing. A specially commissioned painting that hangs in his home indicates that he has at least reached a healthy acceptance of it. In the painting, three generations of Harrington boys – Paddy, Padraig and young Patrick – stand together on a practise green at the back of Padraig's home. There is a flagstick on the green. At first, you could miss the words that are printed on the flag itself; Elysian Fields. This, according to Greek mythology, is the paradise where the gods, the righteous and the heroic go after they die, forever to indulge in what made them happy in their mortal lives. It's a nice thought. Maybe even the one that helped get Padraig back on track and focused on golf again at the start of 2006. As Tadhg told him at the end of that phone call, "It was time to go back to work".

Chapter 2
2006

Padraig once admitted that, after a winter break, there'll be a fear within him that his game has somehow deserted him. "I'll be wondering when I come back out if it's still there," he said. "I play with fear, which may sound odd, but it keeps my mind on the task. I've never had much success with confidence." Given the strains of 2005, a level of trepidation about the new season, which included Ireland's hosting of the Ryder Cup and his likely involvement in those matches, was perfectly reasonable this time. As it turned out, his game held up to the closest of scrutiny. More than that, he flourished, and a strong second-half to the season, including victory at the Dunhill Links Championship and runner-up position at the Volvo Masters, earned him the European Tour's Order of Merit title. He was the first Irish player to win it since Ronan Rafferty in 1989. It was the climax of several years of consistently solid performances. Incredibly, in the seven seasons from 2001 to 2008 – excluding 2005 when he took out PGA Tour membership and was also derailed by his father's illness and death – just three Europeans finished higher than him in the Tour's Order of Merit; Darren Clarke (2003), Justin Rose (2007) and Robert Karlsson (2008).

Thanks to his work with Bob Torrance, he was now a serious force in world golf with a revered, if mechanical-looking, wide-arced swing that belted the ball miles. It was a virtually unrecognisable stroke from the one he'd grown up with and qualified for the Tour with in late 1995. Back then, he'd played with a laid-off, flat backswing and an over-the-top, cutting downswing that chopped out low, left-to-right shots. One reporter compared their trajectory to bowling balls being released down an alley. It wasn't a pretty swing to look at, something he first learned when he viewed a video tape of himself at the age of 15. His long game generally lacked punch and distance. But he found it an easily repeatable motion and one that was mightily successful in delivering ball to fairway, time after time. This consistency, allied to a phenomenal short game, got him by as an amateur. And, because of his easily chartable progress, from underage international to full senior status and finally to regular Walker Cup representation in the early 1990s, he hesitated about embracing change and the sort of major overhaul that would deliver better striking and extra yardage.

It was the Golfing Union of Ireland's Howard Bennett, Harrington's first serious coach from 1988 to 1998, who encouraged him to consider moving to a more powerful draw swing. After his Walker Cup debut in 1991, when he saw the distance that US players like Phil Mickelson were hitting the ball, Harrington lamented his own lack of distance. He talked it over with Bennett who recommended introducing the draw straight away. The advice was declined. So it would be again after the same conversation in 1993 following the Walker Cup matches at Interlachen, Minnesota. In fact, it wasn't until 1995 that Harrington was finally convinced about the necessity of change.

That September, shortly after playing in his third Walker Cup at Royal Porthcawl and turning professional, he was invited to play in the European Open at the The K Club. "Myself and Paddy followed him around the first 18 holes," says Michael Kavanagh, Stackstown professional. "Padraig played with Barry Lane and Costantino Rocca. The two guys were 50 yards past him off the tee each time, on average. It could have been 30 sometimes, other times it was up to 70. Paddy turned to me and says, 'Jesus, you'd worry about the distance he is in comparison to the lads'. Just to try and put his mind at ease, I said, 'Yeah, but look at the driver he's using'. He was using an old Bridgestone driver, which had a short 43½-inch shaft and the guys were using their 44½, 45-inch drivers with bigger heads. And I also said, 'Once he's playing every day of the week, and you know how hard he's going to practise, then I don't know anyone who won't get longer just through that alone'."

It was skirting around the issue, though. And Harrington knew it himself – his cut swing, with all the practise in the world, was only going to take him so far. In January of 1996, just as his new life was beginning on the European Tour, he set the tone for the professional career that lay ahead by taking a massive gamble – he finally moved to the draw. Changing such a fundamental part of his swing so early in his first season went against conventional wisdom. It is often stated that, 'If you haven't brought it with you, then you're not going to find it on Tour'. But he was won over by advice from eminent coach and Tour founder, John Jacobs. They met at the Tour's 'Apollo' week in San Roque, Spain, a sort of induction week for rookie players. It was one simple statement from Jacobs, 'Open the door, shut the door', in relation to the backswing and follow through, that did the trick and turned Harrington from a serial fader to a regular drawer. Gone was the weak cut as he hit a sling hook for the first two years on tour, gaining over 20 yards on his drives. Remarkably, his maiden tournament win came at the Spanish Open in May, just his tenth Tour event. "I was the happiest man out there because I wasn't able to draw the ball as an amateur, and that was a massive change," he said.

Arguably the biggest change of all in this period was one that the public at large didn't even notice – his putting grip. "His strength of mind was something else," says Jody Fanagan, Harrington's Walker Cup partner at Royal Porthcawl the previous September. "I'd been playing with him for four or five years and he was always right hand below left as a putter. And he was a great putter. Would break people's hearts. But all along at home he'd been practising left below right. When the Walker Cup in '95 was over, he went straight to left below right. He played Q-School left below right. So, literally two weeks after winning the Walker Cup, he went the other way. But he'd been practising it all summer. Us not knowing. Nobody else knew. Because he'd been right under left all his career up to then and I can tell you he putted unbelievably well – but this made him better. I didn't even know he was doing it. I was playing with him every day and it was news to me."

Harrington finished his first full season 11th on the European Tour and was a respectable 18th at the British Open at Royal Lytham. But after failing to achieve his aim of winning another individual tournament in 1997, doubts about his ball striking and ability to maximise his potential –

something he's always been led by – began to materialise. The following summer, he turned up for the US Open at the Olympic Club in San Francisco and was damn near broken by the experience of playing his best golf and still finishing 32nd. "I did everything I could," he said, only taking the slightest of credit for getting some extra height into his shots. "I got up and down, holed every putt. I felt I could do no better. I felt totally inadequate."

He and Bennett discussed the situation in San Francisco but parted without any consensus. From Bennett's perspective, the situation wasn't nearly as dire as Harrington made out. He felt Padraig's course management had been good, his short game typically sound and his mental game solid. They agreed to meet again at Royal Birkdale the following month, to talk things over before his second British Open. But straightaway, on the practise ground in Southport, Bennett could sense that Harrington wasn't his usual bubbly self. Padraig broke the news that he was moving to a new swing coach, Torrance, permanently. "People say to me, 'Do you feel upset that Padraig went to work with Bob Torrance?'" says Bennett, now retired and the proud possessor of a PGA Master Professional coaching distinction. "I always say, 'No, I was privileged to work with him for ten years, two years as a pro, eight years as an amateur'. We learn something from everybody. He just wanted a second opinion, if you like. I had no objection to that. We had that thing between us that, if I felt I wasn't going to help him, I would tell him and I would expect him to tell me that 'I've learnt all I can and I'd like a second opinion'. That was how it happened. So we left on good terms, no problems at all."

Torrance's general reputation was for churning out solid ball strikers with plenty of length, a là his great inspiration, Ben Hogan. The immediate problem Torrance recalls about his new student's swing was that it was too flat. But that was only the tip of the iceberg. In a 2003 instruction feature with 'Golf Digest' magazine, the wizened string instructor outlined in painstaking detail the various issues that he and Harrington addressed in their first five years together.

"The first time I set eyes on Padraig's swing, it was obvious we had some work to do," said Torrance. "He had no leverage. He hit the ball no distance. He was a poor striker. The flight on his shots had no penetration. His shoulder plane was too flat. And his right elbow was behind him, not in front of him, on the backswing. I started with Padraig's footwork and leg action. At the top of his backswing, his left heel worked outward, to his left. When he swung through, his right heel worked outward, to his right. Now they move up and in at the same stage. We worked on that for a long time. Then we looked at his rotation, specifically his left forearm to the top of the swing. That move creates speed, cocks your wrist to the swing plane, puts your club in the same position at the top every time and holds your right elbow in. All of those things are desirable. And I learned them all from Ben Hogan. Next was Padraig's connection. If you stand with the upper part of your left arm against your chest and keep it there, you are connected. But if your arm moves away from your body, you have lost connection. Mr Hogan told me the feeling he had was he couldn't get a razor blade between his arm and his chest. That wasn't reality, but that was his feeling." Importantly, Torrance noted that Harrington was, 'prepared to get worse in order to get better. Not many are.'

Thanks to the new regime, Harrington saw out the century by reaching a career high in 1999. The second Tour win he was chasing still hadn't arrived. But seventh in the money list ensured qualification for the Ryder Cup at Brookline and, on October 24, he entered the World's Top 50 for the first time, at number 49. Responding to his progress, Harrington labelled Torrance a 'genius'. "That's my personal view," he said. "I can't say enough about Bob. We have worked hard over the past 18 months on swing changes and I believe I am a much better player. I'm very happy. I'm hitting it further and everything is better." Praise from the innately talented Darren Clarke was a good yardstick to measure his progress by. Clarke beat Harrington in the 1990 Irish Amateur championship final and considered him a good chipper and putter, but not a whole lot more. "I think a lot of my fellow pros would rate Padraig very highly now, much more so than maybe a year and a half ago," said Clarke, who noticed Harrington 'ripping' and 'flushing' irons on the range at the Bay Hill Invitational in early 2000. "When he turned pro, I thought, because of how exceptional his short game was, that he would have a good career, but of late, his swing is improving so much that I think he is going to be a great player."

In 2004, an old pal of Harrington's, Gerard Sproule, travelled down to Mount Juliet in County Kilkenny to watch him compete in the WGC-American Express championship. In all, 56 of the world's top 60 golfers competed for a record prize fund of US$7m. Harrington and Sproule went back a long way, to July of 1987. They first met at the Connacht Boys' championship in Ballinasloe. Padraig was just 15 at the time and had never travelled so far from home for golf. He and his caddy, big brother Tadhg, stayed with a family friend in the west. During one of the practise rounds, Padraig became unnerved by a group of players behind, and one in particular, who was consistently stitching shots in close to the pins. It seemed that whenever Padraig looked around another ball was touching down on the green from a perfect rainbow like arc. The pinpoint player behind turned out to be an even younger teenager from the famous Rosses Point links in County Sligo, Sproule.

Harrington only put a face to the name on the morning of the Connacht Boys' final when the pair shook hands on the first tee box and contested a thrilling match. The young Dubliner made an incredible effort at breaking Sproule's spirit early on with birdies at four of the first five holes. "But I pinned him back over the next few holes," smiles Sproule, recalling an event 25 years ago that he still remembers well. "We were level after 18 so it went into extra holes. It was still going at the 22nd, a par 5. The standard was very high. We certainly wouldn't have been over par, either of us."

Both players despatched good drives at the fourth extra hole. But Harrington blocked his next shot way right, a 3-wood. He lost his ball. Sensing blood, Sproule played the hole conservatively and picked off a regulation par to take the match. "He still made me hole the putt for par though," says Sproule, smiling. "He still made six with his second ball. I'll always remember that." The duo became friends and played regularly on the amateur scene in the following years. They even teamed up as underage internationals and grew closer again when Sproule was in college at UCD with a mutual friend of Padraig's, Ronan Flood. Eventually, they would lose touch when Harrington turned professional. It wasn't until Sproule stood at the back of the 10th tee at Mount Juliet in 2004 and caught the eye of player and caddie that they enjoyed a brief reunion.

Sproule tracked his old adversary's progress around the back nine that afternoon and was stunned by the quality of golf that Harrington produced to finish tied sixth. "I couldn't believe the transformation in his ball striking," says Sproule. "I was flabbergasted. The last time I had seen him play was out at the European Club, before he got his Tour card. At that point, he would say himself, he was a nice striker of the ball but the difference was genuinely unbelievable. I couldn't get over how he'd improved his ball striking. His legs and his upper body probably wouldn't have been as connected in the past. And, from the work he did with Bob Torrance, he would have got a lot more leg action into his swing, a lot more lower-body release. He improved the whole turn and I just couldn't get over how far he hit the ball. It was pure torque, pure coil and it was all so much more connected."

Torrance talks of an occasion a few years back when he got chatting with the Dane, Thomas Bjorn. "Bjorn said to me, 'Harrington had the worst swing on Tour, now he's got the best'," recalls Torrance. "That's what Thomas Bjorn said." Paul McGinley first crossed swords with Harrington on the Irish amateur scene in the early 1990s. They teamed up together as partners for Great Britain and Ireland in the 1991 Walker Cup. McGinley has witnessed the development of Harrington's swing over the last 20 years and concurs with Bjorn's analysis. "I think I'm qualified to say this, that in the history of successful golfers, and I know the amount that Faldo changed his game, but nobody could have changed his game more than Harrington has done," says McGinley.

"I know that Padraig was proud to hear that from Paul," claims Jody Fanagan. "If you look at videos when we played together in the Walker Cup in '95 and you look at him now, it's just two different players. If you look at others and compare their swings from amateur to present day, for example, look at Sergio's swing, it's still almost identical. I think Tiger, in fairness, has changed a bit but certainly Padraig would be one of the most significant ones."

Gary Murphy, another former amateur colleague and subsequent Tour colleague, summarises the changes made by Harrington over the years well with one keen observation: "I suppose the best compliment I could give him is that if his swing was the same now as it was then, you wouldn't be writing a book about him."

Many claim the real magic of Harrington, the X factor he possesses, is his willingness to take on good advice and implement it, to learn and apply. Over the years, this advice has mainly come from his coaches, Bennett, Torrance and, currently, Pete Cowen. But one of the claims continually made is that Harrington also has a unique aptitude for learning from virtually any golfer he comes across, even a jittery 20-handicapper in a pro-am. Interestingly, in his very early days as a golfer, there were no posters of Seve Ballesteros or Greg Norman hanging over his bed. Rather, it was his brothers, a number of whom reached low single-figure handicaps, or his fellow competitors, who did things he couldn't, that he idolised most and modelled his game on. In later years, on the Irish amateur scene, he liked nothing better than to watch and study the short game of Baltray's Mark Gannon, an experienced and renowned competitor. Indeed, his heart almost burst with pride when, on the way to that Amateur final clash with Clarke in 1990, he beat Gannon by out-chipping and out-putting 'one of the greatest short game players on his own course'.

When it came to driving, he would take mental notes while playing with another legend of the Irish amateur scene, Garth McGimpsey, always a solid striker off the tee. Bennett says the beauty of Harrington is not just that he takes on advice and is constantly looking to learn, from whatever the source, but that he is clever enough at the end of it all to retain and implement the mere five per cent that will actually help him. "That's the real skill," says Bennett.

Before that first European Tour outing at The K Club in 1995, Harrington joined McGinley for a practise round. To their delight, they found Bernhard Langer waiting at the first tee, enquiring if he could join them. Harrington carried a deep respect for the German. He admired the calm, methodical way he navigated a golf course. After the practise round at The K Club he was in raptures. According to Bennett, "Padraig said, 'I just can't believe how precise he is and how good his course management is, even in a practise round. He just dissects the place and knows exactly how to get around.' It was strategy, course management. Padraig said, 'I thought I was good at that but Bernhard Langer is at another level. I've got to get to that level'."

To do so, Harrington kept listening and watching. But, most importantly of all, he kept practising. In fact, in the next decade, he practised harder than just about any player had seen. Most of his amateur colleagues had marked him out for a decent career. They felt his short game alone, and his determination, would see to that. There is an intriguing tale of a plus-two handicapper back in the early 1990s who shelved his notions of turning pro after witnessing first-hand in Harrington the sort of intensity and dogged focus required to make it. But a triple major champion? Not too many predicted that. The insatiable appetite for practise and personal development was what got him there in the end.

Long-time European tour caddie Colin Byrne, who looped for US Open winner Retief Goosen, believes Harrington's early years on Tour coincided with a noticeable shift towards higher levels of practise generally. In many cases, he claims, it allowed ordinary players to have mediocre careers and, in exceptional cases, like Harrington, to become world-beaters.

"The Swedes brought it in, not very talented golfers, a lot of them, but they had worked out techniques and ways of becoming acceptable golfers," says Byrne. "I mean there's a big gang of them out on Tour and it didn't come from raw talent. It came from sheer working the system out and playing within that system, which is a way of doing it and of earning a living. I'm not knocking it, but in terms of, you know, you look at Rory McIlroy and you see raw talent. Anyone that doesn't know anything about the game can see there's something special about him, the way he swings and the way he does it. And then you see the other guys and it's like they have a shovel in their hands and they're digging away." As for Harrington, he reckons that, "If you asked anyone on Tour they'd all say he worked too hard for his own good". But he qualifies the remark by stating that, "He may argue that if he didn't work that hard he wouldn't have won three majors. Personally, I always found with players it can be a sign of self-belief when they feel they don't need to keep bashing balls at a tournament. It's the feeling that, you know, 'I'm good enough to get it done'. The best year I had with Retief, for example, he didn't practise that much."

The image of Harrington, huddled in the corner of a practise range at some tournament with his coach and his caddie, has been a feature of life on Tour since the mid-1990s. At his very first Malaysian Open, he finished a morning round, grabbed a quick lunch and then headed for the driving range. He had been warned that he may have slipped back into an old habit of tilting his shoulders. The instructed cure was to hit a 100 or so drivers off the ground, with no tee. He took that figure and multiplied it, by 10. "I must have hit 1,000 balls off the deck and I think I have cured it," he cheerily reported afterwards." He recounted the same story in a different light later on in his career, indicating an acceptance that he'd pushed himself too hard in his early years. "I finished my morning round and then spent four hours on the range hitting driver off the deck," he recalled in 2011. "The other players were in the swimming pool, watching me, saying, 'Who is that idiot?' It was sweltering. I closed every range on the Tour every day for a few years. I got injuries because of it."

Another time, at his first US Open, in June of '97, he spent nearly five hours on the range following a practise round and developed dehydration. Complaining of feeling unwell, he shot 12 over par and missed the cut. Still, there was no preventing him from indulging himself. At the Dubai Desert Classic in early 2001, his wife, Caroline, sat on a chair beside him on the practise ground, watching him pound ball after ball as the sun dipped low towards the horizon. Colin Montgomerie was giving a golf clinic for some sponsors at the other end of the practise area. When the Scot had finished, he walked past the Harringtons, still there practising. Monty threw his eyes to heaven in mock rebuke. "It's either madness or love, one or the other," he said. That Sunday, Harrington finished second again, later admitting he simply ran out of steam on the back nine. "I had just done too much work in the week," he conceded.

Fast forward to the following July and it was a similar scene on the practise ground of The K Club at the European Open. He was lying third going into the final round, two shots behind Mikael Lundberg and apparently poised to strike. A week earlier, he'd finished second in the Irish Open with a closing 64. It meant that, for the second week running, he was carrying the hopes and dreams of a fevered home crowd. Logic suggested he was burning himself up at a terrific rate, physically and mentally, and especially so after practising for seven hours on the Tuesday. But, instead of resting that Saturday evening, he returned to the range with Torrance and his new caddie, Dave McNeilly. They watched Harrington rifle out a couple of hundred mid-iron shots before moving onto his driver. As darkness fell, the little troop were politely asked to move to the end of the roped-off area so the green-keeping staff could prepare the range for Sunday. The following day, Harrington shot 70 and finished second.

Was it all worth it? As Byrne says, only a fool would suggest not in light of the major successes. At differing stages of his career he has ticked all the big boxes a top professional golfer would wish to; multiple major winner, Ryder Cup winner, Order of Merit winner, Irish Open winner, the checklist goes on. Perhaps a more pertinent question is, did he ever have another choice given his hard wiring and compulsive tendencies that were so evident at an early age?

Conor O'Shea, the Irish rugby International and Director of Rugby at Harlequins in England, paints an intriguing picture of early obsession growing up alongside Harrington at Stackstown. "At a very young age he had a ridiculous attention to detail on a golf course," says O'Shea, who reached a single-figure handicap himself and played in a couple of the boys' tournaments. "He'd know the length of the grass on a green and which mower had cut it. To me, that marked him apart and the amount of time he'd spend practising. Years later, I met him in the gym at Friarsland. I was back from London where I was playing rugby and we bumped into each other. He asked me if I fancied playing golf the next day with his wife, or his girlfriend at the time, Caroline. So we played up in Stackstown the following day in a foursomes game with two others. As we started off, Padraig went off to the spare two holes to do a bit of practise. We were golfing for four or four and a half hours and when we finished he was still standing out there on that hole, just driving ball after ball, checking out which driver was the best. I think there's just a certain mentality you need to be a top golfer and it's almost an obsessive compulsive disorder that you need to have, to be able to repeat, repeat, repeat. Because that's what holes putts, isn't it? It's something that he's just always had. He had it as a kid in terms of knowing the length of the grass on a green and what sort of way it had been cut. And I think he just retained it all his life."

It is O'Shea's belief that spending so much of his early life alongside his father and brothers at Stackstown – Padraig rolled in the new 12th green as a four-year-old with his dad in 1975 – may have given him a unique insight into the game which helped him in his career.

"He was almost born on a golf course, wasn't he?" muses O'Shea. "Stackstown was a nine-hole course, became an 18-hole, and his family were central to the whole thing. So he probably saw a lot of the stuff that went into building a golf course. It must be an amazing insight into how greens are laid, made, maintained, preserved, how you speed them up, slow them down. I mean, there was a hole there, the 17th, and honestly, if you went above the hole, or at least above level with the green, you could not keep the ball on the green coming back. It was not possible. Well, he could!"

Gary Murphy contends that, for Harrington, golf is a 'vocation'. "I would say he's totally consumed by his golf and his game," says Murphy. "It's his whole life. It's a vocation for him as much as his job. I think that's the subtle difference with Padraig." But surely that's the same for all Tour pros? "Well, not really," contests Murphy. "Everyone is different. It's impossible to compare one guy with another guy. But I would say his work ethic and his drive to succeed is greater than any Irish player that has ever left these shores."

Harrington eventually recognised a need to reign himself in, however. He maintains the substantive part of his swing overhaul is complete and that, in his early 40s, he is now trying to wean himself off the practise range. Torrance would appear to have been a victim of this fundamental shift. The veteran coach, Harrington once said, 'believes that all the secrets are to be learned on the practise ground'.

As far back as the early 2000s, Harrington began to address ways of bringing down the whole intensity of his game. Partly because it was costing him tournament wins due to over-practising. And partly because he was already swinging well and needed to maintain more than change. But, perhaps most of all, because of the increasing role that sports psychologist Bob Rotella was playing in his career. After the double major winning season of 2008, Harrington intriguingly admitted that, "I used to be 90 per cent Torrance and 10 per cent Rotella, but it's probably the other way round now."

Harrington made one of the most ruthless decisions of his career in 2004 in an attempt to lower this intensity in his game. He sacked his caddie, Dave McNeilly. The Belfast man was, and remains, a hugely experienced, successful and well-liked caddie on Tour. The former bagman of Nick Faldo was initially drawn to Harrington in 1999 by his renowned work ethic. "I would work very hard myself and would be on the golf course until quite late and I noticed that whenever I'd be coming in he was still out practising too," said McNeilly. But five years on, Harrington felt he had made the leap to a new level in his golf career and that a more subtle, refined approach was required. At first, he hoped to bring the ebullient McNeilly with him on the journey. But he claims McNeilly wasn't showing any signs of changing. The situation came to a head in April 2004, at the Bell South Classic in America. Harrington was in the last group that Sunday, three behind leader and playing partner Zach Johnson.

Meticulous as ever, McNeilly spent the morning on his toes, taking down exact yardage measurements around the course for his boss with a laser distance-measuring device. When he clocked in for duty an hour before their tee-off time, Harrington sensed his man was rushed. He claimed McNeilly spent the first 15 or 20 minutes marking the golf balls and completing routine jobs. To Harrington, it felt frenzied at a point in his career when he was trying to move in the opposite direction. It also went against one of his fundamental rules in the player/caddie relationship.

"That hour before the tee-time is my time, I own that time, so my caddie is there to stand there, just be there," explained Harrington. "He's not there to be doing any work, bar just being in my company and if we do that we're more likely to go down the first fairway, and the thought I have is more likely to the same as him." Afterwards, in the car park, Harrington and McNeilly exchanged words and parted on sombre terms. They split up a month later despite finishing second in their last tournament, the Deutsche Bank in Heidelberg. "I probably didn't have any respect for how he handled me at the time but it doesn't make Padraig Harrington a bad person," said McNeilly earlier this year. He is currently caddying for Italian wonder kid, Matteo Manassero.

Despite copping plenty of flak at the time for releasing McNeilly, Harrington was unrepentant. His explanation for the decision shines a light on the mind-set he'd reached in the mid-2000s and which would take him to that Order of Merit success in 2006. "His (McNeilly's) enthusiasm was ... he was bouncing off the walls," said Harrington. "You could be missing the cut by five and he'd (still) be trying his heart out. With him, we parted company because I wanted him to settle down a bit. I didn't want this much enthusiasm. That was very much when I went to a stage ... that was a big change in me. I went from, like ... Dave would always bring you that extra bucket of balls."

More comfortable in his game, and realising that less wasn't always more, the extra buckets of balls that Harrington and McNeilly used to hide out of view, for when the range was closed, weren't required anymore. Not so often anyway, and being named the best golfer in Europe in 2006 was proof positive that Harrington's more refined approach, on and off the course, was paying off. With Rotella's help, he had stopped practising for tomorrow and was playing for now. After 10 years of wearing his grips down to stumps on driving ranges from Stackstown to San Francisco, via Largs, he had crossed a huge psychological threshold by finally accepting that he was good enough to win with what he had on any given day. "For the first time," he admitted, "I turned up for a tournament and played those tournaments as if there were no tournaments the following week."

Chapter 3
2006

Harrington leant down and plucked his ball from the 17th hole at Muirfield. Clutching it in his left hand and displaying a neat row of white teeth in a broad smile, he raised his right hand in the air to the appreciative crowd. He had just recorded his fifth birdie of the day. With one hole left to play in the 2002 British Open he was six under par. Several groups back, Ernie Els was leading on eight under and moving along nicely. Inwardly, Harrington assessed the situation. He reasoned that, having just picked up two birdies himself since the 15th, and with the par 5 17th still to come, the 'Big Easy' surely wouldn't finish any worse than eight under. If anything, Els would probably get to minus nine. There was nothing for it only to try to make a birdie up the last, hopefully post the clubhouse lead at seven under and cross all fingers for the next hour or so. Standing on the tee box of the testing par 4 18th, he pulled out the driver and resolved to go for broke.

The safest way to play the hole was a 2-iron or 3-iron to the heart of the fairway, leaving a mid-iron to the green. That's how his playing partner, Stuart Appleby, had done it and he'd scored a birdie. But then the Australian had been fortunate to drain a 20-footer on the green. Harrington wasn't in any position to rely on a long putt going in. He was struggling with the flat stick. He'd switched from his two-ball putter to a conventional blade after the first round but without any noticeable improvement. While he led the greens in regulation statistics at the end of the tournament – reflecting his virtually flawless long game – he propped up the putting charts in 74th place.

And, anyway, he'd always played to win. Throughout his career he'd rarely shied away from the big shots when there were serious gains on offer. Years earlier, for instance, as a 16-year-old, he'd stood on the 15th tee of the tree-lined Royal Tara Golf Club in the final round of the Leinster Boys' championship. He possessed a decent lead but knew that danger lurked in the testing closing holes. The 15th – now the sixth on the Bellinter nine of the revised 27-hole set-up – is a short par 4 that dog-legs, right to left, around a couple of giant trees around 200 yards from the tee. Many of his tournament colleagues, including playing partner Thomas Reilly, who was trailing him in second place, cracked a 3-wood to the elbow of the fairway. Then they took their chances with a wedge into a green that rises steeply from front to back. Harrington, with his mam and dad watching, went for the jugular with a 1-iron, which he drilled straight over the trees to within 15 feet of the pin. Game over.

He went on to win the tournament by 11 shots from Reilly, the first significant golfing achievement of his career. "It just showed what a class act he was," said Reilly, recalling a perfect 1-iron shot that is mastered by so few. "And then he went and holed an impossible uphill putt on the (par 3) 16th for a two which really ended the competition. I was proud to finish second to him."

Caution could never be described as Harrington's default setting and, at Muirfield, he looked at Appleby, a shot further adrift on five under par, taking an iron for safety up the 18th and was genuinely surprised. 'Why's he playing for second position?' he thought, far more inclined to try to make his own good luck with a show of courage.

"He's always had a lot of bottle like that," says Ireland's former Ryder Cup man Des Smyth, who, at the age of 49, had led the 131st British Open briefly the previous day and eventually finished tied 28th with Tiger Woods. "In fact, I would say he had huge bottle. He definitely wasn't afraid to go for the big shots."

As Harrington stood over his tee shot, however, he found himself struggling to exact his normal routine. Rotella had always urged him to pick the smallest possible target in the distance and aim for it. Aggressive swings to conservative targets. But a small chunk of thick rough about 330 yards away, just off the right-hand side of the fairway and within reach of a good drive, kept popping up in his thoughts, distracting him.

"I won't make birdie from there," went the voice in his head, moments before putting his worst swing of the week on a drive that flew down the opposite side of the fairway and into the face of a deep bunker. After playing out sideways, he eventually made bogey and finished on five under. Agonisingly, as it turned out, a par would have been enough to qualify for a five-way play-off on six under. Els, the eventual winner, had unexpectedly faltered on the way home in regulation play with a double bogey at 16. Speaking to the press, Harrington couched his angst in diplomatic terms, reasoning that he'd have preferred to win with a birdie on the 72nd than in a play-off. Deep down though, the realisation that he'd binned that week's winning lottery ticket must have been unbearable.

The Irishman walked away from the Muirfield experience with his shoulders lowered. Yet he was sure of one thing, that he had the game to win a major championship. He felt he had played the very best golf of his career and, even now, in 2012, after annexing three major titles, points to that performance 10 years ago as the greatest major display of his career, from tee to green. "I played my best ever golf in a major tournament," he said of Muirfield in an interview with Setanta TV. "Best ever golf, ever. I was just in the zone for four days, hit the ball fantastic. But I always considered that week to be an aberration. I didn't know why I played so well. I'd always put it up there on a pedestal. The standard of play was above what I had ever played. I honestly had the ball on a string for a week, which is not something I would have experienced."

Unnerved after staring his full potential head-on without knowing why such stellar form had materialised, he backed away and retreated to his comfort zone to work it all out. He had also reached a career high of eighth in the world. But, again, on the inside, he felt he didn't truly deserve to be there, not until, like Howard Hughes, he could explain how all the parts functioned and what he needed to do to get them firing so efficiently on a regular basis. "In the back of my mind I knew that was the standard I wanted to achieve, though there were many other things I wanted to do first before I'd allow myself to get there," he admitted. Around this time, his dad, Paddy was shooting the breeze about nothing in particular with the club pro at Stackstown when he commented, "I've taught him to be successful, but I haven't taught him to be a winner. Yet." It was a comment Michael Kavanagh has never forgotten. "Padraig was already very wealthy at the time but I distinctly remember his dad saying that to me," says Kavanagh. "He obviously felt there was a bit to work on, that killer instinct, I suppose."

The key questions in Harrington's mind after finishing just a shot outside the play-off at Muirfield were: Why had he played so well? And what did he need to do to make himself produce that form regularly? It wasn't until 2006 that he felt he had cracked it. Away from the course, his life had settled into a comfortable groove by then. He was a husband to Caroline, since December 1997, and a father to Patrick, since 2003. He had replaced caddie McNeilly with his friend and soon to be brother-in-law, Ronan Flood, a seamless appointment, and assembled a crack entourage around him that included the two Bobs, Torrance and Rotella, and fitness advisor, Dr Liam Hennessy.

That April, 2006, at Augusta, when he finished in a tie for 27th at the Masters, he came to the same conclusion about his golf game as he had about his life – that none of it needed tweaking. The jigsaw puzzle that had been the first ten years of his professional career was, essentially, complete. The big picture was there before his eyes and, remarkably, it was just as he'd envisioned it. "There comes a time when you have to say, 'Yes' (I'm ready)," said Harrington, explaining how he'd always planned to peak in the mid-2000s. "When I was growing up, 29 years of age, 28 years of age was a peak. It looks now like your mid-30s is peak time for a professional golfer, up to about 40 years of age."

At the 2006 Masters, Harrington was 34. For the first time in his career he felt there wasn't one single shot in that major championship that he wasn't capable of pulling off. It was his eureka moment and he was confident enough to say it out loud this time. "There wasn't a shot that was presented where I thought somebody else had a big advantage," he recalled of the event in Bobby Jones' back yard. "I said to Bob Rotella afterwards, 'I'm good enough to win one of these'." Those same words he enunciated with even more gusto the following June after finishing fifth at the punishing US Open.

That tournament was held at Winged Foot and despite bogeying the last three holes and finishing two behind winner Geoff Ogilvy – a poor finish rarely recalled by the media because of Phil Mickelson's more spectacular meltdown and, to a lesser extent, Colin Montgomerie's – he was more certain than ever that a major win was achievable. Indeed, when the media teased him about what it might feel like to finally win that one major championship, he'd respond that he was after several of them. He had watched other players struggle for motivation after realising their life's ambition of a major win and vowed not to let the same thing happen to him.

The crucial difference between that US Open performance at Winged Foot, in 2006, and the experience at Muirfield four years earlier, was that he now felt in complete control of his excellence. He was almost serving it up to order whereas, in 2002, he'd been surprised by it and caught off guard. "I realised when I walked away from that (US Open) that I could actually control it, whereas 2002 at Muirfield, I didn't think it was within my control," he said. "2006 at Winged Foot, I said, 'You know what, I actually have an ability here to get my game to peak and, when it peaks, I'm actually good enough to win a major'. I walked away with the most confidence in the world that I could go on and win a major."

He was now utterly transformed as a player, one of the world's great ball strikers. "When you think what Padraig was like when he started with Bob (Torrance), I think it's the best example I have ever seen of what a good teacher can do for a player," commented Nick Bradley, Justin Rose's coach. Fellow pros and analysts even began to describe the player who struggled to drive the ball over 250 yards in his early years on Tour as 'sneaky long', with average drives of over 290 yards in 2005 and 2006. His short game remained as deadly as ever, too. He had the fewest putts per round on the European Tour in 2003, just 28.2 on average, and, in 2005, he led the scrambling stats for getting up and down around the green.

Yet many great players, who are solid in all of these important areas and consistent in the stats like Harrington was, still never win a major. Seven-in-a-row Order of Merit winner Montgomerie stands out as one of the greatest examples of such under-achievement. Sergio Garcia, Luke Donald and Lee Westwood aren't far behind. Harrington could so easily have fallen into this bracket of 'great players never to have won a major' were it not for the work he put in away from the course, with Rotella, on the mental side of his game, rigorously examining the minutiae of his preparations. It was this work, almost as much as the Herculean efforts that he put in on the practise ground alongside Torrance, that would allow him to realise the ambition of every single player that starts out as a professional on Tour – a major win.

Harrington's eyes had first been opened to the power of the mind, and the possibility of manipulating it to help one's golf game, a long time earlier as a teenager. At the time, in the late 1980s, sports psychology was still viewed by many as a dark art pedalled by folk of questionable virtue. Howard Bennett was ahead of his time though. He encouraged his pupils on the GUI's coaching panels, including Harrington, to consider and explore the benefits of positive thoughts. It was Bennett who first handed Harrington a copy of Rotella's ground-breaking book, 'Golf is Not a Game of Perfect'. "Padraig was one who took note when we suggested reading the Bob Rotella books and that kind of stuff, he took to it like a duck to water," says Bennett. There, in print, were many of the ideas and concepts that had already been going around in Harrington's head for years. Interestingly, Rotella would state in later years that Harrington had almost instinctively applied many of the theories contained in the book to his own game anyway. Positive by his very nature, Harrington was consumed by the idea of, as Rotella put it in his introduction to 'Golf is Not a Game of Perfect', "learning to think in the most effective and efficient way possible every day". Rotella described this as "the psychology of excellence" and wrote that he was, "convinced that it is the power of will that separates great golfers from those who never reach their potential". These statements would strike an immediate chord with Harrington whose goal from the moment he picked up a Gene Sarazen Wilson 8-iron with a chipped blue grip as a child at home was to simply be the best player he possibly could.

His first meeting with a sports psychologist came several years before he actually hooked up with Rotella. His father had convinced him to have a chat with Aidan Moran at University College Dublin, in early 1994. At first, he was hesitant about the idea of opening up to a stranger, albeit an expert as renowned as Moran. But his dad was persistent and, after a couple of months, Padraig gave in. The first consultation, in February of '94, came at a time in his amateur career when he was showing incredible consistency, enough to have earned him places on two Walker Cup teams, but without being able to drag himself over the winning line in major amateur championships. Since 1990, he had lost in the final of one of the five major amateur tournaments – the north, south, east and west of Ireland championships and the Irish amateur close championship – twice, and in two semi-finals. His near domination of the prestigious scratch cup, stroke play competitions around Ireland was proof of his ability but he just couldn't transfer it to the tournaments he most wanted to win.

Evidence of mental frailty had been stacking up against him for some time. The deepest wound to his psyche was inflicted in Dundalk in 1990 when he let the Irish Youths championship title slip through his fingers with a closing 77. With just four holes left, he'd been informed that he only needed to par in to the clubhouse to win. But even as he was receiving that information, he could feel the intensity draining out of his body.

He succumbed to that deadly and familiar enemy he has battled his entire career – complacency. He reeled off three bogeys and lost by a shot to David Errity of Hermitage. The ugliest word in the golfing dictionary rang in his ears, 'choke'. At least that's what his pals thought anyway, and he heard them say it. In reality, he felt it had been the exact opposite of choking. He'd actually got cocky and complacent, presuming he was going to win and lost concentration. The following year, with two holes to go in a match against Bobbie Kinsella at the West of Ireland championship, he was two up with two to play but ended up losing on the 19th. Old Mr Complacency had struck again.

The growing list of near misses or, as they were inevitably labelled, chokes, amounted to death by a thousand cuts.

"Do you have any idea how many times I finished in the top four in amateur tournaments and cups between the ages of 17 and 19?" said Harrington in a 1996 interview with the *Sunday Independent*. "24, that's how many. Want to know how many I won? Two. Bloody two. Can you believe that? Numbing it was. Heart-breaking."

His dad's calm assurances that, "You just have to gain experience" barely tempered his frustration. So, he eventually took a seat next to Moran and, as he said himself, "like an overloaded dryer, it all came tumbling out". He told Moran that his problems always seemed to start when he was in front, never behind. He produced his best when up against the wall. But put him in against an underdog, or give him a big lead in a match, and he was liable to struggle. His mind would start racing. He would be scribbling mental notes for his victory speech when, the next thing he knew, he was shaking hands and wondering how he'd just lost. Moran's intervention was vital and almost instantly Harrington felt emboldened. Only weeks after that first meeting, he won the West of Ireland championship at Rosses Point, reserving praise for his new mind coach in what was a rare victory speech. In the following 18 months before turning professional, he contested a remarkable six more amateur finals, winning two of them, the Irish Close and Open championships, in 1995. All of his demons hadn't been fully exorcised and handing victory to David Higgins in the 1994 Irish Close Championship at Portmarnock when two up with three to play hurt like a punch in the kidneys, but it was a noticeable turnaround all the same.

"Aidan helped me with my concentration, helped me stay focused," he said. "And for the last 18 months of my amateur career I never lost a stroke play competition over 36 holes – never looked back."

Initial doubts about the impact a guru like Moran could have on his game were gone. Harrington was a believer and anyone who mocked or chided that sports psychologists were nothing more than charlatans selling snake oil were gently directed towards his increasingly crowded trophy cabinet. In 1998, during his third year on Tour, he finally made contact with Rotella, a move he'd been considering for some time. He and Caroline travelled out to see him at his Virginia home and a personal relationship that, according to Rotella, has ended up with him learning far more from his complex pupil than the other way around, was born. In those early years, Harrington would read summarised versions of 'Golf is

Not a Game of Perfect' three or four times a week. It helped him to learn and reinforce the key principles in Rotella's book or, as the author terms them, 'Rotella's Rules'. The very first of those rules played footsy with Harrington's golfing senses – "A person with great dreams can achieve great things". In 2009, Harrington estimated that he had read these summarised versions, which he would pen himself, several hundred times.

The psychology of human beings, not just golfers and athletes, has always fascinated Harrington. A peak through his book collection offers a revealing window on the intellectual capacity he possesses and applies to life and golf. His all-time favourite book is 'Being Happy', a soft tome that describes itself as "A handbook to greater confidence and security" and is a straightforward, charming read. "It's general psychology," said Harrington. "I read it when I was 18 and it is very simple. A ten-year-old could read it. There are pictures and diagrams, you could read it in a couple of hours and not want to put it down. There is one particular image of a tombstone that says, 'Here lies the man who was going to be happy tomorrow'. So many great things in it. But so simple."

There is a deeper, more cerebral thinker behind those penetrating eyes though as, on another shelf in his office, sits the book, 'Blink', by Malcolm Gladwell, which considers the merits of instantaneous, snap decisions versus ones made after long deliberation. It is an intriguing, complex topic and it is perhaps no coincidence that a golfer with a reputation for stalling and taking too long before hitting the ball would mull over it. In the weeks after his second British Open triumph, in 2008, he found solace in his quieter moments deciphering and decoding the messages within Nassim Nicholas Taleb's, 'The Black Swan', a heavy, college-level read about unexpected events and how we plan for them and interpret them. Two other books he has read which seem to best reflect his approach to golf are, 'Awaken the Giant Within' by Anthony Robbins, and Daniel Coyle's 'The Talent Code', which, at its core, suggests that innate talent is overrated and can be developed and learned.

Filling his head with diverse opinion is what Harrington is all about. He took a lot, for example, out of sessions with the quirky Belgian sports psychologist, Jos Vanstiphout, in late 1999. The new voice led to a sharp rise in form and, after only months, his second Tour win at the Brazil Sao Paolo 500 Years Open. But it was the influence of Rotella that remained strongest in the early to mid-2000s. When making housing arrangements for the British Open at Carnoustie in 2007, for instance, Harrington insisted on his mental coach staying in the same house. "I play the game full-time by the message of Bob Rotella, I have done for 11 years," he freely admitted in 2009. Rotella certainly took on an intense and intriguing client when he said yes to Harrington's request for help back in 1998. That declaration that he has since learned most from their relationship is unlikely to be mere flattery either. For the most part, he has described himself as a sounding board for Harrington to bounce ideas off. At other times he has been responsible for carefully nudging his highly strung pupil away from the red line of over-analysis, none of which sounds overly taxing or ground-breaking. Yet it would be foolish to think that behind closed doors Rotella hasn't disagreed, butted heads and even argued with one of golf's most stubborn and inscrutable figures.

"Harrington's an interesting character in the sense that he loves to interact, to get involved in a discussion," says Irish caddie Colin Byrne. "You could almost say he loves an argument. I don't know if he truly believes it or not, but he likes being the devil's advocate. There's no doubt you see him around the Tour and he's happy. But he's also a moody guy, like all of them. There are times when he's got the blinkers on and he wouldn't even see you. He'd walk by you. I don't know if he's been trained to mesmerise himself or what he does. Whatever condition he needs to get himself into mentally to focus, which is what it's all about, he seems to be able to do. So you have two sides to him, the jovial, interactive side and then the total, don't get in his head, don't get in his space side because he's not in the mood for that. I've seen Harrington practising before he's going out and the expression was, 'I'm not open to anything here. I'm doing my own thing'. Then you'd see him other times, or when you're playing during an event with him, he'll be more open, but it's on his terms and you know that. You'd know pretty quickly if you were intruding."

In an interview with the *Telegraph* newspaper after the 2010 Ryder Cup, Harrington was honest about his relationship with the game and how he risks being consumed by his own perfectionist tendencies.

The writer suggests that Harrington exhibits an "extreme case of golfing obsessive compulsive disorder". The man himself goes along with that assertion saying, "A perfectionist could also be obsessive, I would say I fall into 'obsessive'." Adding that, "One of the keys to my game is to try to get a good balance. If I didn't have a family, a wife and two kids, I'd be a basket case. I do need the distractions. If I don't have something that keeps me away from golf, I'll keep thinking about golf." He added: "I could just about watch CSI on TV, one hour. And even then, if there was an ad break, I'd struggle not to get up and swing a club. I have to be wary. I try to take eight weeks off during the winter. But, in the first week, I'll take my kids to school, come home for breakfast and find I can't sit there, doing nothing. To be a better golfer, I need to have a break. I have to make sure the game doesn't consume me." Summing himself up, he concluded that, "The hardest thing for me in golf is to stop on the Wednesday before an event starts, and say, 'I'm ready'. It's a lot easier to go to the practise ground and hit more balls."

For the first ten years on Tour, Harrington didn't realise that you weren't meant to wake up tired, that you weren't meant to be drained by the work you did yesterday. After working so closely with Rotella, the penny finally dropped in 2006 about the merits of being fresh for play and trusting the work he'd put in on the range. There were little indicators along the way that a more relaxed approach, in body and mind, was the way forward and not, as he'd struggled to accept, a sign of weakness or neglect. In early October, 2002, he pitched up in Scotland for the Dunhill Links Championship absolutely shattered following his exertions at the Belfry the previous week where Europe had won back the Ryder Cup. For once, he gave the driving range a wide berth that week. He won the tournament, shooting 19 under par. By resting and simply relying on his swing, he had shot four rounds in the 60s, including two 66s. He defied all the logic he'd built up around his game that success would only come by throwing himself at the face of the coal pit and digging it out with his bare hands.

He has never explained exactly why he felt he was so comfortable at Muirfield, that same year of 2002 in the British Open, but all the indicators are that he had similarly cut back on the amount of technical work beforehand and found that he played better because of it. It's likely that he was playing in that almost subconscious mode that Rotella espouses, the 'trusting mode', the same zone of concentration he had entered when seeing off Mark O'Meara in his singles match at the 1999 Ryder Cup. It is the state of mind possessed by a player who has no swing thoughts whatsoever in a round and just trusts in what he has done in practise and allows it all to come together naturally. By 2006, after a complicated process of trial and error, and following much consultation with Rotella, Harrington believed he had finally found the way of summoning the form of 2002. He found that to enter into the state of mind where his instinct flourished and absolutely no technical thoughts existed, he had to make a critical change to his preparations exactly three weeks before a major championship. He found that he had to stop working in the left side of his brain and shift to the right. It meant physically moving, from technical to trusting. As Rotella explains in his 2004 book, 'The Golfer's Mind', "To go unconscious, to play instinctively and intuitively, you must trust your swing".

"Bob Rotella advocates playing the game totally in the right side of your brain," explained Harrington. "If you're practising your technical stuff, you're totally in the left side of your brain. It's not a light switch that you can just switch on and off. You have to actually work hard to get yourself into that right side. The right side of your brain is the feminine side, the artistic side, the one that has feel and flow. You'll make good decisions when you're in that side of your brain. The left side of your brain is your mathematical side, your masculine side, the thinking side. You work things out there. So, if you're working on your technique it's all left brain. A good example of this is, if I stood there on the range, and I've seen this happen to my game, and practised my swing technique and worked hard and broke it down, and then walked onto the golf course, I wouldn't read the greens as well as if I'd just worked in the right side of my brain."

To some, it's a baffling concept. The important thing from Harrington's perspective was that it made sense. And it worked. He viewed his results at Augusta and Winged Foot in 2006 having applied this approach of banishing all technical thoughts three weeks before those tournaments, and committing to a far less intensive build-up, as solid proof of this. "It was only when I settled down about 2006 that I started to...well, what actually happened was, I knew what I'd done (in Muirfield) and I was trying it again," he said. "I was relaxed enough to try it again in 2006. I started going into the majors without any technical stuff, no practise, just warm-up play. And at Winged Foot I played majestic again, tee to green, maybe didn't have the best week on the greens but I played awesome."

Like Ben Hogan, and the closely guarded swing secret it was reputed that he kept, Harrington had devised his own way of extrapolating peak performance from himself in major championships. It was a powerful realisation and one of the most important developments in his entire career, one that left him on the cusp of a major breakthrough approaching 2007.

PART 2 2007

Chapter 4
2007

They could have been having the craic on the Las Vegas strip all over again. Their soft chit-chat felt that comfortable, just two pals shooting the breeze. In actual fact, Padraig and his caddie, Ronan Flood, were standing ankle deep in rough off the 18th fairway at Adare Manor in County Limerick, playing for a place in Irish golfing history. It was the first play-off hole of the 2007 Irish Open title, yet the mood was calm and the conversation easy. Bob Rotella would have been proud of them.

"So, who won the Heineken Cup final yesterday?" enquired Harrington, suddenly remembering that the biggest day in European club rugby had completely passed him by. The answer was Wasps, but Flood hadn't known it at the time either. As they waited on play-off opponent Bradley Dredge to play his lay-up shot on the hazardous par 5 18th hole, there was a brief silence. Then, almost simultaneously, they chimed, "But Chelsea won the FA Cup!"

Padraig and Ronan had been friends for many years but now they were also family. The previous January, Flood married Caroline Harrington's sister, Suzanne Gregan. Padraig was groomsman at the ceremony and he and friends celebrated Flood's last days as a single man with a stag party in Sin City, Las Vegas. Pals from home including ex-Walker Cup player, Noel Fox, and Ronan's brother, Kit, joined them at the MGM Grand. They had a blast. Part of the shenanigans included a couple of rounds of golf. Harrington's 'handicap' for one of the outings was that he was only allowed to play with one club. Methodical as ever, even on a stag do, he left nothing to chance. "I'll probably opt for a seven or an 8-iron," he said beforehand, eyeing up the prospect earnestly. "Something to give me a bit of distance off the tee and some loft out of the bunkers."

Flood joined Team Harrington in 2004 after what was widely reported as the ruthless sacking of Dave McNeilly. At first it was a stop-gap measure, like the stint they'd had together before McNeilly came on board. But things worked out so well that the word 'temporary' was soon dropped from the arrangement. "It was like having Bob Rotella on the bag all day," said Harrington after a composed final round that secured victory at the Linde German Masters in September of 2004. "He just kept coming at me and saying the right things." Putting an old friend on the bag was a risky move. They'd grown up together at Stackstown and were Senior Cup team-mates before either of them had ever dreamed about what the future might hold. Eventually, Harrington had turned professional and Flood, a two handicapper who'd competed in the major amateur tournaments around Ireland, turned to banking. Now here they were, cashing in their chips and putting their lifelong friendship on the line with no guarantees at the outset of a pay-out.

"They've got an interesting relationship," says Colin Byrne. "I had it a bit with Goosen where he expected me to spend time with him in the evenings away from golf, too. I know that Ronan tends to stay in the same hotels as Padraig and they tend to eat together a lot so that's a hard, hard thing to do. Obviously they were friends beforehand but a lot of those relationships don't work. A lot of players have brought their friends out and they'd last a month because they see a totally different side to the person. That doesn't suit everyone. The guy who is the friend is all of a sudden being shouted at, or being treated like a bit of a slave. The whole dynamic of the relationship changes so it tends not to work. They're obviously still together now and, with the amount of time they've spent together, I have to respect what they've done because I find that very difficult, to be working all day with someone and then spending all evening with them and probably travelling with them. You'd never get a break from them and everyone needs a break. Then again, that's probably what Padraig wants. In many ways, as a caddie, you've got to realise what the player wants and what's good for him and give it to him. He (Harrington) wanted that kind of friend as well, and that's what he has with Ronan, on top of the advice he gives on the course."

Gerard Sproule, Harrington's nemesis at the 1987 Connacht Boys' championship, grew up playing with both individuals, player and caddie. He wasn't surprised that their partnership blossomed and bore fruit early on, leading to Flood jacking in his day job and taking up caddying full-time.

"I got a golf scholarship at UCD and Ronan was there too," says Sproule, who hosted Harrington at his home in Sligo during the West of Ireland amateur championship and was afforded the same hospitality himself at the Harrington home in Dublin. "I think they've always got on well. There's a chemistry there. Ronan knows Padraig's game and knows what makes him tick from a golfing perspective as well. Ronan's really a very intelligent guy himself. They're a good match and Ronan can be quite good-humoured as well. So I suppose, in intense situations, that may be of use too."

From Harrington's perspective, it didn't get much more intense than trying to win the Irish Open. Flood's measured approach and calming influence was vital. After 10 years of competing in Irish Opens, Padraig knew the drill; turn up, deal with the media's obsession with why there'd been no home winner of the competition since John O'Leary at Portmarnock in 1982 and then attempt to update the history books himself. He'd had plenty of top 10s and come second twice but still the long wait for a home champion went on. So, after blowing a four-shot lead starting into the back nine that Sunday evening in 2007, and finishing level with Welshman Dredge, he could have been forgiven for losing his cool, for succumbing to the pressure that the eyes of a nation and 23,150 on-site fans exerted upon him. Gary Murphy, who reckons he first came across Harrington at a junior coaching day in Woodbrook in 1986, finished third in the 2008 Irish Open and knows the pressures of competing in front of an expectant home crowd. "There's extra pressure but it's a nicer pressure," says Murphy. "It's certainly not a hindrance. For me anyway, I always felt it focuses the mind more."

Thankfully, for Harrington, he found that same focus that Murphy describes as he homed in on victory in Limerick. He was nervous, more so even than in the previous year's US Open at Winged Foot in which he'd contended. But, with Dredge making a meal of the 18th second time around in the play-off he remained composed and unruffled. The intimidating River Maigue that runs down the left side of the hole played havoc with Dredge's plans. Home favourite Harrington was steadier, if not exactly flawless, and, after laying up into high grass, he chipped to the green to leave a long two-putt for a par. If he could make par it would be enough to take the title. The historians were already readying the record books for a new inscription as Flood pulled out the putter and handed it to his man. It was no ordinary putter, but a Torpedo, the name given to the odd looking piece of torpedo shaped paraphernalia attached to the shaft. "It has two lead weights right at the top just underneath the grip and it changes the dynamics of the putter substantially," explained Harrington, who'd started using it the previous week in the US and knocked in 12 one-putts during a 66 at the Wachovia Championship. The carefully positioned weighting was said to increase the size of the sweet spot on the putter face and was recommended to Harrington by biomechanics expert, Dr Paul Hurrion, with whom he'd formed an alliance.

The marriage of Harrington and biomechanics fits well. Given his unique desire to understand in the most forensic way how every part of his body moves during the physical act of the golf swing, he naturally sought out and embraced those who could provide the most detailed information. For several years now he has worked with experts at the Titleist Performance Institute on his long game and allowed Hurrion to advise him on the putting side of things. It is akin to sending a Bugati Veyron car into a tuning house to be refined and improved. Needless to say, the advice that Harrington receives, and the attention to detail he demands, is nothing short of staggering. He has installed Hurrion's specialist Ball Roll Software on his personal putting green at home in Dublin and, after striking several putts, can watch them back on a computer in 260 frames per second clarity. Almost instantly, he will receive a fully digitised analysis of the ball's journey; its speed, sidespin levels, angular rotation, vertical bounce, launch angle and the point at which the ball reaches true roll. The software is said to have proved to Harrington, already recognised as one of the best putters in the world, that he didn't actually accelerate through the ball as he'd always believed, but maintained the same pace throughout the stroke. Upon such information he would gorge himself.

"A point I would make about Padraig is that he's definitely benefited from technology," says Paul McGinley. "I think he's used his intellect to make sure that technology has worked for him down through the years. He's been very clever with that. Not alone has he changed his technique, as we all know, but he's been very aware of technology and I think the changes in technology have definitely worked in his favour and what he was trying to do with his game. He happens to be in the game at the right time when he's able to use that technology to his advantage. He has the intellect to be able to decipher all the information that's out there and put it to good use for himself and his game."

The Torpedo certainly did the trick in Adare. Two putts for a par 5, along with Dredge's dalliances with the Maigue, were enough to secure the Irish Open title. "Who's the champ? You are, Daddy!" chirped little Patrick Harrington on the 18th green. It was fitting, too, that when the moment arrived, Bob Torrance was a few thousand feet up in the air. For he had been playing the role of chess player for more years than he could remember, shifting the pieces in his fingers below into winning positions. He had done it as coach to John O'Leary in 1982 and now, here was another student of his bridging the 25-year gap. Torrance learned of the news aboard a Ryanair Flight from Shannon to Prestwick Airport when the captain announced it over the speakers. "June nearly leapt out of the seat with excitement," he recalls of his wife.

O'Leary had been on hand to congratulate Darren Clarke on his European Open success at The K Club in 2001 – Harrington finished runner-up – and he was there in Limerick to personally pass the baton over to his fellow Dubliner in 2007. Much had changed since he'd left Nick Faldo, Greg Norman, Christy O'Connor Senior and Des Smyth floundering in his wake at Portmarnock a quarter of a century earlier. Harrington's €416,660 prize money dwarfed the IR£13,386 he'd collected, for a start. The apartment he'd bought in London only cost a couple of thousand more than the prize he collected in 1982.

"It's a different world altogether now," says O'Leary, whose golf career was cut short by back problems. "Sam Torrance used to always say, 'We were lucky because we were around before the popular press became popular'. Now, absolutely everything is blown out of proportion." O'Leary wore a famous pair of black and white trousers when he won his national title in '82. "When we played, you were an entertainer and we were quite aware of that," he continues. "Today, they finish one tournament and they're off immediately to another continent to play. That's a totally different existence to the one we had."

The greatest difference of all 25 years on, and one O'Leary acknowledges, is the modern mindset of Irish professional golfers, they feel that they can take on the world. In the 1970s and 1980s, qualifying for a Ryder Cup was the pinnacle of a player's career. O'Leary played against the Americans himself and was a top European player for a spell. Yet the only major he ever competed in was the British Open. The structures at the time simply didn't allow it. The progression of the European Tour and, closer to home, the extra attention paid to developing young talent by the Golfing Union of Ireland has led to a new wave of excellence and a changing of players' psyche. They don't hope any more, they expect. Harrington was among the earliest beneficiaries of expert coaching and has since been followed through the GUI's system and onto the world stage by players like Graeme McDowell, Rory McIlroy, Michael Hoey and Shane Lowry. "A lot of investment has gone in and the proof of it is what's coming out the far end now," says O'Leary. "What the Irish boys have done in the majors in the last few years is mind-blowing."

In 1982, O'Leary had his own majors; The British Open, the Irish Open and the PGA Championship at Wentworth. As much as things have changed over the years, the importance of the Irish Open to its native players remains as strong as ever. Harrington regarded it as his fifth major, a tournament he had attended as a boy on many occasions. Winning it in 2007 meant everything to him. "I had it in my head that it was quite possible I would lose the head at some stage," he admitted. "I felt the pressure out there more than I would probably at any event. So, yeah, it has to be in my head as the fifth (major), the one I wanted to win. It might not be the fifth hardest tournament to win but it's certainly the fifth in terms of pressure that I would feel, and all the expectation about winning it." Referencing his new, less technical approach to preparing for tournaments he also noted, "I'm better able to manage my game to perform when I need it. It's a definite boost to my confidence that I can come into an event that I want to do well in and perform."

Winning at Adare Manor was the completion of an epic journey, from boyhood days at the Irish Open in Portmarnock to national champion. "This 13-, 14-, 15-year-old boy in Stackstown, I don't think any of us dreamed we were in the presence of a guy who was going to take on the world," says Conor O'Shea, a schoolboy friend at Stackstown. "Back then it was all just great fun, playing golf and following golf. You'd go to the Irish Open in Portmarnock or Royal Dublin and get your autographs off Woosnam, Langer, whoever it was. You'd be looking at them going, 'Well, nobody's ever going to be as good as them'. Then, 20 or 30 years later, you see this bloke doing it, your old pal, and it just leaves you going 'wow'."

Harrington had the same reaction himself. In fact, he predicted in the media tent that he would most likely be 'flat' the following week at the BMW PGA Championship as he came down from the euphoric high. He was as good as his word, shooting a jaded 75, 74 on the weekend in Wentworth. The experience in Limerick had momentarily overwhelmed him. Along with overtaking O'Leary in the record books, he'd also moved clear of Darren Clarke as the most prolific Irish winner in European Tour history. The winner's cheque pushed him through the €15m barrier in official European Tour earnings, making him just the fifth player to achieve that feat behind Montgomerie, Els, Goosen and Clarke. And, on the eve of the event itself in Limerick, he signed a new three-year sponsorship contract with Bank of Ireland worth a reported €750,000 per year. It was said to include 'lavish bonuses' that would kick in should he win tournaments like the Irish Open or, whisper it quietly, a major. "We are very confident that the next few years are going to be very successful for Padraig," tipped the bank's Tom Hayes at the official announcement. "I personally believe that a major is not that far away." It was a solid prediction. After winning his 'fifth major' at the end of that week, Harrington's first real major was very close indeed.

Chapter 5
2007

When the stars align in certain positions overhead and two rare golfing obsessions collide, there is the potential for something truly historic to occur. On a stretch of County Wicklow coastline in the summer of 2007, such a collision of like minds took place. The outcome was that they both got to live out their golfing fantasies for brief, but utterly fulfilling, periods as their respective life's labours intertwined. Pat Ruddy believes there is another explanation for what happened to him and Padraig Harrington that summer, a more straight-forward but hugely connotative suggestion – destiny. "To just drift along in life," recalls Ruddy, "then to come close together with greatness and then move on again about one's life, it was a wonderful thing."

It is a cool, windy morning at the European Club links, the sort that demands an extra layer of clothing and a thick woollen cap before even considering venturing outdoors. After a breakfast of freshly made scones topped with rich cream and strawberry jam, washed down with steaming tea, Ruddy offers a tour of the course. This is his place you see, his personal playground. It has been ever since he scanned Ireland's eastern coastline by helicopter some 25 years ago, spied a plot of links land just south of Brittas Bay where a top-class golf course would sit just nicely, and lived out a dream.

It is a more conventional mode of transport he uses now to showcase what has developed into one of the great links courses of his, or any other, country – a beat-up old Nissan car, almost as old as the European Club itself, but powerful and fit for purpose. The big petrol engine roars into life at the rear of the clubhouse and soon it is scaling dunes and points of prominence where no car was meant to drive but which its owner knows will open up a particular aspect on a certain hole that reveals a picture of pure beauty. Throughout, there is a running commentary. Ruddy has bided his time, he explains. He waited patiently for various plots of adjoining land to become available for purchase so that he may apply the finishing touches to certain holes. He has poured every ounce of himself into this land, designing the layout and manning much of the heavy machinery that dug fairways out of barren seaside terrain. Perfectionism becomes him and the reward has been great; the par 4 seventh hole, for example, where Harrington spent hours practising in the run-up to the 2002 British Open, has been named in the World's 100 greatest golf holes. It is also there on a list of the 18 best holes designed since 1970.

Ruddy has designed many other fine layouts too, at home and abroad, though to pigeon-hole him as a golf course architect would be to overlook years spent covering golf worldwide as a reporter and, likewise, his time promoting various championships. A quirk of eccentricity makes him warm, garrulous company. In front of the 12th green, he turns off the engine and gestures towards the green. It is 127 yards long from front to back, the longest in the world. "Whaddya think?" he blasts, to which there can be only one reply, "Two putts would do nicely every time."

It was while working on and around this 12th green that he first spotted, high in the distance between two dunes, a little platform of land just perfect for a golf green. Like an itch that had to be scratched, he eventually took a digger to the area and, in 1999, Hole 12A was born, a 205-yard par 3 and one of two extra holes on the course. Into the wind, he has seen good golfers hit perfect shots with their drivers and still come up short on the hole. "Tiger Woods stood up there with a 5-iron, into the breeze, and put it to about five foot from the pin," he says, recalling the day his course was graced by a famous fourball – Woods, Mark O'Meara, Scott McCarron and reigning British Open champion, David Duval, shortly before the 2002 tournament at Muirfield. Woods shot a course record 67.

It wasn't until 2006 that this record was in danger of being broken. Keen to add a little intrigue to that year's Irish Amateur Close championship, which the club was hosting, and suspecting that one of the participants was capable of matching Woods' score, the Golfing Union of

Ireland suggested using the same tees that Woods had played from, taking the overall yardage up to 7,355. Off these tees, it is one of the toughest tests of golf in Ireland. Rory McIlroy was the player the GUI had in mind. "Let's have Tiger play in the Irish amateur, that was the thinking, because Rory was already playing like him and I was completely up for this, I could see the connection," says Ruddy, visibly excited by the memory. "McIlroy started at the 10th and was three under at the turn. But he put a ball out (of bounds) at the seventh. Because of that he ended up with a 70. But that was as a 16-year-old, off the back tees."

The following year, another idea from officialdom was floated; seeing as how the amateur championship had worked out so well – McIlroy had won it – how about hosting the 2007 Irish PGA Championship? Ruddy felt an affinity with the competition, which he'd promoted in the past. But it was the guaranteed involvement of Harrington, if it was played on a links, the weekend before the British Open at Carnoustie, that commanded his interest. The inference he took from the discussion was that he was being handed the opportunity to, in some small way, prepare Harrington for the rigours of the Open championship.

"I'd been interviewed for a magazine article some time before by a particular journalist, who had been critical of Padraig quite a bit," says Ruddy. "He said to me, 'Do you have any heroes?' This was well prior to 2007. I said, 'It's more difficult to have heroes as you get older because all these guys doing heroic things tend to be younger, for an old guy to view a younger guy as a hero is a bit of a stretch'. But, having read this fella's stuff, and also sincerely believing what I was saying, I told him Padraig Harrington was a hero of mine. And I meant it because he has never put a foot wrong in any respect, in my view. Personal life, professional life, his attitude towards other people, his attitude towards the GUI. Harrington is a fine upstanding young man, as they said in the old days."

So, he agreed to the task. He would, in his own way, help to prepare Padraig. "I said, inwardly, 'Bring it on, let's go'," says Ruddy. "Boom! Straightaway, I'm thinking, let me at this one because 2002 was still in my head, how he'd done a little work here before the Open in Muirfield and played so well. So I was hugely excited by this, without saying it to anyone in that way. I wouldn't have dreamed of saying it to Padraig, or even talking to him about it, because he's a thoroughbred. You don't start whispering to a thoroughbred. You're only going to be a pain in the butt, and the whole thing is destroyed if you do that. So it was the balance of the championship versus the other thing. I went with the other thing, unless someone would rein me in, which they didn't."

The result wasn't quite carnage, though the course that Ruddy presented for the Irish PGA championship was so difficult that it left many participants just making up the numbers. In the opening round, one player shot 105. Only seven players finished under par with Harrington among a trio of joint leaders on two under.

Without making any major issue of it, Ruddy had travelled over to Carnoustie earlier that spring, twice in fact, to consider the lay-out and the sort of difficulties Harrington was likely to experience along the Scottish coastline and to replicate them on his own course. Rough was lengthened up, fairways were taken in and already slick greens were cut to a championship height. A course widely regarded as angelic suddenly assumed a devilish character. The price Ruddy paid was financial and he experienced a drop in footfall around the place as word spread among the green fee brigade that the European Club was a fine place to lose a dozen Pro Vs. Only someone with complete control and ownership of a course and, more importantly, with a mind to do so, could have set up the course as he did, to alienate so many and to help so few.

"I felt it my job as designer/owner and now part of the triangle (with the Irish PGA and Harrington) to present a links which would – subject to the PGA setting up the tees correctly, and I had no control over that – allow him to go to the Open and feel that he'd played off the same turf, roughly the same nature of greens and the same widths of fairways and penalties for missing them," states Ruddy. "The whole thing was that when others would come to the British Open, from wherever they'd played the week before, they'd be shocked by the presentation of the links with every fairway looking like a ribbon. The idea was that Harrington would look down the fairway and see a ribbon a bit bigger than he saw here. The other thing was that he had to win here because if he went over to Carnoustie as a loser, he wouldn't have been as buoyant perhaps."

The European Club hosted the Irish PGA championship three years running, in 2007, 2008 and 2009 and, throughout, was fully committed to the project of preparing a champion. Lost revenue in green fee income at the height of the season, however, and the burden on members, eventually became overwhelming. Ruddy cited these issues in a letter to the GUI explaining why they'd have to find a new host for 2010. "The time has come," he wrote in that letter, "for our members and guests to have a break and to that end we have begun a severe cutting back of our roughs to accommodate normal humans."

The reaction of frustrated participants, annoyed by the difficulty of his course during the championships of 2007 to 2009 didn't overly concern Ruddy. "In a small country like ours especially, you have competitors and holiday-makers," he argues. "So the holiday-makers get beaten up and they shouldn't cry because they should have the wisdom to know that they're holiday-makers. They're just going to the championship. And if it was said to me that Padraig Harrington would play in this championship, if it was played on a links course before the Open, well, you didn't have to be a genius at cracking codes to see that this man was ambitious and was trying to condition himself. I didn't ask him how serious he was, or anything like that, because I already knew him to be a serious young man from coming here with his dad and so forth, and an ambitious young man. It's great that the age is gone when Irishmen would say they love to keep drinking rather than practising and the sort of 'I lost because I didn't try' approach. It was great to be in an age where there were young men like him putting it up to the elites and saying, 'I am bursting my ass to achieve this goal'. I read it that way, anyway, that he was doing this, and to be able to go along with that was a big deal."

Harrington's progress as a player over the years can be measured through his changing relationship with the Irish PGA championship. Competing in 2007 may have been a means to an ends, a warm-up of sorts for the real event a week later. But, back in 1998, when he claimed his first title, it was a significant achievement for him and he viewed it as a vital step in his overall development. He had won just one professional event on the

European Tour at the time and was ravenous for success at Powerscourt Golf Club where the championship was held. Standing on the 18th tee on the final day he only needed to par the hole to take the title from a chasing posse of Des Smyth, Francis Howley and Michael Bannon, now McIlroy's coach. But he chopped his drive into the deep rough and eventually missed a ten-footer for par, resulting in a four-way play-off. Each of the contestants knew a birdie on the tricky hole would suffice.

Smyth felt nicely positioned to do so, and to win the title for the sixth time, when he landed his approach shot eight feet from the pin. "Padraig hit his approach shot past the hole and he had this horrible 35-foot putt across the green, downhill, right to left," remembers Smyth. "I'm looking at my putt down the hill and thinking, 'I have this'. Of course, your man holed it! But you could see he was going to. I could see the look on his face, you know, the eyes bulging and I'm saying to myself, 'This fucker is going to hole this'. Just up there, in his head, he had it. I laughed to myself because I was an older pro and I had won it already. Naturally, I wanted to win it again but it wasn't life or death for me. His career was only just getting moving and it was life or death for him. I could see it in his eyes."

Smyth had sensed something special about Harrington the moment he came out on Tour in '96, not a raw talent sort of specialness but an inherent determination that he's seen in so few players throughout a lengthy career that has included playing in the Ryder Cup twice and winning the Dunhill Cup for Ireland.

"The minute I met the guy I knew it, you could see the determination in him," says Smyth. "I made it my business to go over and wish him all the best when he was starting out. I could see the determination in him straight away. Very soon after that I started to notice the work rate. It was obvious, the guy never left the range. If he wasn't on the golf course he was on the range, and he was the last to leave it. I remember saying to my wife, 'This guy's gonna go places, he's just got this fire in him'. He never struck me as a guy over-confident. But he struck me as a very diligent, hard worker, who, whatever came his way, he was ready to take it. Now that's different from a guy who struts around with a bit of confidence, that maybe isn't as good as he thinks he is. Padraig gave me the opposite feeling to that.

Padraig never felt he was great but he delivered great things. I liked that about him. He delivered results. Anyone who had that determination and that amount of commitment and that amount of hard work, you kind of felt they deserved it. So I could see the difference between him and other players."

Unknown to Harrington, Ruddy had noticed that difference, too, that vital spark. And it was long before the Irish PGA of 2007, or even that practise stint in 2002. A few years earlier again, he'd been commissioned for some design and construction work at Stackstown Golf Club. One of the days, as he went about his tasks knee-deep in muck, he recalls driving rain coming in off a gusting wind so hard that it stung his cheeks. The other worker with him eventually downed tools and retreated for the sanctuary of the clubhouse. All the while, Ruddy observed a young golfer out practising and fine tuning his swing through the worst of the weather. He later identified the saturated golfer as Padraig Harrington.

The stiff challenge presented at the European club in 2007 was just what Harrington was after, something to really focus the mind. While others floundered, he went one better than his opening 69 with a second round of 68. He couldn't quite shake off old ally and Headfort Golf Club professional, Brendan McGovern, though who clung to him like a limpet all week.

The pair went back a long way. The night before Harrington's first event as a pro, the 1995 European Open at The K Club, he'd received disturbing news that his 60-degree Ping Eye lob wedge was non-conforming. McGovern came to the rescue with a replacement wedge that was legal. Some 11 years on, McGovern wasn't in quite so generous a mood and any affection the pair previously shared was parked at the entrance to the Wicklow venue as a ferocious battle ensued. McGovern's 66 in the third round of a weather-delayed tournament left him two ahead and, for all intents and purposes, locked in a two-way battle with second-placed Harrington who was seven clear of the next man, David Higgins.

Ruddy followed Harrington at various times throughout the week. Even in the final round, as he pitted his wits against McGovern for the national title, he says the Dubliner was a picture of serenity and quiet purpose, a model Rotella student. Ruddy and Irish PGA organisers had considered roping off the fairways to keep the crowds back. But, in the end, they put their trust in patrons not to distract or bother the world's number 10 ranked player who, to his credit, engaged with the spectators.

"It was like going to Lahinch for the South of Ireland championship," recalls Ruddy. "Everybody was walking along with the players and Padraig was that sort of guy that it didn't bother him. He has that huge gift, of being a good communicator. He's not as funny as Trevino but he has that same gift of interacting while still concentrating. It's awesome, that he can be inside his head and outside his head at the same time. Most guys have to get in there and stay in there. Trevino could crack a joke and then, like that, he's gone, into the office and hits his shot. Padraig does that too, only in a more subdued way. He liked that about the week and I was pleased because he was amongst friends. There wasn't a man in Ireland who didn't want to see him win a major."

Harrington and McGovern were tied on five under for the tournament as they began the back nine in their final round. McGovern regained the two-stroke advantage he'd started with after a long putt on the 12th, a development which seemed to draw out the true competitive instincts in Harrington who reached the par 5 13th in two, made his birdie and repeated the feat on 14 and 15 to ease a shot clear. When McGovern bogeyed the next to fall two behind with just two to play the classic match play scenario had arisen. Surely, at two up with two to play, a veteran of Ryder Cup successes and massive tournament wins on both the European and PGA Tours couldn't be caught now?

That was the very notion going around Harrington's own head, however, and one which caused him to lose focus and get complacent. It was like the final few holes of the Irish Youths Championship in 1990 all over again. Feeling the job was done, he stood on the 17th tee box lacking the same killer conviction and studious concentration that had driven him to wrestle back control of the tournament. It is a particularly bad place to stall as the space between the 17th tee box and the green is occupied by the narrowest strip of fairway, the sort a millionaire might land a little two-seater plane upon. Dunes encroach from either side and, in the distance, there is the sight of white horses breaking on the Irish Sea, confirming the wind is going to play havoc with your shot. The voice inside Harrington's mind told him to back off the drive and regroup. But he ignored it, drove into the rough and hacked his next shot into a bush, forcing him to take a penalty drop. By the time the madness was complete and he'd three-putted from the edge of the green, he had taken seven shots and trailed by one going up the 18th. "After the 16th it was over, next thing it's on again," says Ruddy, recalling the frenzied finish. "Brendan played in Tour events for many years and is one of those guys who knew how to play. He's a very proud professional, and a very accomplished professional, so it was no surprise he put it up to him."

But even with a surprise one-shot lead on the 72nd tee, McGovern couldn't finish it off. Ordinarily, the par 4 he made would have sufficed but, with his game face back on, and realising that everything was on the line, Harrington flew the water trap in front of the 18th green with a mid-iron and landed 12 feet from the pin, draining his putt for the birdie he needed to force a play-off. He had wavered briefly but now was redeemed.

"There are moments of truth, are you going to play the shot or are you going to back off?" says Ruddy. "Padraig didn't back off. That's for sure. It's awesome to see it happening. The eyes come out, those expressive eyes and the tongue comes out, but it's especially about the eyes. The hunter's eyes. They come out further and you see that happening. If he could only give himself a bang on the back of the head and get those eyes to come out more often, because when they come out, he's in town. It's like the thoroughbred at the races, he's coming to the last fence and then, next thing, whoosh, good night boys!"

Harrington's unlikely up and down at the 72nd was the explosive climax to the championship because the play-off had hardly begun when it was all over. McGovern took four shots to reach the putting surface when they played the 18th again, requiring a penalty drop after a wayward drive. And when Harrington lagged his third shot to the hole side, the match was conceded.

How things would have worked out the following week at Carnoustie had Harrington not birdied the final hole to secure a play-off is open to conjecture. Golfers rarely achieve major gains out of the blue and the daisy-chain effect of one win spawning another is common. In this regard, that up and down at the 18th may have been the most important, yet most unheralded, of his career. He received a cheque for €12,500 for winning the Irish PGA championship, chicken-feed compared to the near €750,000 Gregory Havret banked for winning the Scottish Open at Loch Lomond that same weekend, but priceless in terms of preparation for a British Open. He had prevailed at a links course that had asked every conceivable question of his game. "You can pocket US$150,000 for finishing tenth sometimes," said Harrington. "But it is not as good as finishing first."

After the prize-giving, Ruddy wished Harrington all the best at Carnoustie and reminded him that, "These things are often decided on a putt, maybe one-hundredth of an inch." He told Harrington, "You can do it," and, perhaps in light of events on the 17th tee box, added the rider, "But concentrate all the way."

"That's all I really said," recalls Ruddy, "that everyone can apply the broad brush strokes but be in town for the little strokes, they're the ones that add up." Ruddy never discussed with Harrington the way the course had been set up that week, with him almost exclusively in mind, or of his own personal pleasure at the role he'd played. In light of events at Carnoustie the following week, he reckons he might never have that chat, that they share an unspoken knowing, which is enough.

"I know and he knows, I think…" says Ruddy, trailing off. "But, look, he did it, he did it all and I wouldn't like to go beyond that .001 per cent that we might have given him. But I burst my ass trying to produce that. Whether it did help or not you can't prove, but one thing is sure, there's a set of stats there which fairly convinced me that something happened."

Destiny? You'd better believe it. Ruddy certainly does.

A week after beating McGovern in the play-off, Harrington would need to get up and down again on the 18th at Carnoustie to get into another play-off, which he did, and which he also won. In front of the 18th green at the European Club is a water feature. It used to be a pond but, taking inspiration from Jean Van de Velde's troubles at Carnoustie's notorious 18th hole in 1999, Ruddy decided to turn it into his own version of the Barry Burn, the wandering creek that would play such a central role in Harrington's own challenge for the Open a week later.

The following year, 2008, Harrington won the Irish PGA championship at the European Club again. This time it was by four shots and, at Royal Birkdale the following week, he won the British Open championship by four shots. Still not convinced about Ruddy's destiny theory? Well, consider the following – months before the idea of staging the 2007 Irish PGA at his club was even mooted, Ruddy was offered €40m to sell his course. The offer was made at the height of the construction boom in Ireland and the plan was to include the course at the centre of an ambitious, high-end development. He thought long and hard about the offer, remembering the early days when he'd cashed in just about every asset he'd owned to create the place. Everything in his name had gone into the pot back then, the pension plan, the fancy car, the mortgage-free home. And here was the payback upon a golden platter, the chance to live out a stress-free retirement of luxury.

He had 40 million reasons to sell but turned it down, reasoning that to sell what he'd spent the greater portion of his life striving for since learning in 1958 about Jack Burke's and Jimmy Demaret's ambitious plans for a Champions' Club in Texas, and taking inspiration from such grand plans, would be to sell himself.

"The only thing I could think of wanting that money for was to build a golf course," he says now, six years later and five since the most spectacular property crash in the history of the state, which has reduced the value of his property by a large fraction. "I'd spent since 1958 meaning to get a golf course of my own, not necessarily even a golf course, just a place to hit balls. That was nearly 50 years of aiming at one spot. Then I'd just got there and to leave it all behind would have been tough. To this day, I'll never know if I was lucky or mad. People will say mad but maybe I was lucky – lucky because this Harrington thing happened and because we consolidated this place in the mind of the world as not a bad golf course. But, certainly nobody in Britain and Ireland I suspect has paid €40m for a golf course. That's what I did by turning it down. But, look at what it's given me. I mean, it's a nonsense in a way, that Tiger Woods, the best golfer in the world, would come into your field of business. That he would have come in and the next thing, Harrington arrives, and you have a chance to play any peripheral part in helping your own do something so special. Wow! If nothing else ever happened again, that's a lot."

Chapter 6
2007

On the eve of the Open championship at Carnoustie, one prediction about the tournament had gained widespread approval – Jean Van de Velde was going to look a whole lot better by the end of the week. The inference was that, after eight years ruminating on the Frenchman's spectacular collapse at the 1999 championship, a new tragic golfing figure would be ordained. Exactly who that would be was for the monstrously difficult links to decide. It definitely wouldn't be Van de Velde again, for he was laid low by a mystery virus the year the championship returned to Carnoustie. It was feared at one stage that he might be battling leukaemia, though he explains now that the illness was eventually diagnosed as a rare 'mutation' of the glandular fever virus he'd previously suffered with. Either way, he didn't play much golf that summer and, despite the desire to return to Angus and purge the demons of '99, he wasn't even up to taking part in the qualifying tournament. It left him to consider the runners and riders at Carnoustie from the comfort of his home. As he did so, he placed new Irish Open and Irish PGA champion Harrington high on his list of contenders. Not for a moment did he consider that Harrington would be the player that followed him into sporting infamy by tripping up along Carnoustie's fiendishly difficult 18th hole.

Harrington and Van de Velde are old friends, as European Tour colleagues in the 1990s whose relationship was smelted in the furnace surroundings of the controversial Ryder Cup at Brookline in 1999. "I know Padraig extremely well," says Van de Velde. "Unfortunately, I don't see him now as often as I would like. He's playing and continuing with his life, and I'm continuing with mine, but he's always been a person that I've enjoyed spending time with. He's a very likeable character and a very interesting person. I think Padraig has always had his feet on the earth. He's very rooted to his origins, very well-mannered, a great guy. I like the fact that, yes, he's got a brain and he thinks about many things. Maybe people possibly think he can over-think things a bit but it doesn't matter to me. He's a guy you can have a good conversation with, and a good debate, whether you agree or not."

As for Harrington the golfer, Van de Velde had been a paid-up fan club member ever since watching him get up and down at the 18th hole in the '99 BMW Championship to seal his place on captain Mark James' Ryder Cup team. Asked when he first suspected that Harrington might be a player with major-winning potential, the Frenchman traces his thoughts back to that terrific chip and putt. "I think, yes, that (major) potential was there from the way he qualified for the Ryder Cup in '99, knowing what he needed to do in the last hole in that tournament in Germany," recalls Van de Velde. "He had to make up and down, on the last hole, from the left-hand side. I remember it perfectly. First of all, he hit a great pitch to about six or eight foot. If he didn't make the putt, and he knew this at the time, he knew where he was on the leader board, he was going to miss out on the team. He knew in which position he needed to finish. He did all he had to do to make the team. That revealed the kind of character that the man has. That's what makes great champions – somebody who is not going to back off when the challenge is there."

Perhaps, that August afternoon in Germany, Van de Velde saw a little of himself in Harrington's dashing finish as he went for it on the 72nd hole of a massive tournament with everything on the line. It was just over a month since Van de Velde had taken his own infamous pot-shot at golfing history and came up agonisingly short, before the eyes of the world at Carnoustie. Possessing a three-shot lead after 71 holes of the British Open championship, he elected to go out in style and finish the tournament off in the same maverick fashion he'd displayed all week. He opted for a driver from the final tee and so began a tale of woe that, in Van de Velde's own estimations, will be retold for another 20 years. After spraying his drive right on a hole that is bisected by the meandering Barry Burn at three different points, Van de Velde got lucky by staying above ground with his ball. With his second shot, he went for the green but his brave 2-iron carved away right towards the grandstand. That was until a piece of metal railing attached to the stand, no wider than the width of the ball itself, got in the way, redirecting the path of the ball and, as a consequence, his life. If the ball had simply landed in the stand, he would have got a drop and almost certainly finished with a double bogey, or better, to win his first major. But it didn't. "We play a game and there's an element of luck," reflects Van de Velde now. "You can say whatever you want, 'Oh, Jean, you should have just hit an 8-iron from the tee, then another 8-iron, then another 8-iron'. Fine. We could all argue that. But, I mean, hitting a piece of metal that was the size of a golf ball, coming backwards, landing in the hazard on a stone and then coming back another 30 yards into a terrible lie! It could easily have stayed in the hazard, then I would have just dropped out. So many things could have happened. It was a traumatic time, a traumatic experience. I'm sure it was hard for everybody that was watching as well. When people see something like that happening, they must think, 'Wow, what is going on here!' It's just, 'Wow!'"

It is fitting that 'flog' is an anagram of golf, for Van de Velde suffered a public flogging that afternoon. Curtis Strange was commentating for a US broadcaster and labelled the Frenchman's folly "stupid", a cutting assertion by the norms of tame golfing analysis. After his ball had ricocheted off the railing into the burn and then cannoned out into thick rough, he went for the green again but decelerated into the ball with his wedge and duffed it into the Barry Burn. The worst of his suffering was still to come.

With the ball sitting atop a layer of silt deposit in the creek, he decided that he could probably play it, like a sweeping bunker shot. But, by the time he had removed his shoes and socks and jumped down into the water, the ball had shifted slightly and was now submerged. As the crowd cheered at the bizarre spectacle, Van de Velde finally saw sense, put his socks and shoes back on and dropped his ball. He hacked his next shot into the bunker from where he got up and down for a triple bogey seven. It did earn him a place in the play-off alongside Justin Leonard and Paul Lawrie but, after all that had gone on he never stood a chance. Lawrie played majestically in the extra holes and took the title. In doing so, the Aberdeen man became the player who won the Open that Van de Velde threw away, a moniker he struggled with and railed against for many years. That was the legacy of the 1999 British Open and the indelible background that Harrington would compete against in 2007.

Gary Player won the 1968 British Open at Carnoustie. "There is nothing charming about Carnoustie," he claims in his book, 'Don't Choke'. "It is a bleak course in a bleak town." He is right, about the town anyway. On a spring morning borrowed from summer, 37 years on from the South African's two-stroke win over Jack Nicklaus and Bob Charles, there is not a cloud in the sky. Yet it is hard to envisage this grey, old town inspiring any poetry. The main street is narrow and claustrophobic, pockmarked with local business that the big chain stores haven't bothered to encroach upon. There is no hint that, just a few hundred yards away, resides a golfing cauldron where dreams have been made and hearts, more often, broken.

Outside the information centre on the main street is a large sign, detailing points of interest around the locality. The main picture on the sign is of Harrington, crouched down, holding the Claret Jug aloft. A little further up the road, back towards Dundee, is the Carnoustie Golf Shop. So golf really does exist here. Turn off left, down Ferrier Street, towards the ocean that runs parallel to the main street, and the scent of golf gets stronger as you pass The Nineteenth, a local watering hole. Walk on still further and there is an almost inner city feeling as you pass through the thick stone tunnel beneath the Dundee to Arbroath railway line. Then, as you emerge back into the light, and the vista of the wide open seafront and golf course comes into view, there is the first tangible sign that there may just be magic in this town after all.

Harrington knows Carnoustie well. It has not always been kind to him. It is likely that his first experience of the venue was while playing there in the 1992 British amateur championship. That was a watershed tournament for the host club. "I came here in 1985 from St Andrews," says course superintendent, John Philp, who was honoured with an MBE after the '99 British Open. "The course hadn't been in great condition but '92 was a turning point in our efforts to turn it around." In 1995 and 1996 it hosted the Scottish Open. Harrington competed in '96, his first season on the European Tour and used the event as a tune-up for the British Open at Royal Lytham and St Anne's a week later. "I remember Padraig sitting on the wall outside the Carnoustie Club, devastated," recalls Philp, a Scotsman full of native bonhomie. "He had just failed to qualify for the final two rounds by, I think, a shot or two. He was absolutely devastated, a young man just out on the Tour. I went down to check around the course that evening and who's on the driving range hitting balls on his own, in the grey dark? Padraig Harrington! After missing the cut. That struck me as, 'There's a man, utterly dedicated and realising that, okay, I'm putting that behind me now. I'm going to make sure I'll be a better player because of it'.. That attitude struck me hard, way back when he was that young."

Fellow professionals were also taken aback by this aspect of Harrington, how he would miss a cut on a Friday yet stay on at the course and use its practise facilities to iron out his faults. Others who missed the weekend action would be taking advantage of the time off, or availing of the quickest possible exit strategy. But Harrington would simply walk on out to the range and perform a rigorous self-examination of his deficiencies that could go on for hours. Only when he felt he had got to the root of his problems, or was bound by some pressing engagement, would he leave. "Nobody else does that," says Stuart Cage, a 1993 Walker Cup partner of Harrington's who was runner-up in the 1995 Irish Open. "Nobody else. If you miss the cut on a Friday afternoon the first thing people do is pack their bags and go. Padraig will go to the range on Friday afternoon and hit balls. That is one thing he does, and I'm not sure I've ever seen it before. But I've seen him do it on a number of occasions." Harrington found something in the sandy dirt of Carnoustie's practise ground after missing the cut at the '96 Scottish Open because he shot a pair of 68s the following week at Lytham and went on to finish tied-18th in his first major.

Carnoustie had clearly sharpened his links game in '96 but, as a course itself, he found it tough to master. He shot 76, 78 there in that Scottish

Open that Philp speaks of. And, after emerging from pre-qualifying at nearby Panmure for the British Open three years later, Harrington tallied three 74s and a 77. In his defence, the '99 Open was played after weeks of unseasonably warm weather that left the rough thick and hazardous and which played havoc with the scoring. Sergio Garcia fell into his mother's arms and sobbed after shooting 89 in the first round. That was Carnoustie, capable of reducing men to tears. Philp was blamed for 'tricking up' the rough with fertilisers and chemicals that year, a charge he still claims was bunkum. He blames the stiff wind that blew across its trademark, narrow fairways for the chaos, particularly on the famous sixth hole, 'Hogan's Alley'.

Even when the wind isn't blowing hard, Carnoustie is not easily tamed, bludgeoning would-be conquerors with a mean spirit that replicates the grim surroundings of the seaside town. "Don't get me wrong, every golf course is difficult," says Van de Velde. "But it has some really strong holes. I have to say that, from 9 to 12, and then as you finish into the breeze, or across the breeze, with 15, 16, 17 and 18, they are savage holes. I don't know any of the links courses up there that are easy, certainly not the ones that are on the rotation of the British Open. But, to me, probably it and Muirfield would be the strongest ones."

The 18th hole is Carnoustie's last, and cruellest, instrument of torture. Put Van de Velde's name into a YouTube search and see for yourself. It is a crude but beautiful former par 5 that was converted years ago into one of the most challenging par 4 closing holes in the game. From the championship tees it stretches out to 499 yards. The out-of-bounds fence all the way down the left which divides the course from its sister track, the Burnside links, awaits a hooked tee shot and explains why so many drives end up flirting with the section of the Barry Burn on the opposite side that divides the 18th from the 17th. The famous creek first comes into play on the 10th hole but poses no great risk to players until the 17th and 18th when it snakes back and forth across the two fairways, heading beyond the out-of-bounds line on the left of the 18th before coming back into play about 15 yards short of the narrow green, the point where Van de Velde jumped in.

"You've heard of Bernard Darwin, the golf writer of yesteryear?" asks Philp. "Well, he had the ideal words to sum up the Barry Burn. He described the Barry Burn as, and to me this is just brilliant, the 'ubiquitous circumbendibus'. Now think about that, the ubiquitous circumbendibus! It described in two words this serpentine thing that winds its way every way between these two holes, the 17th and then the 18th. It is everywhere and it is bendy. Perfect!"

Van de Velde played 71 holes of brilliant golf in '99. But the 18th, with the Barry Burn coiled and poised, ate him up.

Unbeknownst to many, it had bitten Harrington badly over the years, too, on several occasions. He closed out the '99 Open with a double bogey on the hole. But the incident that affected him deepest occurred seven years earlier, during the 1992 British Amateur championship when he hooked a crucial shot out of bounds on the 18th. It is easily done. There is just 18 yards between the left edge of the green and the out-of-bounds line. It is an amazing statistic that, in the nine times Harrington has played the 18th hole, between the 1999 and 2007 Open championships, he is a collective 10 over par. He has made par there just twice in that period. "Ah, give me a break!" exclaims Van de Velde, defending Harrington's reputation against the damning statistic. "It's a brutal hole. Padraig is 10 over par, yes, but 10 over is not that much of a disaster for nine times there. It really plays between a par 4 and a par 5."

With all that history playing on his mind, more drama on the 18th was perhaps inevitable for Harrington in 2007. For his part, Van de Velde had his friend marked down as one capable of coping with the stiffest of tests. "You've got to think that, if you were put in a position where your life depended on somebody making a five-footer for you, you probably would put Padraig in the top three people you'd want putting for you," says the Frenchman, now a popular TV analyst. "He's smart, he's a great player. He can work the ball any way. His short game is phenomenal and to be able to contend at that level you need to have that sort of game. You can't rely on hitting great shots one after the other. Going into majors you know you're going to have bad patches when you are going to be frustrated. In major championships and, particularly the Open, you always know that there's a time when the wave is going to come at you and try to drown you, and you've got to survive that with what you have. He's got the ability of making the shots and he's also got a tremendous temperament and the ability to make up and down from anywhere you can imagine. That is a great combination. I don't know how much more compliments I can give him without sounding like a sucker! But that's truly what I believe about Padraig. I believed it before the 2007 Open and I still believe it."

Playing like a major champion and thinking like one, it was time for Harrington to tackle his Carnoustie demons.

Chapter 7
2007

Monday

On the first morning of British Open week, Nick Faldo and Seve Ballesteros enjoyed a working breakfast with journalists in the Carnoustie club house. They were promoting the Seve Trophy, which they would contest later that year as non-playing captains at The Heritage resort in Ireland. Between them, they possessed 11 major titles and, given the week that was in it, were asked why they felt no British, or indeed European, player had won a major since the Open was previously held at Carnoustie, eight years earlier. In that time, 31 majors had been contested with Americans coming out on top in 22 of them. The rest of the winners hailed from South Africa, Fiji, Canada, New Zealand, Australia and Argentina. Not one was European, let alone British. According to Faldo, it was because his successors were 'too chummy' with each other. They 'are all having lunch together', he said, contrasting this against the apparently more sombre existences of the leading players of his generation, like 'Seve, myself, Langer, Woosie, Sandy Lyle and Olazabal' who chased major silverware with a blinkered, tunnel vision at the expense of close personal relationships. Faldo maintained that he and his peers kept their cards close to their chests and were the better off for doing so. "The bottom line is the six players I've mentioned won 18 majors and on the other side you have none," he said.

These days, Faldo could be described as a bit 'chummy' himself, rarely in less than loquacious mood when charming US TV viewers in his role as silver-tongued golf analyst. As a player, though, he was moody and introverted, often described as a 'loner' who got on with his own game and wasted little time buttering up his rivals or the press. It was an approach that served him well as, with half a dozen major titles to his credit, he is up there with Harry Vardon and Seve as one of the greatest European golfers ever. The performance of his European team in the 2008 Ryder Cup at Valhalla, however, indicates that his outlook on modern performance, and what it takes to win, may be a little out of touch with reality.

Eschewing the success of predecessor Ian Woosnam's arm-round-the-shoulder strategy of 2006, captain Faldo went in the opposite direction and told his European players, including Harrington, to prepare for the Ryder Cup as they would any normal tournament, which was as individuals. It appeared to be born of the same sentiment he expressed at Carnoustie, that team-room back-slapping and high-fiving was all very well but nice guys generally finish second while Ben Hogan and Tiger Woods make off with the trophies. What transpired, however, was that Faldo sent out a team of individuals in Valhalla who lacked overall leadership and were comfortably beaten. "We weren't a team," reflected Harrington of the experience. As if to hammer home the folly of Faldo's rant about 'chummy' European players, seven of the next 18 major championship titles would be annexed by Europeans. And Harrington would be central to the turnaround.

Tuesday

Faldo's observations left the top British and European players with the task of sticking their chests out throughout Tuesday and defending their impugned reputations. Harrington, fourth favourite to win the tournament, offered a typically thoughtful response to the claims, while attempting not to tread on Faldo's toes in the process. "Does a person want to be... How do you want to live your life?" he asked pointedly. "As much as I want to win a major, you don't want to... I don't know how to say... Look, we all have different ways of going about our things. I don't believe any of the players, just because they're nice guys, that they can't win a major. Sure that doesn't stop you winning a major."

Whether or not Harrington was in Faldo's thoughts, only he knows. The effervescent Irish man certainly fitted into the category of 'nice guy' and, over the years, has gone out of his way, within reason, to answer any requests made of him. These requests, usually for a piece of his time, increased as his profile soared in the early to mid-2000s. One such call came from the Dublin football team in 2004, a side Harrington may have been part of had golf not intervened in his life.

Paul Caffrey was part of Dublin's management team at the time and explains that they asked for a ten or 15-minute motivational speech from the world's tenth- ranked golfer, to rally the players early in the new season. He stayed for nearly two hours. "He explained that he was an ordinary golfer, talented, but ordinary," recalls Caffrey. "He reckoned he wasn't extraordinary, not compared to the talent of players like Darren Clarke. But he acknowledged that he was the hardest-working professional that was out there. And he said he'd been the hardest-working amateur as well. So his point was that the reason he had got to the level he'd got to, was through pure persistence, hard work and dedication. They were the things that he enthused about, dedication to your game, self-analysis, setting goals for yourself. It was no magic wand theory he was coming in with, just graft, graft, graft. But I have to say he was hugely admired by everybody in that room. He fielded a questions and answers session then which went on for about 40 minutes. I think Jason Sherlock asked him about ten questions! We all walked away thinking it had been a pretty phenomenal discussion."

The really interesting thing was that, for the first few minutes as Harrington addressed the players, he was noticeably nervous and jittery. He was outside his comfort zone, staring back at a room full of highly tuned and ambitious young footballers. "I'd say it was early in terms of Padraig going out doing these public talks and maybe himself, given his own dad's background, he was a bit in awe coming into a Dublin dressing room and giving a talk," says Caffrey. Harrington would never have admitted it but he'd probably have preferred to have been at home that day, spending time with his young son or even practising, instead of breaking out in a cold sweat in front of a room full of strangers. But he put himself out. Maybe he was a little too nice, a bit 'too chummy'. But, like he said in Carnoustie, it's about how you want to live your life.

He gave another speech on the Tuesday evening at Carnoustie, at the Association of Golf Writer's annual banquet. It was described as a 'moving oratory'. This time, his subject was Bob Torrance, who'd been handed a distinguished service to golf award. Harrington regaled the gathering with a story about workaholic Torrance who once boasted, "I've just had a personal best on the range – fifteen and a half hours. I started at 5.30am and finished at 9pm". Then came Torrance's own speech, which he admitted was the first he'd ever given in public. Halfway through he left the podium, kissed his wife June and returned to finish. "That's not just the most romantic thing he's ever done – it's the only romantic thing he's ever done," she smiled. It was a grand night and the Scot described the award as "one of the proudest moments of my life". Yet, within days, he would enjoy an even prouder moment as all the hours he invested in fine tuning Harrington's swing, over nearly ten years, paid out a stunning dividend. "I first saw Padraig as an amateur at Dornoch," Torrance revealed in a 2008 interview. "I asked someone who the young guy was and he replied, 'If you want someone to hole putts for your life, that's the man'."

Wednesday

Harrington met Paul McGinley in the early afternoon for a final practise round before the championship began. They skipped the first hole, a relatively straightforward 405 yard par 4, and began instead on the second, a tough dog-leg par 4 of 460 yards, named Gulley. Using an old driver with just seven and a half degrees of loft, which he'd put back into the bag after breaking his normal club, Harrington drilled a penetrating low drive out over Braid's Bunker and into pole position to attack the long, narrow green. He would eventually make a routine par that gave little indication of the storm he was about to whip up in the coming four hours or so.

McGinley and Harrington went back a long way, longer than either of them even realised. As kids, they were raised in blissful ignorance of one another in the Dublin suburb of Rathfarnham before their paths finally crossed as students at Colaiste Eanna, the local secondary school. "I remember a GAA training session when I was on the school senior team and he was on the junior team," recalls McGinley, almost five year's Harrington senior and a fine Gaelic footballer until a knee injury forced him to turn to golf. "He was playing in goals. That's actually what I remember mostly about him from then, he had this red tracksuit that he used to wear all the time and throw himself around the goals in. To be honest, I was aware of him rather than knowing him when we were in school."

It is truly an amazing coincidence that two golfers, who would go on to play together in the Walker Cup, World Cup and Ryder Cup grew up just a few hundred metres from each other. "Yeah, very ironic, yeah," agrees McGinley. "Incredible, really. He lived in Ballyroan Road, I lived in Barton Drive. As the crow flies it's less than a mile apart."

Though they didn't know each other for the first 20 years or so, the pair would make up for lost time, firstly, as competitors, then as partners in both the amateur and professional ranks. By the time they reached the back nine at Carnoustie in their practise round on Wednesday, they exchanged knowing glances about each other's respective games, which they realised were in good shape. The following day, McGinley opened with three birdies in his first four holes and finished day one of the Open in second position after a sparkling 67. It was telling then that, even by those lofty standards of excellence, he still hadn't been able to match Harrington's scoring in the practise round. In a 12-hole stretch between the fifth and 16th holes on Wednesday, Harrington had fired off seven birdies and an eagle, finding the sort of groove before a major championship that he could only have dreamed about. He still wasn't happy, though, and, in a strange sort of way, perhaps that was a good thing. For, as he has always admitted himself, he has never had much success with confidence, often producing his best scores in spite of his swing as opposed to because of it. On this occasion, he complained that he was coming out of some shots too early and losing them to the right.

When he and McGinley were through with the round, he hit the range for an hour. He tried to keep technical thoughts to a minimum. On the eve of the British Open it was all about finding a level of feel and tempo that he was comfortable with. "I have learnt over the years that things can feel bad on a Wednesday and, by Thursday morning, they are back to normal," he told reporters.

Thursday

There are some shots in golf that you'll only ever find on a links course. During his amateur career, Harrington attempted to find as many of these as possible, throwing down balls in wicked lies and awkward positions when out practising to prepare himself for whatever tournament play might throw at him.

"You'd be playing in a foursomes match and he'd be in the rough somewhere," says Jody Fanagan, who formed a near unbeatable amateur partnership with Harrington that took them to the Walker Cup together in 1995. "Now, you know the way the rough grows so wild on links courses, the grass might be growing across you or into you or whatever, but he'd always say, 'Okay, this is the way the ball is going to come out'. It was amazing that he'd always know, but he would, because that was the way he'd practised it. For most of us, you went to a tournament, went back to work, went on to the next tournament and that's how it was. But he would stay on whenever he got the chance and keep practising all these weird shots. So, that when it came to it, in the crucial situations, he knew what way the ball was going to come out." Harrington was presented with one of these difficult situations just two holes into the 136th Open championship. The old cliché holds true – that you can't win a major on a Thursday afternoon but you can sure lose one.

Harrington sensed the potential to put up a disastrous early number in the tournament as he found his approach shot had landed tight up against the left edge of the greenside bunker on the left of the second hole. There was no way to get his club at the ball, at least not by normal right-handed means. So he improvised, twisted the face of his wedge around and began taking full practise swings left-handed. It was a risky shot with a low margin for error, and the chances of the ball remaining in the bunker or shooting 20 yards over the far side of the green were about equal. But, drawing on all those years of experience and practise, he carefully manufactured a swing that shot the ball into the opposite face of the bunker and hopped it out onto the green. He required two putts to get down for a bogey but, in the circumstances, it felt more like a birdie.

David Higgins was one of the first starters on Thursday, rising at

4.30am to be in position for a 5.52am tee time. The Kerry man, who beat Harrington twice in major domestic amateur championship finals in 1994, shot a 79 and was left battered and bruised by a course dubbed 'Car-nasty'. "The weather that day reminded me of going back to the amateur days, of the likes of myself and Padraig playing in Lahinch, Portmarnock or wherever we were," says Higgins. "It was real Irish weather. Looking back now, you can see why the Irish lads did well that week and why they often do well, like Darren Clarke winning it a few years later. We certainly had an advantage playing in that kind of wet, damp weather and Padraig always did well in the Dunhill Links Championship as well. It was just really difficult, very demanding and, in those situations, you have to be strong mentally and just get stuck in. You're going to hit bad shots but you have to battle on." The bogey at the second was Harrington's only dropped shot all day as he braved the cold, wind and rain of a Scottish summer's afternoon and invented shots to get himself out of sticky situations. It must have felt a lot like being back at the West of Ireland amateur championship all over again, the site of his first big amateur win in 1994. That competition is played around Easter each year over the Rosses Point links. Snow and hail are regular obstacles to be overcome and Harrington would laugh to himself each year as amateurs turned up at the gruelling early season event with little or no winter practise behind them and shot in the 80s and 90s.

"Of course those experiences stood to him going to a place like Carnoustie," says Higgins. "The big thing about professional golf is hitting shots that you're comfortable with. Nobody likes hitting shots they don't actually see or feel. I think that's why Irish guys do well in bad weather. It's just kind of an instinct thing where you go back to doing what you did when you were younger, at places like Rosses Point. You see the shot. It's not a mechanical shot, it's more a feel shot. And you can't teach that to guys. We grew up playing in that and you learn the different ball flights and strikes. I think that was definitely a huge advantage for Padraig and the Irish fellas going into tournaments like that."

Harrington's opening 69, that included three birdies and just the one bogey, left him sitting pretty on two under par. The fact that McGinley scored two better than him, and that an amateur named Rory McIlroy carded a 68, meant there was no great fuss created about the score which left him four shots back from leader Sergio Garcia. "I did a lot of good things and 33 for the back nine is pretty good," he said before heading back to Poppy House, the bed and breakfast just minutes from the course on Dalhousie Street where he'd been staying since the previous Sunday with his family and Bob Rotella.

Friday

Inside the pro shop at Carnoustie, on the wall across from the main counter, hangs a putter, framed and enclosed in decorative casing. It is the Never Compromise putter used by Jean Van de Velde in the 1999 championship. "Jean completed the four rounds in a total of 290, which included 101 putts," it says on an accompanying plaque. An average of 25 putts per round – better than nine one-putts each day – is some achievement around Carnoustie and a display of excellence unfortunately eclipsed by his difficulties at the 18th hole.

As Van de Velde put it, there comes a time in all major championships when the 'wave' will hit you. All that stands between you and the middle of the chasing pack is a hot putter. Good putting can hide a multitude of sins further away from the hole, something that Harrington found to his pleasure as he attempted to back up his opening day 69 with another solid score. His driving was shocking that second day. The push shot he'd battled against in the practise round with McGinley had somehow turned into a hook, the loose shot that pros fear most as it has the potential to do most damage. He was hooking all of his shots but by far the worst offender was the driver, which, with only a few more degrees of loft than his putter, was an unforgiving tool. Every time he pulled it out, he feared the ball going left and the day turned into one long battle not to shoot himself out of the tournament. He only just avoided the out of bounds after a pull on the par 3 eighth where the pin was tucked temptingly in against the left edge of the green, about 20 yards from the OB line. He went left again, into the sand trap beside the par 5 ninth green and had to take a drop after a terrible drive on the 10th. Another hooked tee shot let him bunkered off the tee on the famous Spectacles 14th hole and he was back in the sand with his drive on the 15th. When he finally drove off on the 18th, where out of bounds awaits anything hooked, a big push right that ended up on the 17th was at least understandable, if hardly acceptable.

The tale of wayward hitting is out of sync with the widely held opinion that Harrington must have been swinging at his very best all week to have scored so well over the four days. But the truth is that, on Friday at least, an excellent display of chipping and putting to almost rival what Van de Velde conjured in '99, bailed him out. In the first 36 holes, he needed just 55 putts. "Myself and Padraig were working on something, a good while after Carnoustie," says Bob Torrance. "I was looking at his swing and I said, 'That was just like your Carnoustie swing'. And he said, 'I never want that swing again'."

Torrance had grown used to such comments. During the 2002 Ryder Cup at the Belfry, Harrington had also felt he was struggling and asked captain Sam Torrance, Bob's son, to be left out of the Saturday morning session. He spent hours on the range and in the afternoon partnered Colin Montgomerie to a 2&1 win over Phil Mickelson and David Toms. Still things didn't feel right though, specifically his transition from backswing to downswing. "He got two buggies down to the practise ground that evening, put the head lights on and that was it," says Torrance. "It was dark but we were up there until 10, 11 o'clock at night." The next day, Harrington beat Mark Calcavecchia 5&4 in the singles. "He said to me, 'Ah, Jeez, Bob, I played rubbish'," smiles Torrance. "He'd just beaten one of the best players in the world 5&4 and he says, 'I played rubbish'. How could you say that? Maybe things just didn't feel right to him but the shots were all right."

Harrington felt the same again at Carnoustie after a day of missed fairways and great escapes. He shot a creditable 73, just two over par. Given both the poor conditions and the state of his long game, it could have easily been a 75 or 76. That afternoon, he hit the range again. Wilson built a driver on site for him, with an extra degree of loft, and it worked a treat. After a couple of hours he was hitting it long and straight again and the hook was eliminated.

Saturday

Harrington finished 'moving day' as he started it, six behind pace setter Garcia. Despite the feeling of standing still on the leader board, it was a day of veritable gains, some more tangible than others, as he shot 68, to sit among a clutch of players, including McGinley, on three under par for the tournament, joint third position. The day started for Harrington with a birdie, one of the most important holes of his entire weekend. It was his first since finishing up on Friday evening with a double bogey. For all of his good work with the putter on Friday, he'd missed a bogey putt of just 20 inches on the 18th after what seemed an eternity of standing and deliberating over the ball.

After a day of grinding it was a sickening blow and he dropped from under par in the overall tournament, always a nice psychological position, to level par. Worse still, the 18th had tripped him up again, indicating that it now held some sort of debilitating force over him as the weekend approached. That evening, Rotella got to work. "One missed putt isn't going to affect the outcome of this tournament," he stressed, over and over and, when Harrington opened with that birdie on Saturday morning, it was clear he'd regained his focus. He followed it up with three pars before birdieing the fifth and adding another at the sixth, the famous par 5 Hogan's Alley. A level par back 9 ended with a morale boosting par at the 18th and, while no ground had been made up on Garcia, there was at least just one other player now between Harrington and first position.

In outright second place was Steve Stricker, who'd fired a course record-equalling 64 to haul himself into contention. But it was a fleeting show of genius from Stricker and Harrington was confident of reeling him in on Sunday to put the pressure on Garcia. "I actually picked Padraig Harrington to win on that Saturday night," says Van de Velde. "When I don't play golf I usually don't watch it on TV. But I remember watching a bit of it on Saturday, and, of course, Sunday. But, on Saturday, believe it or not, I told everyone who wanted to hear it that Padraig was going to win." Strangely, so did Harrington. Where once self-doubt existed in the mind of a player who had aspired to no greater station than journeyman professional, now there was a striking clarity about his prospects. He would win the British Open and, like Van de Velde, he was telling it to anyone who cared to listen. He gave the range a miss after the third round, something he'd agreed to do if in contention for the tournament, and spent the night with family and friends.

Throughout his career, he's strictly adhered to a policy of not disclosing his personal ambitions. At the start of each season, for example, he would power up his laptop and jot down his targets. But they would be for his eyes only. The notion of actually predicting victory at any stage was anathema to him. So, when he spoke on Saturday night of how he was going to win the British Open the following day, those closest to him were shocked. "I hope you've taken Monday off work," he told one friend, implying that his pal would be partying deep into Sunday night. "At first, Padraig said it in a joking tone," revealed Rotella in his book, 'Your 15th Club'. "But as he repeated it to me and to others I could tell that he was trying the idea out, not only on his friends, but on himself. For these folks who knew him well it was a startling statement. Padraig had always been one to shy away from predictions about himself, particularly predictions of victory. But here he was doing precisely that."

Rotella stood back and listened. Normally he'd discourage the sort of predictions that might heap unwanted pressure on a player and distract from the important business of routine and acceptance. But after a week in Harrington's company at the house they shared together, just a few minutes from the course, he knew his man was in the right frame of mind. At one stage that week, Harrington confided that he'd entered that zone of 'soft focus' on the greens where he was so 'into his target' that he was simply swinging and holing. He was allowing the putting stroke to come almost instinctively to him. The bookies still reckoned he was a 20/1 long shot for victory but to those around him he was perfectly positioned to strike decisively the following morning.

Later in the evening, Harrington advised Rotella of a change he was going to make to his game on Sunday. He would stick to one specific shot shape all afternoon, a draw, which he felt came most naturally to him. Under the sort of pressure he expected, it would be a familiar feeling that he could lean upon to support his charge for victory. Rotella told him it was a wise move.

Des Smyth had been in with a shout of winning the 2002 British Open himself, for a while at least before winding up 28th. That turned out to be the last of Smyth's 22 appearances in a tournament he came closest to winning in 1982, when he finished fourth. On the eve of the final day's play in 2007, he couldn't help thinking of Harrington and, specifically, an incident at the Boyne Valley Hotel in Drogheda just a few months earlier, in April. He'd asked Europe's Order of Merit winner to be his guest of honour at the Des Smyth Drogheda Youth Foundation's annual gala ball, just after the Masters. An appearance fee was never suggested by Smyth nor asked for by Harrington, who turned up resplendent in a black suit, white shirt and bow tie and gave of his time freely. "He sat up on stage and must have talked for an hour," says Smyth. That wasn't what struck him, though, on the Saturday night in July when he recalled the occasion. It was what Harrington had said when asked about how he thought he'd fare at the British Open after a good showing at the Masters that was foremost in his memory. "He actually told everyone that night that he fancied himself for the Open at Carnoustie," recalls Smyth. "I just hope they all backed him when they had the chance."

Sunday

When Torrance began working with Harrington he crushed his new pupil with his opening observation, "You're never going to swing it like Hogan." Aware of Torrance's reverence towards the American, Harrington was cut by the remark. But what had been taken away in one hand was restored by the other as Torrance followed up with, "You're just going to have to hit the ball more like Sam Snead."

Harrington found himself straddling the legacies of both players on the front nine of his final round at Carnoustie as he swung it like Snead and scored like Hogan. A full 54 years since Hogan had shot 34 for the opening nine en route to winning his third major of 1953 – he didn't compete in the US PGA because it clashed with the British Open – and completing the 'Hogan Slam', Harrington would go one better with 33. "Hogan wasn't frightened of winning and Padraig's got that too," says Torrance, raising his finger to his heart. "He's got it in here."

Having tracked Hogan around Carnoustie in '53, Torrance now stood behind Harrington on the range before play began on Sunday and said little, allowing his player to slip into his own relaxed zone. Harrington had woken up in the middle of the night with a neck spasm but his mind was set at ease as he made it through his warm-up and practise routine pain-free. He was ready for play and when he demanded his five wood off the first tee, an ambitious play given the proximity of the solitary fairway bunker to his likely landing spot, he displayed a confident state of mind. He nailed the tee shot and eventually tapped in for a par 4 that steadied any lingering nerves.

Overhead, the clouds cleared after a watery start to Sunday and Carnoustie was bathed in sunlight. Harrington birdied the third after a big drive before stepping into the shoes of Hogan on the sixth for his second birdie.

Back in '53, Hogan had entered Scottish golfing folklore by driving down the left of the long par 5 between a couple of pot bunkers, in the middle of the fairway, and an out-of-bounds fence barely 25 yards to the left. Before then, everyone had gone right of the two bunkers, taking the out-of-bounds out of play but leaving a much tougher, blind second shot into the green over gorse and Jockie's Burn. In 2007, the fairway was cut so as to encourage courageous drives down the left, though it was still a high-risk shot. Anything hooked toyed with a two-shot penalty. Harrington played an aggressive drive left and was rewarded as he found the ideal position down Hogan's Alley, allowing him to reach the green in two and pilfer another birdie. When he holed for his third birdie of the day on the ninth from 15 feet, he closed to within one of a stuttering Garcia. A magnificent short iron on the 11th then sealed his fourth birdie and left him and the Spaniard tied for the lead.

David Higgins was already back in Ireland having missed the cut despite a good second round of 71 and was left to ponder the sort of pressure that must be bearing on his long-time colleague, who had moved into contention on the back nine of the oldest major in golf. "I honestly have no idea what that pressure must feel like," says Higgins. "I've never been in that situation where I'm trying to win a major. I can only imagine it's pretty nerve-wracking." Nobody knew better than Higgins that Harrington hadn't simply arrived at the moment however. While the young Argentine, Andres Romero, had emerged from left field as a possible winner after a blistering run of 10 birdies in 14 holes, Harrington had paid his dues as a seasoned professional, slowly but surely building his career towards this point. A full 20 years earlier, he had given an indication of his realisation of the fight that lay ahead of him, stunning GUI coach Howard Bennett as a 16-year-old with the assertion that, "As iron sharpens iron, so one man sharpens another".

At almost the same time that Harrington was draining an eagle putt on the par 5 14th, following a brilliant long second over the Spectacles bunkers to the green, Romero was doing his own Van de Velde impression, blasting a 2-iron off the walled face of the Barry Burn on the 17th and watching as his ball flew away out of bounds. The South American double-bogeyed the hole and bogeyed the 18th to leave himself on six under. Harrington, nine under overall, led the tournament. Garcia pegged him back with birdies on the 13th and 14th but a dropped shot at the next handed the initiative back to his former Ryder Cup team-mate who tapped in for pars on 15, 16 and 17, each hole carrying the potential for ruination. As Harrington made his way to the 18th tee box he was leading by one again.

It is just after 9pm in Russia when Stephen Dundas answers the phone at his splendid home outside Moscow, three hours ahead of the clocks in his native Glasgow. The passing of time since he won the British Amateur Championship as a teenager at Carnoustie in 1992 has been good to him. He looks as fit today as when he became the first Scot in 35 years to annex one of the world's most prestigious amateur titles. In achieving that feat in '92, he earned himself a place at the British Open and the US Masters. But it was a career in coaching he ultimately pursued and he is currently Director of Golf at the luxurious Pestovo Golf and Yacht club.

He is warm and courteous and, having once put his hand up as the great white hope of Scottish golf, he jokes that it is only from time to time now that his phone rings with requests to discuss that amateur win.

He reveals how that week started with a private and rare prediction to his father, much like Harrington's before the final round of the Open, that he would win the tournament. Dundas was as good as his word in '92 and, as the likes of Lee Westwood, Gary Wolstenholme and Ireland's Raymie Burns fell by the wayside in the match play format, Dundas virtually cantered to victory, beating Stephen Gallacher in the semi-final and overcoming Bradley Dredge 7&6 in the final. The toughest match he encountered throughout, and the one he should have lost, was against Harrington.

"I think Padraig was the only one I went to the last hole with at Carnoustie," says Dundas, who remembers the fourth-round match vividly. "I was playing well all week, really good and was two up after nine, then I just lost my rhythm. I missed a little 18-inch putt on the 15th and that put Padraig one up. That was the first time all week I'd been down in a match. Then he hit an awesome shot at 16, the long par 3, a little four wood or something to about 10 feet. I landed in the bunker and chipped out to just inside him, about eight feet. He left his putt short, which would have put him two up, and I got mine. Then he kind of just screwed up the last two holes. He went six-six. I won them with two fives and finished one up."

Losing that match at a time in his career when he was showing strong consistency on the amateur scene, but without being able to apply the finishing touch, upset Harrington greatly. "I've always looked at that as being one of the tougher moments of my career," he admitted. It was an incident on the 18th hole, when the match was at all square and perfectly balanced, that affected him most. He had drilled a solid drive to the fairway, just short of Johnny Miller's Bunker before coming to realise that negotiating the Barry Burn off the tee is only half the battle on the treacherous final hole. Weighing up the proposition of shooting to a narrow green that is bunkered on either side, with out of bounds tight on the left and the burn short, he pulled out a 6-iron and clasped it nervously in his hands. That match was all square.

"He has probably never hit as bad a shot since," recalls Dundas of what transpired. "It didn't even land in bounds. He missed the green by probably 40 yards with only a 6- or a 7-iron from the middle of the fairway. Obviously for me that was good but, for Padraig, it wasn't. It was just one of those bizarre situations that fell in my favour. He hit a shot that he probably would never have hit in any other circumstances. From what I remember the pin was back right, probably a similar position actually to where it was during the last day of the Open. But, as I said, it didn't even land in bounds. It was just one of those freak shots. It happens from time to time."

It was a self-inflicted wound that never truly closed and Harrington's record of playing the 18th hole in 10 over par throughout the 1999 and 2007 British Opens, even allowing for its extraordinary difficulty, can be traced all the way back to that day in 1992. During his third round in 2007, he boomed a drive from the championship tees just over 300 yards to the front of the same bunker he'd skirted with in '92. When he reached his ball, the memory of the dreadful 6-iron came flooding back. "I think it's sitting in the same divot," he said to his caddie with gallows humour. This time, he hit an 8-iron, instead of a 6, but the result was almost the same as, in his own words, the ball was once again 'heading out of bounds but somehow landed softly' and stayed in.

Early on in Open week, Harrington and Rotella discussed the 18th hole, the inherent brutality of it and how all of the history associated with it, his own and that of Van de Velde and others, might best be dealt with. Rotella's conclusion was that routine and good planning were vital to help reduce the variables that might lead to disaster. For example, an iron could be taken from the tee if he was in a comfortable position. Harrington concluded the talk by telling Rotella he felt he had an advantage over the rest of the field because of his experience of the hole and indeed the course. Harrington had remained blissfully ignorant of what those around him were doing all day Sunday, until the 14th hole. Flood handed him a five wood on the tee. They had previously agreed that he'd only hit a driver if he was more than three shots off the lead. Immediately, he realised he was in contention. He still made eagle anyway and, in doing so, took centre-stage in the tournament.

The pre-arranged plan for the 18th was to hit driver from the tee if he was within a shot of the lead, either leading or trailing. So, with a one-shot lead after 71 holes, he pulled the club out as planned. After tossing some grass up in the air, however, he noticed that the wind was blowing right to left, pushing a straight shot towards the out of bounds line left. He decided to hit a fade and to hold the ball up against the breeze. It went against his plan for a draw all afternoon but seemed like the sensible decision.

As he took his stance and began to swing the club back, he got the slightest feeling of a closed clubface, promoting a hook, and contorted his hands and body mid-swing to compensate. The result was that his hands and arms came in ahead of his body and he pushed the ball out way right. The blocked shot flew towards the section of the burn that divides the 18th from the 17th and danced on his boyhood dreams as it tiptoed across a pedestrian bridge, teasing for a moment that it may cross to the other side, before skipping off right, into the water.

It was a blow, certainly, but not a fatal one. A five was still a good score and could be achieved, piling the pressure on Garcia, a shot back and standing on the 17th tee, to make an unlikely birdie coming in. Garcia hammered a long iron down the 17th before Harrington's very eyes and, as they made their way to their respective second shots, they met in the middle, crossing the bridge. It was an awkward moment. Garcia's natural buoyancy appeared to compel him to make a light-hearted gesture. But Harrington wasn't in receptive mood. The only TV camera that caught the exchange was trained on the back of Harrington's head. His steady, unbroken stride past Garcia told its own story.

After his penalty drop he was left with a horrendous shot, 229 yards to the green, over the section of Barry Burn that is only yards from the putting surface and coming from an angle that brought the out of bounds on the left into play. Hitting from the fairway is difficult enough, as Harrington could attest, but he'd left himself with an even more hazardous proposition, under the greatest pressure of his life, shooting to a green that had never been welcoming. "I was thinking, 'I hope he doesn't screw up like he did against me'," says Dundas, recalling how he sat entranced as TV pictures beamed out the story of the Open's climax.

Harrington tried to cut his shot into the wind again but fatted a long iron and plonked it into the burn for a second time. It wasn't just 1992 all over again – this was far worse than that. Emotions he'd rarely felt on a golf course flooded his mind. Disgust welled in him. He was embarrassed. "I felt I'd lost the Open," he admitted. "Not alone did I feel I'd lost the Open, I felt I'd messed up and lost the Open. I felt embarrassed. I felt like I'd choked. I was hanging my head as I walked away from that second shot."

The exact effect that the 1992 incident had on him 15 years later is hard to quantify. Only Harrington truly knows. But Dundas was surprised to hear him discuss and reflect on the amateur meltdown so many times that week. "I didn't think for a minute that he would be thinking about it," says Dundas. "I mean, that was 15 years earlier but, in various different interviews, on TV, in newspapers, I think three or four times during the week he actually mentioned the incident which, well, it just showed you how much he wanted to win the British Amateur at the time and how much it affected him. He was obviously very, very disappointed and thought about it a lot longer, I guess, than I thought he would have."

As Harrington hung his head and walked away from the scene of his own personal Waterloo, he thought of Van de Velde. The Frenchman dominated his thoughts followed by a terrible conclusion, am I the new Van de Velde? "Every day I walked down 18 in practise and every day I walked down it in the tournament I thought about Van de Velde," he later admitted. "This is the thing about Open Championship golf – you carry the baggage of other players with you."

Van de Velde wasn't surprised to learn that his image was franked upon Harrington's brain at that perilous moment as the ball dunked into the Barry Burn beside the bridge, yards from where the drama of '99 had played out. "Well, you try to keep these things out of your mind, but Padraig was playing at the same hole where my trouble happened," says Van de Velde, shrugging. "Really, what happened to me was a fluke. But the thing is, nobody can say, 'This is never going to happen to me'. Nobody can say that. Because anything can happen on that hole. We play a game and there's an element of luck, irrelevant of strategy."

The difference between 1999 and 2007 was that Harrington ultimately redeemed himself. Van de Velde had the chance, in a play-off, but blew it. Flood was integral to the redemption process eight years on. For the first 50 yards as he walked towards the green, Harrington was utterly inconsolable, lost in a world of negative thoughts. Flood knew the deal. In the past, when he'd seen his boss get overly down on himself like this, he'd ask, "Do you want me to iron your hands?" a reference to the character, Dobby, from Harry Potter who'd iron his hands when he felt he did anything wrong. They'd always have a laugh then, snapping out of the moment. Harrington once said that having Flood as a caddie was like having Rotella on his bag and on yard 51 the bagman kicked in with the psychology. "He came out with all the clichés, all the one-liners, he kept going at it," said Harrington in a 2009 feature interview for BBC TV's Inside Sport programme. "After 150 yards I was starting to believe him. By the time I got to the ball I believed him. And by the time I hit the shot I was more in the zone than I've ever been."

That shot was a chip of 48 yards, off a tight lie. A play-off win was now Harrington's best chance of victory but he needed to get up and down to stand any chance of qualifying. "Van de Velde made seven, Ronan," he said to Flood confidently. "Let's make six."

Years of work on his mental game allowed him to regain the focus required to pull off what was a near-perfect shot. Gripping down to within an inch of the metal, he hit an aggressive shot that took the spin from the club face, bounced twice on the green and pulled up within five feet of the hole. Analysts and commentators who'd tut-tutted about the size of Harrington's elaborate practise swings beforehand, and speculated on his brittle mental state, now hailed the feathered touch of a craftsman. And he held his nerve with the putter, finding the middle of the hole and retreating with his card to the official recorder's hut. Behind him, Garcia, now a shot ahead, played up the 18th.

Clive Brown, Harrington's Walker Cup captain at Royal Porthcawl, was working as a scoring official for the R&A, the governing body that organises the British Open. He was one of the friendly faces that greeted

Harrington in the hut. "He came in and he was absolutely shell-shocked after taking the six on the 18th," says Brown. "But what he did, I thought it was very professional, he just sat in the recorder's hut. There he was, thinking he'd just blown the Open but he sat there and asked for the TV to be put on, but with the sound off so he couldn't hear any comments by Peter Alliss or whoever the commentators were. There wasn't one word said in that time. That was just the tension of the occasion."

Garcia left himself with an eight-foot putt to win the tournament but, wielding his belly putter, hit what seemed a perfect effort a fraction left which spun off the rim of the hole and away. "You got the impression, with Padraig, of a person who felt that perhaps his chance had gone," says Brown, recalling when Harrington first walked in. "We all thought that anyway. Obviously, when Garcia lipped out the play-off was on. So he was up and out then and you could see he was a lot more positive."

Harrington met Rotella on the putting green as he warmed up for what would be a four hole play-off. "If you ever wanted to know if you had the ability to hit your absolute best shot, under the greatest conceivable pressure, you just found out with that pitch shot," said Rotella. Padraig would later tell him that acceptance and routine had saved him. It had helped clear his mind to achieve that brilliant up and down.

As they walked to the first tee for the play-off, he felt like a prisoner just released from a life sentence of torment. "If Sergio parred the last and I did lose, I think I would have struggled to come back and be a competitive golfer again," admitted Harrington that evening. As it was, he embraced the momentum of the situation, which was on his side after Garcia's miss. "When you see me waving to the gallery during the play-off," he whispered to Rotella as they walked, "you and I will be the only two who know that I'm not really waving to the gallery – I'm holding the Claret Jug and raising it to the sky. That's the way I visualised it last night and every night for months."

McGinley shot 73 on Sunday and finished 19th. He'd planned for a quick getaway to join his family on holiday in Portugal. That was until he learned of the play-off. "I had a flight that night, a charter flight, from Edinburgh," recalls McGinley. "I remember phoning my wife and saying,

'I'm gonna miss this flight'. I said I had to go and watch Padraig in the play-off because there was no way I could imagine him not winning. I said to her, 'He's gonna win his first major here'. I was that confident he was going to win because he had got away with making his mistake yet he was still in the play-off. I thought there was no way he was going to leave two chances behind him to win the Open."

The TV cameras homed in on McGinley and Miguel Angel Jimenez supporting their fellow countrymen. "You've got to remember the psychology standing on that tee box," reflects McGinley. "Padraig is on a high because he's after getting a second chance. He feels he's got a second bite of the cherry whereas Sergio was very much on a low because he's hit a world-class putt on 18 and somehow it found a way of lipping out and not going in the hole. So he is quite distraught standing on that tee. Psychologically, Padraig was at a massive advantage."

Play-offs are won by bold acts of heroism. What clinched victory for Harrington was an aggressive iron shot at that very first hole. After watching the Spaniard bunker his approach shot, Harrington went pin seeking and, unlike Muirfield five years earlier, was rewarded for his courage. He was 162 yards out and drew on the experience of playing during the evening at the Irish PGA Championship eight days earlier. He remembered how the rapidly cooling seaside air seemed to demand an extra club. He hit a 7-iron. Normally, that would fly 180 yards but this time it landed just about exactly where he expected it to, 12 foot left of the flag. When Garcia failed to get up and down and Harrington drained his putt, he immediately assumed a two-shot lead. Despite a decent showing by Garcia over the four holes – and indeed, the four days – he was unable to recover from that early two-shot swing and Harrington had the relative comfort of playing for a bogey on the 18th to claim his first major title.

Little Patrick jumped into his dad's arms when it was all over. The three-year-old talked of putting ladybirds in the Claret Jug, as if they might slip away later and use it like a jam jar for catching insects. It was a delicious moment devoured by the media. How Padraig would have loved to have fallen into his own dad's arms.

His acceptance speech as he held the trophy for the first time was a perfectly delivered oration, picking out all those who'd helped him along the way, from R&A volunteers to Torrance, Rotella, Paul Hurrion, Caroline, Tadhg, little Patrick and his mother, Breda. His voice only gave way when he mentioned his dad, buried in Kilmashogue cemetery exactly two years earlier. The crowd cheered as he blew his cheeks out and composed himself.

He knew Paddy was close. "I totally believe he was there, he was," he insisted in a 'Golf Digest' interview the following February. He'd felt even closer to his late father the previous weekend at the European Club. With the Wicklow links opened up to the galleries to fall in behind the players, Padraig was continually reminded of his dad, who'd accompanied him among the crowd during big amateur events in years gone by. "Every time I turned around I expected to see him," he admitted.

If the hug from young Patrick was warm and familiar, the one he received from his caddie, Flood, after the winning putt had been sunk, carried deeper significance. "It's the strangest time to be sharing a private joke but that's what Ronan and I were doing with that hug," he admitted in an interview with *The Independent*. "We've always had this thing that the closest we'd ever come to hugging each other after winning tournaments before was a handshake. It never seemed enough to go for the full hug. But, suddenly, this time it did and we really went for it. Like I say, it was an odd time to be fooling around. But we always knew it would happen some day."

That certainty of impending major gains had sustained him through the low points, the years of second-place finishes and the moments of self-doubt. In reality, he'd been planning for Carnoustie for longer than just weeks or months, but years. As far back as 2002 he gave an insightful interview that uncannily addressed the key issues that cropped up that week in 2007. "Talk of choking doesn't bother me," he said, blindly considering the exact circumstance he would find himself in five years later on the 72nd hole. "In fact, Caroline keeps telling me that the winner of a tournament is often the guy who chokes least." Another observation he made that also addressed his difficulties on Sunday evening in Carnoustie was that, "The difference between a good golfer and a great golfer is that a good golfer can play great golf when he's in the right mood – a great golfer can play great golf when he wants to." Sure, it wasn't as if he'd wanted to put his ball in the burn, twice. But when he'd needed to play great golf under extreme pressure to get it up and down and reach the play-off, he'd done it.

Perhaps most poignant in the 2002 interview, however, was his piece of critical self-analysis, which just about summed up the story of his first major triumph. "I'm a very complex individual," he accepted. "I think far too much for my own good, which generally results in making things difficult for myself. There are players who seem to have the confidence to do what's expected of them, but not me. Nothing in golf has ever come easy to me. I've always taken the difficult route."

That night, at his rented accommodation, the party kicked off. As close friends and family made hasty arrangements, belatedly getting around to booking that Monday off work that had been advised 24 hours earlier, Harrington slipped away from the celebrations and took a breather, in the shower. The water was warm and relaxing on his tired limbs. The sheer simplicity of the moment was a welcome break from the intensity of the links, of the wind, of the crowd's expectations and of the ecstasy that had followed the agony on the 72nd hole. Suddenly, as if the water had turned freezing cold on his face, a thrilling realisation dawned upon him. Overpowered by the moment of exhilaration, he rested his palms flat against the suds splashed tiles and steadied himself as the words dripped slowly from his tongue. "Oh my God, I've won the Open!"

PART 3 2008

Chapter 8
2008

The golf club car park was as busy as young Padraig had ever seen it. It was Sunday, September 11, 1983 and Stackstown was alive with activity. Little groups of members and familiar faces gathered around the main entrance of the new clubhouse, which they were there to officially open. And still the cars kept streaming in, climbing the steep road up towards the clubhouse before veering off to fill the remaining spaces at the bottom of the parking area.

The sound of clinking champagne glasses and women's laughter carried on the stiff breeze. Padraig was just 12, and only by a matter of weeks at that. He was intrigued by the occasion and the excitement of it. It was obviously a big deal. He sensed it by the body language of the club officials. He recognised club captain, Aidan Brown, and president, Oliver Nugent, being co-ordinated for a series of pictures in front of the clubhouse. They were standing either side of two men, both golfers, Christy O'Connor Senior and Peter Thomson. Those names meant next to nothing to Padraig at the time. He was aware that they were there to play an exhibition match and that his dad, Paddy, would be the match referee. But their significance in the world of golf went right over his head. He has said that he was probably more interested in chasing rabbits around his home course than figuring out, as the match got underway, how Thomson was capable of dispatching such perfect, low draws beneath the strengthening wind.

Of the two players, Padraig was more aware of Christy Senior. Just about every young golfer in Ireland in the early 1980s had heard of 'Himself' to some extent. Lee Trevino described him as a rare breed of player who 'looked entirely natural swinging a golf club'. Christy Senior shot 75 that afternoon, a three-over par total that included 11 pars and two birdies in windy conditions. It was golf played at a level few in Stackstown, including Padraig, had seen before. Still, at 58, Christy's best days were behind him and it was a full quarter of a century since he'd been crowned world champion by winning the Canada Cup team event for Ireland alongside Harry Bradshaw.

That win came in Mexico City, way back in 1958. It wasn't until Harrington and McGinley teamed up in 1997 to represent Ireland in the World Cup – the Canada Cup's modern incarnation – that the feat was repeated. They did it on North American soil this time, at Kiawah Island, the site of the famous 'war on the shore' Ryder Cup battle of 1991. "It was a nice thing for myself and Padraig to be able to say, 'world champion'," says McGinley. "It wasn't done individually. It was done for Ireland, and that's what made it so special. If it had been a world event or something that we'd won individually it wouldn't have had the same feeling, but the fact that we were representing Ireland and it was on live back home on TV was a big deal for us."

McGinley was on a good run approaching the event. He'd won the Irish PGA and then shot 22 under par, including a low round of 64, to win the Oki Pro-Am. His solid ball striking was what convinced Harrington to cut his ties with Howard Bennett and begin working with McGinley's swing coach, Bob Torrance. "I was hitting a lot of the fairways and a lot of the greens and Padraig was missing them, but every time he was chipping up to a short distance and making the putts," recalls McGinley. "That was giving me as much of a boost as if I'd made a birdie myself, to see him display an array of short-game skills which were phenomenal. And, with his competitiveness, I just knew he wasn't going to let me down. I had that much faith in him."

Both players would later point to Harrington's gregarious caddie, John O'Reilly, as a crucial ingredient in their winning formula that week. 'Wily' best describes O'Reilly, the Tallaght man who'd spent 14 years on Des Smyth's bag and, before that, seven on Peter Townsend's. He was one of golf's great characters and, in his autobiography, 'The Life of O'Reilly', describes how he once overheard Nick Faldo telling his caddie, Fanny

Sunesson, to 'Keep an eye on that old Irish geezer – he would buy and sell you'. Faldo's suspicions were well warranted.

During a British Open at Muirfield in the 1980s, after Smyth had missed the cut, O'Reilly and a caddie pal pulled off an ingenious scam. The entrepreneurial duo bought two entry tickets and a tennis ball. For months, O'Reilly would retell the tale of how they'd sold the same tickets over and over again to dozens of Scottish golf fans who, after entering Muirfield, were instructed to stuff the tickets inside a hole in the tennis ball and toss it back over the fence.

They were never rumbled. Though, on another occasion, O'Reilly did have to own up to Harrington when he set fire to one of his expensive cashmere jumpers. It was after a rain-soaked round that he'd had the brainwave of drying out the jumper with a hairdryer only to see the garment catch fire. "Here, give it to me," said another caddie, taking a pair of scissors to the smouldering sleeve and hacking it off. "Now tell Harrington to send the 'bleeping' sweater to The Fugitive!"

O'Reilly was a joker who smoked and loved a drink. But he was a reliable caddie, an old-school bagman who never mis-clubbed a player and had a natural eye for distances and yardages. For example, Harrington had pulled a 7-iron for his third shot into the long 11th in the final round at the World Cup. O'Reilly insisted that he back up to an eight. He struck it perfectly and the ball stopped pin-high, securing back-to-back birdies. It was this vast experience that had convinced Padraig's dad, Paddy, to first set up a meeting between O'Reilly and his son, in the Spawell bar in Templeogue, shortly after he'd turned pro. O'Reilly lowered several pints of stout in front of the two Harringtons in what was effectively his job interview that afternoon but still got the gig. He even got away with asking his new boss for a sub straight away. "He gave me IR£20 ," said O'Reilly, "and from that day on was always asking me if I had enough money to get myself home, or whatever." At Kiawah, more money changed hands and O'Reilly was again the beneficiary. "The more difficult the situation that Harrington was in, Johnny would come up to me and have a little bet," smiles McGinley. "He'd say something like, 'Harrington will get up and down here, watch this!' And surely he would every time."

Harrington's attention to precise detail got on the grizzled caddie's nerves at first. He found the rookie pro fussy and too inclined to pace out the distance to greens and landing points instead of simply referring to the yardage chart. He would learn that it was Harrington's way of coping with the pressure and the tension of a big moment.

O'Reilly would crack jokes to lighten the mood. On the 12th hole on the final afternoon of the World Cup, as Ireland closed in on the winning line, O'Reilly teamed up with CBS commentator David Feherty to keep the players relaxed by setting them both a riddle: "What's the most stupid creature of all?" he and Feherty asked Harrington and McGinley, leaving them to think about the answer during the tournament.

The two players were in such a calm and comfortable mental place that they produced their very best golf. Harrington's lob wedge responded precisely to his touch on the 13th and 14th for a couple of crucial pars. McGinley contributed with birdies at 15, 16 and 17 to give Ireland a five-shot lead coming up the 18th. A pair of pars on the last hole sealed a 545 aggregate score and victory on 31 under par.

"It was a great achievement because it's a hard bloody tournament," says Dunhill Cup winner Des Smyth. "I never won the World Cup and I had some great partners. We played some great golf but it just demanded two players playing at their peak at the same time, which is the really difficult bit."

Harrington was asked about the value of winning the tournament in the absence of Tiger Woods, the then Masters champion, as well as Greg Norman and Nick Faldo. "I honestly believe we would have won, irrespective of who was put in against us," he said. "Even Tiger. When it's your week to win, nobody can take it away from you."

Team Ireland celebrated in a local bar in Charleston that evening. Harrington and McGinley pulled O'Reilly aside after a couple of drinks. "So, what's the answer to the riddle?" they asked. "The sardine," said O'Reilly. "What other eejit would lock himself into a tin can and leave the key on the outside!"

Back in 1983, when Harrington had watched Christy Senior beat Thomson by seven shots around wild and windy Stackstown, he probably wasn't even aware of the Canada Cup win all those years earlier. It had secured Ireland's hosting of the international event two years later, in 1960, when literally tens of thousands turned out at Portmarnock to watch Arnold Palmer and Sam Snead carry off the trophy for America. That event left a feel-good factor about the sport in Ireland that lasted for years, broadening the game's appeal and earning the World Cup a special place forever in Irish golf.

By '97, however, Harrington had long since learned what the big deal was all about and of the shoes he was filling when it came to Christy Senior. "I used to play a lot of golf in Royal Dublin and the Spike Bar there must have 10 photographs of Christy O'Connor Senior up on the walls," he once said. "That was some heritage that was always there and I was very conscious of it when I was growing up and playing myself." Later again, in December 2010, he gave an intriguing insight into his respect for 'Senior' when he was asked to submit a list of the top five sportspeople who influenced him growing up. There, at number one, was Christy Senior, ahead of soccer goalkeeper Pat Jennings, hurler DJ Carey, distance runner Eamonn Coghlan and boxer Barry McGuigan. "Christy O'Connor Senior (is at number one) because I met him and knew him and knew what he'd done," explained Harrington. To mark the '97 World Cup win, the Lord Mayor of Dublin hosted a banquet for them at the Mansion House in Dublin City when they got back. A lavish feast followed a cocktail reception. During a speech that he gave, Harrington is said to have stopped for a moment, looked across at McGinley and in front of the crowd said, "We're bonded forever now."

Other bonds simply had to be broken though, for the sake of progress. Harrington's partnership with O'Reilly, for instance, only lasted until the end of the following year, 1998. The veteran caddie claimed that a couple of incidents at the 1998 British Masters precipitated the breakup. In danger of missing the cut, and having been put on the clock by an official for slow play, Harrington apparently became agitated and accused O'Reilly of rushing him. Then, at a long par 3 over water, he called for a 4-iron. "Are you on drugs?" retorted O'Reilly, insisting on a 2-iron and noting that playing partner Jose Maria Olazabal had hit a 1-iron. They met in the middle. Harrington hit a 3-iron and the ball came up short in the bunker. He eventually took a bogey, shot 73 and missed the cut by two. "I think it is time we took a break," uttered Harrington as they left the 18th. O'Reilly was heartbroken. Retirement may have been a sensible move after 25 years of caddying but he reckoned Harrington's decision was influenced by his advisers. "I am convinced that what finally undermined our partnership is that Harrington's management team, IMG, was simply looking for a more 'businesslike' image and wanted a younger, more photogenic guy at Padraig's side when he was in front of the TV cameras," claimed O'Reilly, who passed away in 2008. "I did not fit the image they were trying to create. I was too old and scruffy looking, even though I wore cashmere as expensive as the next guy. Some fellows look cashmere. I did not."

Harrington explained in an interview with Setanta TV, in the winter of 2011, that cutting O'Reilly loose had nothing to do with his image, but his performance. "Johnny O'Reilly was brilliant at the start," he said. "He knew the ropes. I didn't have to worry about him and he was very relaxed on the golf course. He kept a very good demeanour on the golf course and was super. Eventually, I parted ways with Johnny because he was too relaxed. He was also getting older and losing interest. He was second-to-none and, when the pressure was on, I can't ever remember him pulling a wrong club. He would stand there and give his opinion, an honest opinion."

Ronan Flood filled in briefly after O'Reilly's departure before taking on the role full-time when he quit his AIB Bank job in 2004. Harrington's old Stackstown pal was the right man, in the right place, at the right time and has since been rewarded in many ways, not least of which financially, for his decision to drop everything for life as a professional caddie.

"Everyone's arrangement is different," says major-winning caddie, Colin Byrne. "It (Flood's deal with Harrington) is probably somewhere between five and 10 per cent (of winnings). I actually don't know what half the guys are getting. But that's kind of the standard. Yeah, he's probably done very well. There's plenty of us who have been out there for years. Some have done very well. Some have just got by. If you're with a top player you're privileged, as a caddie, to get the chance to both earn and perform at the top level. You've got to make the most of it because who knows how long it's going to last. But, yeah, I'd imagine he has done well."

Harrington and Flood approached the 2008 British Open at Royal Birkdale in the mood to make their major winning form last as long as possible. Harrington handed over the Claret Jug at the start of the week and was only half joking when he told reporters that, when he got it back on Sunday, he hoped the box that it came in would be smaller, so he could carry it with him on airplanes in future. He never said it but, that week, as he weighed up the challenge that Birkdale presented and the rich history associated with the venue, he must have been reminded of that exhibition match 25 years earlier in Stackstown. The connection may appear tenuous until you take a look back through the British Opens played at the Southport venue. The first, in 1954, was won by Thomson, the five-time Open winning Australian who struggled at Stackstown in his match with Christy Senior and shot a disappointing 82 several years after giving up full-time golf. But what tied Christy Senior and Thomson together so inextricably was the 1965 Open championship. Again, it was played at Birkdale and, when O'Connor Senior posted a final round 71, he set the clubhouse lead. But holding his nerve behind him, Thomson came in with the same 71 score for a four-round total of 285 and took the title by two shots from the Irishman who finished second. Jack Nicklaus and Arnold Palmer were some distance back from them in the pack.

Harrington hadn't realised it in 1983 – how could he possibly have known what fate had in store for him? – but, standing there in the crowd, watching that exhibition match, he was the third point in what would prove to be an intriguing major championship triangle centred around Royal Birkdale. As a 12-year-old just as interested in soccer, Gaelic football and hurling as he was in golf, he would have been shocked to realise that he would one day emulate Thomson as an Open winner at Birkdale and that he would not just repeat Christy Senior's World Cup winning heroics but also outdo him in the Open championship that meant so much to Ireland's golfing patriarch.

Chapter 9
2008

Maybe it was the double-bogey finish. Maybe it was the slight of being outscored by a 46-year-old Philip Walton in the final round of a competitive championship. Or maybe it was just his indefatigable spirit kicking in once more. Whatever the reason, Harrington made the short trip home from the European Club after capturing the 2008 Irish PGA Championship title planning a long evening of practise. He had, again, used the national championship at the seaside venue as preparation for the British Open the following week. On the face of it, a four-stroke victory in, at times, terrible conditions represented another successful warm-up mission.

"It was an excellent exercise," he said after the win, agreeing with Pat Ruddy's observation that, "Birkdale is going to look a lot less intimidating in the crucial, scoring areas – if you can score here, you'll score there." Yet as he made the 40-minute drive back up the N11 from Wicklow to his Rathmichael home, he mulled over where he might improve. He felt he'd lost concentration on the last couple of holes, dumping his approach shot to the 18th green into the Barry Burn-like water hazard. With Walton, his playing partner and nearest challenger, parring the hole, it meant the 1995 Ryder Cup hero had finished with a 70 compared to Harrington's patchy 72. Walton admitted it himself that a major winner and top Tour player like Harrington should have been outscoring him by at least two shots. A four-shot swing then left obvious room for improvement.

Harrington also wasn't fully happy with an alignment issue that had been bothering him. So, while others might have celebrated the win with a stiff drink, or even a night out, he was to be found that evening deep in practise mode in the purpose-built facility at the rear of his home.

"It's a fine place," says Stackstown professional and long-time friend, Michael Kavanagh, of Harrington's personal practise area. "He was telling me that he has room to hit a 6-iron about 170-odd yards. Depending on the breeze it could be a 6-iron or an 8-iron. Then he has permission off the guy who owns the land beside him to hit drivers out there." Padraig practised outside for two hours until the last of the light had drained from the day. Still his work wasn't complete.

Next, he headed for his indoor practise area in the basement, to invest his muscles with the memory of more solid swings. The high-ceilinged room allows for full, free swings and there is a giant net to catch golf balls. To the rear of the teeing area is a large mirror, the sort that can be found at most public driving ranges. But the hand-painted mural that adorns the right wall is completely unique, a little piece of golfing indulgence. It is a painting of the 18th hole at St Andrews and includes all of the old buildings along the right of that hole which frame it so superbly, giving his basement the feeling of a cauldron of golf. There is also a wooden golf club holder in the corner of the room with hundreds of old irons and wedges, more strategically-placed mirrors, several golf bags and a flat screen TV. It is the full GTI version of the cramped golf room he used to practise in as a kid in the family home in Rathfarnham.

"I remember going into Padraig's family house for the first time and the room on the right side as you went in was a putting green," says Gerard Sproule, his old amateur colleague. "So, where you'd normally walk into a house and there'd be a sitting room on the right-hand side, he had a putting green! It was an artificial surface and it was about ten foot in length with a hole at either end. It wasn't just an ordinary carpet. It was a kind of wooden platform with an artificial surface on top. It was a kind of golf room, with putters and wedges. I remember seeing that and thinking it was pretty cool."

One of the other items that Harrington also has in his personal golfing laboratory is an impact bag. It is a simple device that can be as straightforward as a thick bag full of towels. When hit with a club, it gives the feeling of solid contact and helps to promote full compression of the golf ball where the hands and shaft are ahead of the ball at impact. Harrington had pummelled his impact bag thousands of times. After driving balls into the net for a while that Saturday evening, he decided to round off his Irish PGA 'celebrations' by giving the bag another going over. Only this time it wasn't so forgiving. And, as he released a full-blooded swing into it, a jolt of pain shot up through his right wrist and forearm. In the split second that it took for the pain to register with his brain and for the club to fall from his hands, a library of thoughts invaded his mind. Had his grip on the Claret Jug just weakened? Had he just sabotaged his chances of playing at Birkdale the following Thursday let alone winning there?

He walked hastily to the kitchen and grabbed an ice pack to keep the swelling down. With his left hand, he picked up the phone and called his physio, Dale Richardson. They agreed to meet up the next day and assess the injury. The pain was much worse on Sunday and Harrington was unable even to support the weight of a club in his right hand. Richardson administered ultra-sonic and laser treatment and diagnosed the injury as a first degree strain of the pronator quadratus, a muscle in the lower forearm. "Probably just one swing too hard, just maybe slightly off-line into the impact bag and bang! jammed up the pronators," reflects Harrington's long-time fitness advisor Liam Hennessy. "The next thing, it's a big problem."

As well as physio Richardson, Harrington also called Hennessy that Sunday. A Tipperary man, the fitness guru and ex-international pole-vault champion, was walking into the Gaelic Grounds in Limerick where Tipp and neighbours Clare were about to contest the Munster Senior Hurling Championship final when his phone rang. Harrington explained how the injury had occurred and the diagnosis he'd received from Richardson.

"It was a sprain or a spasm in the pronator muscles of the forearm," remembers Hennessy. "But, look, it's happened so we're talking away on the phone, dealing with it. I'm saying, 'Okay, you've got an issue, holding the club and striking the ball is an issue'. But personally, I'm delighted! Because I know he won't go and practise now. We're talking on the phone and I'm saying, 'You're working with Dale to manage it and you'll try it out afterwards. Okay, that's all fine'. Inside, I'm thinking, 'I know the man. I know this man is going to play regardless. I know that nothing is going to stop this man. Yes, he'll be distracted by the injury but he's got such a capacity to deal with these things that he'll say, 'Right, I've just got to get that ball into that area there, whatever it takes'. That's what he's going to do. Even when it happened, and I remember this, going into the match I was at and thinking to myself, 'You know, this is going to be good for him. Now he's just focused on how he's going to get that ball from A to B. He won't be distracted by technical things or what's happening around him. He's just going to get that ball from A to B'. I just felt that, you know, this is actually a good thing. The fabulous thing about Padraig is that these things don't hold him back. They force him into focusing much better on what he has to do and simplifying what he has to do."

Padraig didn't practise at all on the Monday. That wasn't a huge problem, for he hadn't practised on the Monday at Carnoustie either. Worryingly, things weren't much rosier by Wednesday evening. He declared that he had just a 50-50 chance of being fit to complete the 72 holes and defend his title.

The issue was always going to be how the wrist responded to heavy contact with the turf. Would it jar and spasm or would it hold firm? The look on Harrington's face was as much disappointment as pain when he felt a strong twinge during practise on the Wednesday. He'd decided to play the back nine but didn't even reach the 10th green. Two separate attempts to play the hole ended with darting shots of electric pain through his forearm, the first after an iron shot, the second when he returned to the tee-box following treatment and hit his driver. He abandoned the session. He told the media his plan was to rest up for the evening, go through his normal warm-up on Thursday and pray that he was okay to play.

Trevor Immelman set the tone for a year of injury-affected major championships when he won the US Masters in April. The South African's victory came just a few months after he'd undergone surgery to remove a benign tumour from his diaphragm. "When I was diagnosed I thought maybe I wouldn't be able to play any more majors," said an emotional Immelman after the win. In June, the golfing world was left even more stunned by Tiger Woods' epic US Open battle with Rocca Mediate despite the searing pain of anterior cruciate knee ligament damage and stress fractures in his tibia. Each evening after play, Woods received hours of intense treatment on the knee, though, as he got deeper into each round, the discomfort increased leaving him grimacing in pain. Heroically, Woods beat Mediate in a play-off. Then he 'shut it down' for the year. He underwent surgery and sat out the final two majors, the British Open and US PGA championships. Woods' absence at Birkdale impacted on the marquee status and appeal of the event and, when champion Harrington publicly considered pulling out also because of the wrist problem, the very credibility of the oldest major was in jeopardy.

Was it ever likely that Harrington would actually withdraw? Only he knows for sure if the 50-50 assessment erred on the side of caution. The chances are, as Hennessy suggests, it was never truly going to happen. The whole issue certainly wasn't a smokescreen or contrived in any way. The injury was real. But it definitely helped in the context of reducing expectation on him as defending champion.

A few months earlier, he'd been invited to the *Irish Examiner* Junior Sports Stars of the Year awards as a guest speaker. He told the large gathering that he hadn't prepared a speech but, instead, would speak directly to the youngsters and give them general tips and advice. "There'll be times," he told them at one point in the 20-minute talk, "when even those closest to you will doubt your ability, and no doubt you'll give them plenty of cause to. But, as long as you can maintain your own belief in yourself, everything will work out in the end."

At Birkdale, he was in that place himself, the one he'd described to Ireland's brightest young sports stars. He had been backed into a corner of sorts – and it was a position he relished. The alternative was to come into the tournament carrying all the baggage and pressure upon a fully fit defending champion. So, while injury was his enemy it was also his saviour. Somehow, despite being Open champion, he had managed to take all the pressure to perform off himself. "I'm not the sort of person to build up my own chances," he told a magazine writer just days before the event. "I've never really had that confidence or arrogance, or whatever you want to call it."

Self-confidence, killer instinct – he was touching on a sensitive topic here. It was an issue that went to the heart of his uncanny run of second-place finishes in the first decade of his professional career. This bridesmaid's tale of consistently coming second is worth recounting now if only to highlight the mental hurdles he jumped before finally developing that crucial killer instinct necessary to become a major champion. He has finished second 35 times as a professional, with 14 of those coming in just three seasons between 1999 and 2001.

The beginning of this curious period in Harrington's career can be traced back to the Italian Open in '99. After that tournament, he insisted that bogeys at 16 and 17, which saw him finish second, were the result of a neglected short game after so much work with Torrance. But, when at the end of October he found himself explaining away his fifth second-place finish in only six months after a late blow-out at the West of Ireland Classic, a pattern had clearly emerged.

On the one hand, his consistency in challenging for titles was remarkable. But his failure to convert more of them into outright wins began to weigh him down. In March of 2000, he travelled to Brazil for the Rio de Janeiro 500 Years Open off the back of six runner-up finishes in seven months. It proved to be a significant turning point. Again, he finished second, losing out this time to journeyman Roger Chapman, though the sight of Chapman claiming his maiden title at the 472nd attempt, nearly 20 years after arriving on Tour, put his own issues into context. Sports psychology played a major role in finally getting Chapman over the winning line. His guru at the time was Chris Linstead, the man who'd secretly helped out Bernard Gallacher's Ryder Cup team in 1995.

Already deeply consumed by sports psychology himself, it seemed more than coincidence that, the following week, Harrington ended his own losing streak by winning the Brazil Sao Paulo 500 Years Open. "Even a blind pig finds a trough every now and then," he joked.

The headline writers proclaimed the good news – 'Harrington Breaks Hoodoo'. And his third professional win came in October, at Club de Campo, the site of his Spanish Open win in '96. This time, he won the Turespana Masters there. With all sorts of personal demons seemingly exorcised, he looked forward to a 2001 full of promise. But it was a return to the ranks of runner-up as he finished second seven more times. Again, it was another astonishing show of consistency. From the Malaysian Open in February to the two events in Ireland in July – the Irish Open and the European Open – right through to the beginning of winter, his form was as constant as time itself. He didn't miss a single cut in Europe and his stroke average of 69.23 was the best on Tour. He was second in greens in regulation, tenth in sand saves and regularly banged his drives over 300 yards. But, if there were stats kept for 'tournament conversions when in contention', he would have propped it up. "I just don't seem to be able to stumble upon a win, whatever I do," he said after handing victory to John Daly at the BMW International in Munich after finding greenside water on the 18th.

Frustration turned to rage when he blew the Cisco World Match Play Championship five weeks later. He'd hammered Nick Faldo, humbled Darren Clarke and then beaten Sam Torrance to book a final spot with Ian Woosnam at Wentworth. The Welshman displayed all the qualities of a past US Masters champion but he still couldn't touch Harrington, who shot a record 61 in the morning round of their 36-hole final. Records tumbled like dominoes as Woosnam hit seven birdies in a row at one point. Between them in the opening round, they carded a better ball 56. When Harrington led by three with just 12 to go in the afternoon, he looked to have survived the best that Woosnam could throw at him. The biggest victory of his career was close. The Irish reporters who'd travelled over explained to their British counterparts that Harrington always loved match play because it demanded his fullest concentration and guaranteed his focus. To everyone's shock, his game fell asunder on the home straight. By the time they walked onto the 32nd tee, Woosnam had turned the three-hole deficit into a lead and finished off a 2&1 victory on the 17th.

Harrington looked shocked as he gripped Woosnam's hand and shook it. "Are you angry, Padraig?" asked a reporter in the media tent. "Disgusted would be more the word, anger doesn't cover it," he responded. "With three or four of these events, I certainly had my nose in front. If you look back at them, it's clear that I am not finishing the job off. Something is changing as I am coming down the home stretch. Without doubt, something is happening."

As the room cleared, he remained in his seat for several minutes, digesting the gravity of his words. Eventually, his wife led him out. "I really did think I choked," he later admitted. "And, when that happens, you start wondering if the same thing is going to happen again and again. I felt so down. It is a horrible feeling when you believe you've done that. You think that people are starting to point the finger and have a little snigger." After a long postmortem, he concluded that his diet had been to blame at Wentworth, that he hadn't refuelled for the afternoon round and lost all his focus. "I started getting that rushed feeling where your mind has a thousand thoughts and you just can't seem to stop it thinking that way," he revealed. "It helped my game. Without a doubt. I learned to recognise when I am losing focus and how to correct it."

To some, it was a dubious explanation. Yet, to Harrington, it made perfect sense and, in the final European Tour event of 2001 just a month later, he won big, taking the Volvo Masters title. He shot 66 in the final round and holed out from 25-feet on the 18th green to win by one from McGinley. The funny thing was, before the final round of that tournament at Montecastillo, he'd actually joked to his wife about finishing second again. "You know, Caroline," he said mischievously, "if I finish second again today, I could possibly be second in the order of merit, second in the stroke average and second in the greens in regulation."

Experience and an iron will ultimately allowed Harrington to turn the corner on this frustrating period in his career. Improved technique and greater fitness played their part, too. But it was his ability to stand back from the situation and realise it was all a learning curve that made him a better player. Some never take that step back and, as a result, never overcome their issues.

"It's like a lot of guys who don't realise they don't like winning," Harrington once said, "because they don't want the focus or the attention or the pressure – which is why many guys sabotage their game early, so they'll be in the middle of the field."

That wasn't the case with Harrington but it shows that, in the lonely world of professional golf, there are many battles a player has to fight. By accepting his lot, and realising that when he didn't win, even when he finishing agonisingly short in second place, he was still learning, Harrington finally developed that killer instinct he craved. "Mistakes don't define the game, it's your ability to recover," is his constant mantra. Ironically, when he won the European Order of Merit title in 2006, he clinched it with a second-place finish.

This 10-year period between 1996 and 2006 was one long learning curve and not, as some believed, proof that he was destined to be remembered as a serial runner-up. By his reckoning, most leading golfers are truly competitive for around 20 years. In football terms, he had only reached half time at the end of that season when he was crowned best golfer in Europe. The following year, the first year of the second half of that 20-year period, he won his first major and buried the bridesmaid issue for good.

The reaction of the public and the media to his period of runner-up spots also convinced him of another central truth – that other people's interpretation of his play and results was to be discounted and ignored. "For me, self-confidence is knowing that I prepared right, knowing that I set my strategy right, going through my routine and accepting," he said. "They're the little mantras. If I can do those four things, I can walk away from a tournament (happy), regardless of the result. Because results in golf can be so fickle at times."

His first major, competing on three straight Ryder Cup winning teams, becoming European number one and even winning the Irish Open, his fifth major, all erased any lingering doubts in Harrington's mind about his ability to close out tournaments.

Still, at Birkdale, it was better to be the hunter than the hunted, the position he had neatly manoeuvred himself into by talking down his chances after damaging his wrist. On the Tuesday night, deep in the throes of concern over his injury, he attended the Golf Writers' Association Annual Dinner. He was there to accept his Player of the Year award. Peter Thomson, the five-time Open winning Australian whom he'd followed around Stackstown in 1983, presented him with the trophy. Harrington thrust forth his left hand, offering his apologies that he couldn't give a normal handshake with his right but afraid to chance it.

It was the same on Thursday on the first tee. He'd felt discomfort in his wrist a few minutes earlier when warming up on the range. But he swallowed anti-inflammatories and painkillers and resolved to play. When tournament announcer, Ivor Robson, gestured to shake hands, he put forward his left hand again, carefully protecting the right wrist until the very last moment he had to put it into action. Then, with that famous old brogue, Robson piped up, "On tee from Ireland, the defending champion, Padraig Harrington". It was the point of no return.

Flood, Harrington's caddie, joked that the wrist would be fine as long as he didn't hit his ball into the rough all week. The sort of long, wispy rough grass that grows on Birkdale and most links courses has the potential to grab a club face and turn it over, twisting the grip and placing an injured wrist in real danger. Despite his good intentions, he proceeded to push his opening tee shot right, straight into that heavy rough. "We'll soon find out if it's going to stand up to it," he told Ronan as they walked towards the ball.

Chapter 10
2008

Ben Hogan reckoned that golf is "20 per cent talent, 80 per cent management". In plainer terms, talent will only get you so far. Harrington is the living embodiment of Hogan's theory, making his way in the game by trading on substance more than natural style. His wife, Caroline, ribs him that, when they started dating back in 1989, there was little fame or grandeur to speak of as he couldn't even make one of Ireland's underage panels. "I wasn't considered to be in the best 20 golfers in the country who were under 21 years of age," he recalled. "So I was absolutely a nothing at that stage." He wasn't blessed with the natural talent of a McIlroy or a Garcia and, tellingly, as an amateur, was never once invited to play in a professional event.

The real talent he possessed was a rare ability to bleed every last drop of potential out of himself and to accept that his golf game would be a long-term work in progress. It was this mature approach and commitment to gradual improvement that allowed him to eventually breathe the same thin air as the truly talented.

It was a different sort of wave that Greg Norman rode. Flamboyant and fearless on the golf course, the Australian surfed a wave of raw skill that reached its peak on the seaside links of Turnberry and Royal St George's and only broke in the late 1990s after occupying number one spot in the world for 331 weeks of his career. With Norman the 20 per cent was never in question, though, had he managed the other 80 per cent of his game a little better, he would have won more than just those two major titles at the 1986 and 1993 British Opens. He famously gifted the Masters to Nick Faldo in 1996 and finished second at least twice in all three of the major championships that are staged in America. Harrington would surely agree that Norman underachieved for, when he came into contact with 'The Shark' himself, he saw the brilliance of the man at first-hand and must have wondered how he didn't win more.

In July, 2002, Harrington agreed to play Norman over 18 holes of match play to mark the official opening of Doonbeg Golf Club, a new links course on the south-western coastline of Ireland that Norman had designed. The novel match between one of the game's most iconic figures and Ireland's number one player, drew a large crowd, though no one was quite sure what to expect. They knew that Harrington always loved playing in County Clare, particularly at nearby Lahinch, and that he was in excellent form. He was fresh off a second-place finish at the European Open 48 hours earlier at The K Club and, generally, was enjoying an excellent season. Failing to win at The K Club had been a bitter pill to swallow. He'd needed an eagle at the par 5 18th to reel in Michael Campbell and gone for the green in two but landed in the water. He'd lost the contest, yes, but his game had never been in better shape. And, after finishing inside the top eight at both the Masters and the US Open, he was using the Doonbeg match as vital links preparation before the British Open at Muirfield nine days later.

The great conundrum was Norman who, when fully tuned in, could still match the best. But he was doing so less often as he gave more of his time to his burgeoning business interests. He had slid to 140th in the world but, by the first green, the audience trailing the match realised he was there to play. From the tee, he showed why he was once regarded as the best driver of a golf ball in the world before nailing a long approach on the par 5 to within 30 feet of the pin. The hole was eventually halved in birdies and an epic battle ensued.

On the fifth, a par 4 into the wind, Norman produced the dead-arm strike of an expert links player, punching the ball low through the wind to a couple of feet for a conceded birdie. Still, Harrington was holding up his end of the bargain and gave the Aussie a run for his money. On the par 3 ninth, the home favourite almost scored an ace and his birdie brought the match back to one up. The masterful Norman generally held the whip hand, though, and with the agility of a fly fisherman contorting his hands and wrists, was able to manufacture the most sumptuous of seaside shots. He effectively ended the contest on the par 4 15th. There he dispatched a 6-iron with so pure a strike that it bored through the crosswind before landing softly beside the pin, like the helicopter that touched down next to the 18th green an hour or so later to whisk him away to a holiday in Rome. Norman wrapped up a 2&1 win on the 17th. He was six under par for his round, compared to Harrington's minus three. "When he's interested, Greg Norman can really play," Harrington later reflected. "He knocked the socks off me in Doonbeg and you could see he wanted to play golf that day. I've seen him at other times turn up at golf courses that he's looking at the design of and he's got other things in his mind. When he wants to do it, when he puts his mind to it, he can certainly play."

Norman arrived at Royal Birkdale in 2008 once again in the mood to play. That he was ranked outside the world's top 600 players at the time and was a 1000/1 shot for glory didn't affect him. No competition rewards the touch and feel of an innately talented golfer like Norman more than the British Open, with its fast-rolling fairways, gusting winds and quirky holes that place a premium on precision over power. Robotic players that lack skill and imagination will never win a British Open. But the truly gifted will always stand a chance. It is why a near 60-year-old Tom Watson almost won the 2009 Open at Turnberry, and why Norman, 53 the year before, knew he, too, was capable of living off his natural talent and contending, even if nobody else gave him a snowball's chance in hell.

As ever, the weather at the 137th Open Championship imposed its own will. Peter Thomson once described Birkdale, the venue for two of his five Open wins as, "Man-sized, but not a monster". In 2008, it really was a monster. Strong winds lashed rain across the competitors. "A combination of wind and the course tossed the golfers around like Godzilla with a handful of popcorn," wrote a reporter. Ernie Els played through the worst of the weather on the first day and carded 45 for his back nine. Rich Beem played nine holes in 12 over par and walked in. Sandy Lyle lasted a hole longer and caused a storm of controversy by also quitting. "It was just brutal," recalls Jean Van de Velde who shot 73, three shots better than the average. It was incredibly tough. The wind was blowing so hard, the rain was lashing. It was as tough as it can get, no doubt."

Even without the freakish weather the course was playing more difficult than 1998 when it had previously hosted the Open. That was the year Justin Rose confirmed his rising talent by finishing fourth as an amateur, behind winner Mark O'Meara. Harrington had shot 73-76 and missed the cut then. "They hit the ball out about 300 yards now whereas 10 years previous to 2008 they were only hitting it out about 260/270 yards, so things needed changing to make the golf course play as it was designed to be played," says Birkdale's head greenkeeper, Chris Whittle. One of the more intriguing changes, and one which played a central role in the destination of the title on Sunday evening, was an alteration to the 17th green. "The green was moved back about 30 yards," continues Whittle. "It was a new green but further back."

With 19 players shooting rounds in the 80s on Thursday, including Els – who fought back to finish tied seventh – Vijay Singh and 1995 champion John Daly, who shot 80-89 on the first two days, Whittle accepts that conditions were 'on the limits' of fairness. "On any links course, you don't want a calm championship," he says. "You want the course to be testing but not silly either. It was on the limits with the wind speeds, definitely. I mean the gusts were quite severe, particularly over the weekend, they were up at 30 miles an hour and into the 40s at times. They were very lucky not to suspend play. We were right on the edge of it but we got away with it."

To a grinder like Harrington, the conditions were perfect. The sheer ferocity of the weather took his mind off his damaged wrist and demanded his full attention over each and every shot. He reasoned that, in such a testing environment, a section of the field were out of contention before a ball was even struck because they lacked the mental toughness to cope.

His former coach, Howard Bennett, used to tell him that "50 per cent of the field aren't prepared to play in those conditions and the next 50 per cent aren't capable", leading Harrington to decipher that, "On a bad day, most of the field just won't be able to raise it". In situations like this, even going as far back to qualifying school in 1995, he had often taken advantage. "His brother, Tadgh, caddied for Padraig at qualifying school," says Harrington's former Walker Cup partner, Jody Fanagan. "He (Tadhg) said it was just an unbelievable experience. He said most of the guys were just white with fear. Apparently, he said to Padraig, 'Look at those guys, they're in tatters. Half of them have no chance'." Harrington qualified at his first attempt and never had to return.

Colin Byrne watched Harrington from close quarters over the first 36 holes at Birkdale, as caddie to Retief Goosen, who partnered the defending champion. Byrne's eyes were fixed on Harrington's face for the slightest sign of pain or discomfort as he struck his second shot in the championship, an approach to the first green from the thick rough where his opening tee shot landed. Harrington got an iron to the back of the ball, dug it out with a chop and walked away reporting no problems. It was a load off his mind, though Byrne felt that it wasn't until nearly the half-way point in the round, at which stage Harrington had taken three bogeys, that he was finally starting to trust the wrist. To Byrne, Harrington looked defensive and uncommitted, not trusting his right hand fully and failing to release the club head properly as a result. But, after a birdie on the eighth, he settled down and enjoyed a bogey-free run of five holes on the back nine as he finished with a worthy 74 in atrocious conditions. Byrne describes the occasion as 'a battle for survival' and recalls how the third man in their group, Justin Leonard, played out of turn at one stage even though he was 50 yards ahead of his colleagues. He was just that disorientated by the onslaught of wind and rain. He describes Harrington's short game that day as 'supreme' and recalls several terrific up and downs from inside 80 yards, a chip in and some vital par saves on the greens.

"If you have respect for people who just have the attitude 'never give up', and just being able to make it happen, somehow, then Harrington has got to be top of your list," says Byrne. "If you respect that sort of, I'm not saying scrappy or untidy, but that doggedness, that sheer unmitigated belief that, 'I can get it done, I don't care where I hit it, I'm going to get out of this trouble, watch me get up and down'. Because he did that, not just that day but all the time. He hit it left, right and centre but he would get up and down and make a score. There's not many people that can do that. So I have the utmost respect for him doing that, over a long period of time, with what looked like, on occasions, a limited game. He just squeezed that game dry every time he stood up on the first tee, which is a very hard thing to do. It's a special mind that can do that, day in, day out, instead of going, 'Jesus, I'm hitting it shit. I'm sick of trying'. But never once did he say that or take that attitude."

Michael Kavanagh saw the determination in Harrington at Stackstown from early in his career. Intriguingly, Kavanagh isn't surprised to hear Harrington claim that his determined streak actually comes from his mother, Breda, more than his dad, who was the talented sportsman. "I'd well believe it," says Kavanagh. "Padraig's mam was always straight as a rush. I can see he has a lot of his mother's ways. I remember she came into the shop one day and somebody said, 'You must be very proud of Padraig and everything he's done'. Quick as a flash, she says, 'I'm proud of all my sons. There's no difference there. I know he is what he is, but there's no difference between any of my boys'. Just a very straight person she is, and a lot of determination there, I'd imagine."

Byrne's man, Goosen, carded a 71 on the opening day, while Mediate went two better with a 69, breaking into a grin as he admitted he would have been happy with 73 or 74. The most unexpected score of all was the level par 70 shot by Norman. When he matched it in the second round to claim outright second position, two shots clear of Harrington who followed up with a superb 68, it was confirmation that the choppy waters of the British Open were once again 'Shark' infested. Norman's position strengthened with a third round 72. It left him in the lead on two over par for the tournament, two clear of defending champion, Harrington, and KJ Choi, heading into the decisive final round. Statistics backed Norman's bid to become the oldest ever major winner. Since 2000, six of the eight winners had held the lead, or been tied for the lead, on Saturday night. "The players are probably saying, 'My God, what's he doing up there?'" accepted Norman, essentially a part-time golfer who hadn't played in a major for three years. The only reason he'd even entered the British Open was to warm up for a couple of senior majors that were coming up.

Harrington was keenly aware of the growing clamour to support Norman and push him over the winning line. The thousands of spectators who lined every fairway and queued for hours to fill the grandstands around the course, wanted to witness history and be part of it. After all of Norman's major heartaches over the years, they felt he deserved a final day in the sun, like Nicklaus had enjoyed at Augusta in '86. The media reported the fantastical tale of a sleeping giant awakening from years of slumber. They painted colourful pictures of his natural aptitude for links play, like one classic knock-down 5-iron that he hit into the teeth of a 40-mile-an-hour wind on the fifth on Saturday. It landed just where he wanted. Norman had turned the egg-timer on its head for three magical days and only the stonehearted, or those with a vested interest in the other competitors, wanted anything but the fairytale conclusion on Sunday.

It was a situation Harrington could hardly have expected or prepared for, to be going head to head with a boyhood idol who was loved by all. Earlier in his career, it was a battle he might have convinced himself he couldn't win, back when he was stuck in that rut of second-place finishes. In fact, for long spells into adulthood, Harrington privately wondered if he'd been hard-wired the same as his dad, who was best known in his sporting career as a runner-up, too. Worse still, he wondered if he'd inherited a condition that left him fearful of killing off opponents and being in some way sympathetic to their cause. Padraig thought about that long and hard. He wondered why his dad had never been plagued by losing the All-Ireland finals he played in with Cork in 1956 and 1957. Padraig expected angst and regret in his father's eyes but it was never there when he went looking for it. He and his brothers would tease their dad about the All-Ireland final losses when they were growing up but his brow never furrowed with lament or disappointment. "Ah, sure it was good while it lasted," he would say back to his boys. "He never seemed disappointed enough," thought Padraig.

And everyone used to say that Padraig was a real chip off the old block. He and his father looked alike. They had that same distinctive walk. And an intriguing story from childhood confirms that they even thought alike. One evening, as a kid, Padraig was sitting at the dinner table with his brothers and his mother. Of his four brothers, he was closest to the next oldest, Fergal, but, on this occasion, they were quarrelling. Beneath the table, Fergal was aiming kicks and punches at Padraig, the runt of the litter.

Padraig told him to stop. So did his mam. But Fergal didn't listen. In an instant, Padraig lost his cool, picked up a potato and fired it at his brother, hitting him squarely on the head. He says it's the only time in his life he's properly lost it. They were picking up pieces of potato around the kitchen for six weeks after. Before Fergal knew exactly what had hit him, Padraig was up on his feet and darting to the bathroom, which was the only room in the house that he could lock himself into. He stayed in there for an hour until his dad came home.

He prepared himself for the biggest lecture of his young life. "Well, if Padraig did that, he must have been provoked," reasoned his dad after hearing the tale. "That was it," recalled Padraig. "There was no retribution." Paddy understood Padraig, for they were one and the same. But, then, if they really were the same, did Padraig also lack that vital killer instinct? "I got his temperament," Padraig once admitted. And that was exactly what worried him for many years.

Padraig often recalls another story about his dad, who was a keen boxer. He won a national title at his weight level within the police force but, in doing so, administered a terrible beating to his opponent in the final. "The guy he beat in the final was badly outclassed but just wouldn't go down," recalled Padraig in an interview with 'Golf Digest'. "My dad hit him, and hit him, and hit him and hit him. The guy was determined not to fall. Dad won comfortably on points but he felt so bad about the beating he gave this guy he never boxed again." It was a noble gesture from Paddy. But sentiment had clearly clouded his sporting judgement, compelling him to back away.

Years later, were the sins of the father being revisited upon the son when it came to all those second-place finishes with Padraig? Was he afraid, too, to throw that crushing knock-out punch? "I always wondered if I was like my dad, all those second places," said Padraig. "It (killer instinct) was a thing I always worried I didn't have. That's what worried me about Birkdale; I looked at Greg and everybody was sympathetic to his story. It was going to be, 'The great swan song of Greg Norman'. And it would have been great, but not when I was there. I'd spent a strong part of my last 20 years trying to find that killer instinct. I'd got better. I'd moved on."

Late on Sunday morning, an email dropped into the inbox of the golf writers. The subject line read: 'A few early notes in the event of a Greg Norman victory'. The scribes that were sympathetic to Harrington's cause were glad to see that fate was already being tempted. Norman, of course, had also held the lead, a six-shot cushion, going into the final round of the Masters in '96 before blowing it. So, when he opened his final round at Birkdale with three straight bogeys the word 'choke' was heard among the galleries again. It seemed he was being hauled right back across the hot coals of Augusta. But, when Harrington closed out the nine just as badly as Norman had begun it, with a three-in-a-row of bogeys himself, the Australian moved back into a one-shot lead.

Harrington won his first major championship fair and square at Carnoustie. He shot 67 in the final round and conjured some stunning golf in the play-off against Garcia. Carnoustie greenkeeper John Philp says he's very proud of the fact that it was a technical golfer, a deep thinker and an expert in course management that ultimately came out on top. It would have annoyed him had a long-hitting bomber just overpowered the place and ignored all its subtleties. "Yes, without a doubt," says Philp, acknowledging the fact. "Strategy-wise, course-management wise, he was a deserved winner. We're proud of that very fact."

Inevitably, not everyone agreed that Harrington's was a victory for the ages, or anything like it. For all of his excellence in getting up and down on the 18th, he'd still found the water twice on the final hole of a major championship. And he had only got through to the play-off because Garcia had failed to take advantage and missed a putt to win the tournament. Harrington was quick not to get caught up in the idea of winning another major as a means to somehow validate his win at Carnoustie. But among his ambitions for 2008 was to win another major title and, surely, to do it with a strong finish this time that eliminated any doubt about his credentials.

On the 13th hole of his back nine at Birkdale he began to produce the sort of golf that saw him realise that ambition. From the middle of the fairway, he knocked a 5-iron to 15 feet and holed the putt for his first birdie of the day. "That was a very important birdie because of the set-up at

Birkdale, it puts you on the front foot approaching the run-in which has two par 5s," says Whittle. Norman, in contrast, caught a sand trap off the tee and finished two shots worse off after a crushing bogey. Harrington followed up with a par on the 14th before a stunning three wood into the par 5 15th green that started out over a copse of gorse before straightening out on the wind to set up another birdie. Norman birdied the 15th too but, with seven bogeys for the day already, he'd fallen to eight over par, three behind Harrington. Unbeknownst to Harrington, a charge from native peacock, Ian Poulter, several holes ahead had taken the Englishman into contention. Poulter was even tied for the lead at one stage before posting the clubhouse lead at seven over.

Completely in his own zone of excellence now, Harrington parred the 16th and, after a good drive on the par 5 17th was left with 272 yards to the pin. He hadn't looked at a scoreboard all day but sensed he was leading. He was, by two. Caddie Ronan suggested the lay-up. But viewing it as the perfect opportunity to finally kill off lingering Norman, he decided to go for the green with a five wood. A BBC TV commentator described it as an "aggressive play" given the strong left-to-right crosswind, the narrow landing area and attendant dangers of sand and gorse. Ken Brown suggested Harrington was taking "a bit of a risk in this wind". And Peter Alliss, the doyen of British golf broadcasting, gave the official seal of disapproval as he told viewers that Harrington would have to aim his five wood shot at the grandstand 30 yards left of the green if he was to ride the left-to-right wind. "He's aiming into the grandstand virtually on the left, two shots ahead… " muttered Alliss as Harrington began his backswing.

A couple of days after turning 20, in early September, 1991, Harrington stood on the first tee at Portmarnock Golf Club, in Dublin, and prepared for the biggest shot of his life, his opening drive in the Walker Cup. He stood there longer than normal, staring down at the ball on the tee peg below him. His mind was a jumble of mixed messages, old dos and don'ts about the fundamentals of the golf swing that he'd recited a million times over, 'Left arm straight, full shoulder turn away, complete the backswing'. Yet one thought was all that was getting through, 'Don't hit the clubhouse!' The warning entered his head like a Trojan horse and refused to leave, unloading battalions of little soldiers to attack his golfing senses. It was a throwaway remark from another player during practise after noticing the clubhouse just left of the opening tee box that had caused the torment.

Jay Sigel, America's most capped player ever, was standing there waiting on Harrington to hit. Sigel's foursomes partner, Allen Doyle, one of the sweetest strikers of a golf ball you're likely to come across, was by his side. Harrington was so consumed by dread that not even the silent well-wishes of Great Britain and Ireland playing partner, Paul McGinley, registered. "I can actually understand him having a fear of hitting the clubhouse there because it's on the left and he started everything down the left and hit a fade," says McGinley. "At that stage, he hit a flat fade, it was the only shot he had."

"By the time I went to swing the club, I definitely couldn't see the golf ball," recalled Harrington many years later. Operating on autopilot, he got his shot away safely, avoiding the clubhouse with a curving fade that spun through the air and came to rest on the fairway.

Nearly 20 years later at Birkdale, his swing looked nothing like the old scything motion of his Walker Cup days. As he swung back his five wood on the 17th fairway, his powerful, wide arcing plane line was capable of delivering a shot of virtually any shot shape or height. It was ironic then that the shot he dispatched away down the left of the hole towards the grandstand, and which rolled out past the left greenside bunker and up onto the green to within a few feet of the pin, was a ringer for that opening tee shot at Portmarnock. The wind had provided the fade this time, but the shot of a lifetime that he summoned to secure the eagle he needed to win the title at Birkdale, was literally the shot of his lifetime. It was the shot he was born to play. It'll never be repeated either because shortly afterwards, the 17th green was altered again.

"It was a hell of a shot," says Whittle. "That green has been rebuilt again since. We felt it just needed a few more subtle changes." A routine par on the last sealed Harrington's successful defence of his title. He won by four shots, the exact same margin as the previous weekend at the European Club, further endorsing his preparations. Norman could only par the 17th, two strokes worse than Harrington's eagle and a bogey on the 18th dropped the Australian to tied third for the tournament. For 71 and a half holes, Harrington hadn't allowed sentiment to affect his concentration but, as they walked up the 18th he finally dropped his guard. "He congratulated me," revealed Harrington. "I said, 'Greg, I'd love if this was your week but I couldn't get caught up in that'. And I genuinely meant that."

In a rare moment of showmanship, Harrington held his left hand up to the photographers afterwards and stuck out two fingers – two British Opens. In his other hand, he had a firm grip on the Claret Jug, his for another year. It was the same hand that had given him all the trouble, the right one.

Harrington's brain is truly a fascinating organ. At one point on the back nine, he had felt the cold chill of the early evening sea breeze but refused to put on a jumper, for fear he might somehow jinx his good play. Ultimately, all it took to get the best out of that complex brain was a little diversion in the form of an injured wrist.

"I need a little bit of tension, I need something to keep me focused," he said. "The wrist was a great distraction for me. I have to look back and say that there's no question that having a wrist injury pushed everything about coming back to defend this title to one side. It took a lot of pressure off me. It took a lot of stress off me. It was a good distraction to have. The wrist injury was a saver for me, really."

Chapter 11
2008

The putt had hardly dropped when Paul McGinley's left arm was hooked around Padraig's neck, embracing him like a boxer in a clinch. As they hugged, the first strains of 'You'll Never Beat the Irish' rose up from the huge crowd, gathered around the 15th green at Oakland Hills Country Club. Irish tricolours were proudly stretched aloft as a green wave of bodies closed in on the pair. Harrington's hat was whipped off – revealing a dubious crop of bottled blond hair – and replaced by a green one with a shamrock badge. Sensibly, the local police and marshals stood back. For over an hour, cries of 'Ole, Ole, Ole, Ole' hung in the Detroit air. Team Ireland, Harrington and McGinley, had just pulled off their biggest success since the 1997 World Cup victory and the party was one to savour.

Harrington's putt had been for a birdie, which wrapped up a Saturday afternoon foursomes' victory at the 2004 Ryder Cup. The 4&3 win came at the expense of none other than US captain Hal Sutton's strongest home pairing, Tiger Woods and Davis Love III, both ranked inside the world's top five. It was the last match of the day and sealed a gigantic 11-5 lead going into the final session of singles. Europe's demolition of America for the second successive Ryder Cup was virtually complete.

"My two outstanding moments from playing with Padraig on a golf course were the World Cup win and the Ryder Cup in Detroit," says McGinley. "We were two down very early in that match against Davis Love and Tiger. I remember Padraig had been playing in the morning. He'd been playing with Colin Montgomerie and they'd lost, which was his only dropped point of the week. He pulled his tee shot on the first hole and we made bogey. Then, after a good drive down the middle on the second, we didn't make birdie. Tiger made an eagle. We were very downhearted after two holes to be two down against such a strong pairing. We had a chat on the third hole. I just said, 'Let's forget we're playing Tiger Woods here. Let's play the golf course and see what score we can shoot'. It was like flicking a switch because we ended up playing the golf course as we'd agreed. We played some wonderful golf and beat them 4&3. Padraig holed about an eight-foot putt to win it on the 15th. There were so many Irish people around the green, and all the other matches had finished. Between doing interviews and the Irish crowd not letting us go, wanting to sing all the songs like 'Molly Malone' and 'You'll Never Beat the Irish', we were at least an hour there before we went in. We just had great fun with the Irish fans. So that's a really outstanding moment for me with Padraig. To share that together in front of a very noisy four or five thousand Irish fans around the green, after beating Tiger, who was on top of the world at that stage, it was a very special moment for both of us."

The next time McGinley and Harrington paired up against Woods was at The K Club in the 2006 Ryder Cup. McGinley only recalls the event to highlight the contrast between the two episodes. "We played Tiger again, though with Jim Furyk this time, in 2006," he continues. "I remember myself and Padraig having lunch together before we went out playing in the afternoon. Somebody who had played Tiger in the morning, I forget who it was, announced to the table, 'Jaysus, you two will take him handy, Tiger's playing terrible'. Padraig says, 'That's the last thing I wanted to hear. Because there's no way he's going to play terrible two rounds in a row'. That's exactly what happened. The two of them played fantastically and Tiger played especially well and they beat us 3&2."

It is a strange statistic that, in 2004, on the alien Oakland Hills track, Harrington enjoyed by far his greatest returns as a Ryder Cup player. He won four of his five matches, an 80 per cent success rate compared to the solitary half-point that he extracted at The K Club. The K Club was a course he knew well and had played many times, stretching all the way back to his first professional event there in 1995, the European Open. It is even harder still to fathom why Harrington struck out so badly, in scoring terms at least, a matter of weeks before he was crowned Europe's number one player and only months before the landmark major success of 2007. The obvious conclusion is that, saddled with the expectation of an entire nation at The K Club, he simply wasn't able to cope. Des Smyth, European vice-captain to Ian Woosnam in 2006, agrees that the burden of pressure placed upon Harrington's shoulders at the Straffan venue was immense.

"I actually was appointed during that week to take care of Padraig during the practise rounds," says Smyth. "Because he was in huge demand. Being the personality that Padraig is, he doesn't like to say 'no' to people. He's a really nice guy. During the practise rounds I used to have a laugh with him. Because we had to get them done in a certain time-frame. We had to get back in and there was no leeway. There were other functions to be done so they were only given four and a half hours for their practise rounds. And, of course, if you let Padraig sign all the autographs it would have taken six hours. So I had to be the minder and tell him to move on. Of course, the spectators were giving me a load of stick. But I'd get to the next tee and he'd wink at me and say, 'Thanks for that'. Because he can't say no. I had to be the spoilsport for the spectators."

While acknowledging the demands on Harrington, the highest-ranked Irish player at the time, ahead of Darren Clarke and McGinley, Smyth insists that Harrington managed to deal with the hype, despite scoring a meagre half-point from a possible five. "He was in the top match the first day, him and Monty against Tiger Woods and Jim Furyk, so he was up against the very best in the world," claims Smyth. "They just lost that match by one hole. The quality of his play was great. But that doesn't mean you're going to win at that level. You can play great and never get a point and, for me, that's how it happened with Padraig that week. He just got beaten by greater golf. There was a lot of that going on. Tiger Woods played Robert Karlsson. Robert played fantastic. But Tiger played better. You could go out there that week and shoot six under and be beaten 2&1, that was the standard you were at. I'd say Padraig felt disappointed. In fact, I know he felt disappointed. He'd tell you himself, he said to me, 'I don't know why they're praising me out there. They're all clapping me. I only got half a point'. But he was a great team player and that was as important. The younger players would go and talk to him. You'd see them sitting around watching him and listening to what he said. He played that role in the team room very well. He was a leader at that stage and he knew it."

After his excellence at Oakland Hills in 2004, Harrington went 10 Ryder Cup matches without a win. He beat Jay Haas 5&4 in the singles in Detroit but failed to pick up another win until 2010 when he partnered Ross Fisher to a foursomes success over Phil Mickelson and Dustin Johnson at Celtic Manor. The barren streak came at exactly the same time he was experiencing his greatest personal successes in the game, 2006 and 2008.

"Some people would say that the Ryder Cup they lost in America when Faldo was captain (2008) was because people stayed too quiet in the locker room," says Jean Van de Velde, who made his Ryder Cup debut in 1999 with Harrington at Brookline. "But you can only learn from experience, and I'm pretty sure Padraig would have learned that lesson. He carried that experience into the Ryder Cup in Wales in 2010. He didn't play that well there but I'm convinced he was a great asset in the locker room."

Colin Byrne was caddying for Edoardo Molinari at Celtic Manor in 2010. He witnessed Harrington take on the role of "a statesman, a senior figure" in the locker room. "That's the funny thing about the Ryder Cup," says Byrne. "You're asking these guys to perform that role. But the thing is, they're islands, guys like Harrington, all of them, they're used to playing by themselves, week in, week out. Then they come to these rare occasions when they're playing for 11 other guys. It's interesting to observe how they last the week doing that because, really, what they're good at is looking after themselves, not other people. So you see little glimpses of them where they're looking out for their team-mates. It's actually quite a unique insight into them because they're not normally like that. The game doesn't demand them to be like that, the more selfish you are the better, normally. With Harrington, the little bits I did see of him there's no doubt he did have a strong presence there. He was leaving a strong, positive impression on guys around him. I mean, he's such a grinder that other plays can't but feel that. Even when he's walking up the stairs he's grinding. That's his nature to squeeze something dry, even if it doesn't look like it's there. It's a great mentality for match play."

Byrne has no immediate explanation for why Harrington's Ryder Cup results dipped so violently in tandem with his most successful period as a professional. But he reckons that, generally, there is too much analysis of results and scoring in a competition that is a basic sprint to the winning line over 18 holes or less. If, somehow, Ryder Cup scoring had been based on four-round singles' scoring at the time, like normal tournaments, then Harrington, and Woods, would most likely have had a far more impressive record.

"You know, I think there's too much talked about the Ryder Cup," says Byrne. "When it comes down to it, it's the guy that makes the most putts over 18 holes of match play that wins. In those terms, anyone can beat anyone and you consistently see that happening. It's not 72 holes of stroke play. The element of 'one good day' with the putter is ruled out in stroke play. But it's what wins points in the Ryder Cup. I also think there's an awful lot of guff talked about why someone is a good captain. Was Monty a great captain in Wales? He won, so that makes him a great captain. Faldo lost, so that makes him a bad captain. I know you can argue that he puts them out in their positions, almost like the director of a movie. But, personally, the most inspiring thing I saw at the Ryder Cup in Wales was when Ian Woosnam came into the team room and gave a bit of a rabble-rousing speech after a defeat one afternoon. That was the most inspirational moment I saw all week, and he was there as a past captain. I think Monty was like Monty is – if he plays badly his head's down and if he plays well his head's up."

As for Harrington's own explanation of his poor contribution at The K Club and Valhalla, he is typically honest. "Look, I can explain it very easily," he said. "Essentially I was burnt out at the (2008) Ryder Cup, coming off the high of the summer. At the previous one in Ireland I had some tough matches, and by the time the singles came around on the Sunday it was a non-event. But I'm definitely aware that my match play hasn't been good. I think it's because I've knocked the edges off my game in the last four or five years, whereas, previously, I was very erratic, and that's a lovely way to play match play. My style of golf suited match play incredibly well earlier on in my career. I've become more conservative."

With that more gung-ho attitude as a younger player, Harrington performed well on his debut for Europe at Brookline in '99. When he recalls that event he is consistently drawn back to an image on the 16th tee during the Sunday singles session. He was playing Mark O'Meara in a potentially decisive match to the overall outcome. It was a par 3 and he was undecided on what iron to hit, a smooth six or a flat out seven. He called captain Mark James over for advice. "My only thought," wrote James in his book 'Into the Bear Pit', "was that this could be the first time a captain had ever misclubbed a player to lose the Ryder Cup. It was not a nice feeling. I thought, 'My God, I'm going to be responsible for the whole thing right here'."

Harrington sensed James' unease and, for a moment, stood back and observed the pressure cooker they had fought so hard to submerge themselves in. "I kind of laughed and said, 'We actually wanted to be here, we actually worked to get into this position, nobody held a gun to our heads'," recalled Harrington in a 2001 interview with the *Sunday Independent*.

"I mean, an enjoyable experience is a good movie at the cinema but you haven't lived when you've watched a good movie at the cinema – you've enjoyed two hours of eating popcorn and drinking Coke and that was the experience. But, when you've played in a Ryder Cup, you know the week is going to be etched into your memory forever. It's like jumping out of an aeroplane with a parachute – you know you did something."

Harrington eventually went with the 6-iron at Brookline and found the green. On the next hole, he ran a gauntlet of abuse, riling the raucous US home support by pacing out the full yardage of his wedge shot to the green. It was viewed as a stalling tactic from a player with a reputation for slow play, to unnerve O'Meara. A US TV commentator reflected the spectators' anger by dryly suggesting that Harrington's walk, "gave new meaning to the Boston marathon". They halved the hole and Harrington claimed the match with a win on the 18th, thanks to an adrenaline-fuelled, 150-yard wedge to the green. "I was on the greatest high of my golfing life after beating Mark and, within five minutes, I ran down the 18th fairway to get to the match on the 17th green (between Justin Leonard and Jose Maria Olazabal)," said Harrington. "In fact, I didn't run – I glided. I sat down at the 17th and, within 30 seconds, Justin Leonard holed that putt and I went from the biggest high to the biggest low." That putt was, of course, Leonard's raking effort that won him the match and sealed USA's overall win, sparking wild and controversial celebrations on the green as Olazabal was preparing for his putt.

Brookline will always be special to Harrington. But it was at Oakland Hills where he truly came of age as a Ryder Cup player and enjoyed his greatest success. In August, 2008, just weeks after becoming the first European to retain the British Open title since James Braid, in 1906, he happily headed back to Detroit to contest the US PGA championship. It was the fourth and final major of the year and, after Birkdale, and in the absence of Woods, nobody expected anything but Harrington to lead the title charge. Doing so would mean going against the habit of a lifetime.

"Whenever I get on top of things, I don't use confidence very well," he once admitted. "Even though it is inside me, I don't use it very well in the immediate aftermath. I don't go on runs of playing well for six or eight weeks. I tend to win, and for some reason – I don't know if it is expectation in my own head or that I try too hard – (winning again) just doesn't happen."

Yet, it was impossible not to feel that he had turned a corner on all that had gone before. His win at Birkdale had simply been that impressive. He was now ranked third in the world and had not so much ground out his win at Birkdale as wrestled it away from his closest challengers, with a level of golf that none of them had come close to matching. He was the real deal, the complete major player.

"I'll tell you one thing, his performance at Birkdale, what he did there was unbelievable," says Van de Velde. "Because I was there, I finished 19th. It was incredibly difficult. But after no practise round, after thinking about maybe pulling out because his wrist was injured and the performance that he put in there, well, my hat goes off to him. Because he was ahead, miles ahead of everyone else, a head and shoulder higher than anyone else."

After years of private self-doubt, Harrington now believed in himself fully. "I played fantastic, solid golf," he reflected of Birkdale. "I got the wrong side of the draw, played the best golf, swung the club the best, did everything like you would imagine as a kid, if you were dreaming about winning the Open, you know, everything is perfect, whereas in Carnoustie obviously the 18th hole meant everything wasn't perfect. I did play well at Carnoustie, I really did hit it well, but I think the 18th hole, the 72nd hole, always left some detractors, some doubters. But, Birkdale, I played solid all week. I was in control. Even though I wasn't leading going into the final round I was the favourite and I delivered. It was exactly how you would imagine it as a kid."

Two weeks later he travelled out to America. On virtually any other course he would still have been many people's favourite to win, given the circumstances. At Oakland Hills, the scene of his greatest triumph in the game before his major breakthrough, he never looked in better shape to succeed. "Yeah, I have good memories of the course," he said upon his return. He was about to make even better ones.

Chapter 12
2008

Liam Hennessy was sitting in his car after a fitness session with the Irish rugby team in Cork when the phone rang. It was Padraig. Hennessy wasn't expecting the call. After a decade or so working with the golfer, he sensed that all was not well. The pitch of Harrington's voice immediately concerned him. He sounded anxious and disorientated. He was speaking faster than normal. He had completed two rounds of the US PGA championship but all was not going to plan. Oakland Hills was meant to be his course, his field of dreams. But, after reaching the half-way point of the tournament just four shots inside the cut mark, he was drifting upon a sea of confusion, hopelessly lost.

A 71 on Thursday had been a decent return in tricky US Open-like conditions. He'd been relatively happy with that opening score, if a little fatigued. But, on Friday, he just swung it plain badly and limped home in 74 strokes. Worse still, he felt emotionally drained and plain out of control. "I was mentally fried, my co-ordination was gone and I didn't know where the ball was going," he later admitted. "On the eighth, I hit a drive that made my tee shot on the 18th in Carnoustie look straight. It ended up in a hospitality tent. Then on the ninth hole I pulled my 4-iron 40 yards left of the green and again made a bogey." After that second round, he went straight back to his house and slept for a couple of hours. When he woke he went in search of answers and dialled his long-time fitness advisor, Hennessy.

"I knew straightaway that he was searching in his own mind, going 'What on earth is happening?'" recalls Hennessy. "But he wasn't able to articulate it to me as well as he normally would. He wasn't right at all." Nobody knows the inner workings and routines of Harrington's body better than Hennessy. Over the years he has amassed a detailed collection of statistics and body patterns that tell him exactly how Harrington is functioning from day to day. "You've got to know the individual and get to understand them," says Hennessy. "In order to understand, you have to measure and monitor. So we would have, from day one, seen that as part of our daily routine with Padraig, measure and monitor. At least then you know how you're responding to what is being done and we have continued that throughout our time working together. I learned all about his adaptations and responses to all kind of situations."

Hennessy can't say for sure but reckons it's coincidence that Harrington first sought him out to address his physical conditioning around the same time that Woods came on the scene, in 1997. Until then, golf was viewed as a sport for middle-aged men with saggy bellies. Fitness fanatic, Gary Player, used to draw quizzical looks from his peers for his devotion to training, often rising at the crack of dawn and waking hotel owners for the keys to their gym. And, while Jack Nicklaus was forced to confront the reality that he was overweight early in his career, pulling himself into impressive shape, it still didn't impact on the game generally. But, when Woods emerged as an athletic young golfer in the mid-1990s, hitting the ball miles and talking the gym language of 'reps' and 'workouts', a revolution had begun.

Harrington, never one to ignore new developments in the game, noted the change with interest but, in truth, was some way off rivalling Woods as an athlete, or of even being physically fit. His first aim was simply to lose some weight so that he'd have a little more energy on the last few holes of rounds and on the weekend at tournaments. "I weighed 15 stone, about 210 pounds," the six-foot, one-inch Harrington said of his early years on Tour. "I was fat, no question about it." As a child, he was nicknamed 'Pudge' by his brothers. Food was his passion but also his poison. While he never drank much as an adult, barely at all in fact, until he cut himself some slack in more recent years and began celebrating wins a little more wholeheartedly, he always liked his food. He once stated that he never travels anywhere without a bar of Cadbury's milk chocolate in his bag. He says his favourite food is pork chops and baked potatoes and he has been known to celebrate milestone successes in his career, such as becoming European number one and winning his major titles, with a cheeseburger and chips.

"My problem is, I put on weight and if I start with the treats I'm in trouble," he said in December 2008. "My first year on tour I was 15 stone and I went down to eleven and three-quarters stone through exercise. I've stayed at 13 stone for the last four years but now I'm creeping up to 14 stone. So I've got to work on that." By the middle of 2010, he revealed he had got back down to twelve and a half stone and appears to have settled in around this athletic weight. "I wear a monitor and it measures exactly how many calories I burn up each day," he said. "It kind of stops me obsessing. I used to be always thinking, 'Have I eaten enough today? Did I get enough energy in?'" According to the *Irish Independent* report that carried those Harrington quotes, his heart pumps at 40 beats per minute, about half the rate of the average man his age.

"Before his first victory in Madrid, in 1996, he was a totally different character," says Colin Byrne. "You could almost say he was a bit portly back then, definitely unfit. He came on tour, won within weeks and then everything seemed to change. He turned into a different being after that. He'd seen what was going on around him. You would have thought, 'He's won, why's he changing?' But, obviously, it was a great decision. And, of course, not only did he change his physical make-up by getting much fitter, he changed his swing and everything else."

Of all the data that Hennessy has collected on Harrington over the years, the most revealing details how his heart responds to the various situations he finds himself in. Put him on the first tee of a major tournament and it'll beat away with the efficiency of a metronome as he assigns each shot a low level of importance and swings away. But place him in a room with even just a couple of other people, where he is expected to speak on a topic he is interested in, and the graph of his heart rate will spike and crest as he gets deeper into conversation. He gives so freely of his time, and is such a good communicator, that he is consistently asked to fulfil all kinds of engagements. His chat with the Irish rugby team just a few months before their historic Grand Slam of 2009 was described as hugely influential and he has taken time out for one-to-ones with boxers, golfers and various other Irish sports people.

Earlier this year, he even branched out and gave a motivational speech to a group of musicians. "Just some young musicians going into competition, pianists, actually, they were," he revealed. "Somebody asked me to have a chat with them. Their big issue, and it was interesting and I didn't realise it until I sat down, (is that) they're country cousins of the Russians and everybody in classical music thinks the Russians are going to win because of heritage, and it's very hard for an Irish person to be seen as the best. Automatically, they'd be walking into a room feeling below the competition because of its history. It's trying to give them the self-confidence that just because (other competitors) were good ten years ago doesn't mean they have a right to win this time." Imploring the young musicians to aim high, he was speaking from his own experience of starting out in the world of golf as a virtual unknown outside of the Irish amateur scene. Regularly, he will talk to people about anxiety under pressure. He tells them to embrace nerves because you won't achieve anything worthwhile in life without those butterflies in your stomach.

He thinks long and hard about what he is going to say. "Yeah, Padraig engages," says Hennessy. "That's probably a really modern word but Padraig is really into the understanding of, 'Look, what exactly is going on?' In terms of himself, there is that forensic, detailed monitoring of how he responds to x, y and z and all that helps him to understand his own game better. As I said, we've been doing that for years and we've kind of profiled him and we know how he responds to any kind of given situation. Interestingly, the most stressful situations that he encounters are not on the golf course, they're more to do with the corporate work that he might do, the commitments, the talks. He gets so involved, so engaged, he just loves the banter and the conversation. He just loves the opportunity to stand up and describe and talk about the game and that in itself, because he goes so deep into it and because he's so passionate about it, it sends the little red lights flashing on the monitoring systems that we use with him. It's like, hold on, this is more stressful than competing in 30 degrees out in tournaments, in one of the majors or whatever."

With such a breadth of knowledge of his client, it didn't take Hennessy long to figure out what the problem was when a frenzied Harrington called him mid-way through the US PGA. "Funnily enough, I was just leaving the squad session where we'd done some measurements with the rugby lads that included measuring their hydration levels in the middle of the day and then when they'd finished training," reveals Hennessy, who was Director of Fitness with the Irish Rugby Football Union at the time. "So, we'd given them their feedback and made sure that the guys were hydrating well and ready for their next session. Then I'm in the car, travelling somewhere when Padraig rang. He'd just had a horrible last few holes, well, his 36 hadn't been great really. Knowing his routines, and knowing that the weather is pretty warm out there, I'm listening to him chatting to me and describing how things have gone very badly. As I say, he's not articulating himself the best. I said, 'Padraig, how many times did you go to the toilet, how many times did you have a leak during the round?' He says, 'I didn't'. Ahhhh. Right! Okay. So we see what we're dealing with. 'If you didn't, then it means you didn't have the fluids on board, and if you didn't have the fluids it sounds as if you have the effects of dehydration. So, let's start there. Let's get that right. That means you can't go back out practising. You go now and eat something and while you eat, you drink, and then you rest. Because you must give yourself time to restore. You need restoration time'."

Hennessy adds a crucial addendum to the tale; as much as he suspects so, he can't say for certain if the diagnosis of dehydration was actually correct, not when over 3,000 miles separated him from a proper examination. But, rightly or wrongly, it did the trick. By buying into the theory that he was dehydrated and then following all the steps to address it, Harrington's methodical mind was put at ease. He was satisfied that he had identified and addressed the problem, and it was no surprise that he produced some stunning golf across the weekend.

It is a critical part of his make-up that as long he believes he has found the answer to a problem, whether he actually has or not, then he will often benefit. By the sheer force of his powerful mind, he will make the change work for him. It is a character trait that swing coach Bob Torrance instantly identifies.

"You see, he gets these feelings," says Torrance. "It's not always right (what he thinks) but he believes it's right. And if he believes it's right he'll do well."

Hennessy agrees. "Yeah, you're right," he nods. "Again, nobody can say whether it was or it wasn't dehydration but, from our discussion, and from what Padraig described, it's very likely that this was the issue. So, fine, let's sort it out. That in itself puts the mind in the best place, as in one of control, and, therefore, he's in control and feels confident. And because of the situation he's not outside doing additional practise which would drain him further."

Playing at almost 7,400 yards and with rough so dense it was described as being 'on steroids', Harrington hadn't shot himself out of contention at Oakland Hills despite lying five over par after two rounds. The course was playing tough. "The 'Monster' has its teeth back, and they're sharp," bragged a club official before the tournament began, a nod to the changes that were made to make it more like the 'Monster' Ben Hogan described when winning the US Open there in 1951. Harrington was six off the lead going into the third round and the process of 'restoration' and hydration of his body was helped by a weather delay that meant he only played nine holes on Saturday. He showed enough in those few holes to hint that he was back in the scoring zone. When the hooter sounded for the suspension of play, he had just picked his ball out of the hole on the ninth green after scoring his third birdie. "I knew it would come down to mental strength more than golfing ability," he said. "I had to try and convince myself all week that I was jockeying for position until Sunday afternoon, and all I wanted was to be in with a shout for the back nine on Sunday."

For the second major championship running, the course stole the limelight from the players such was the severity of the test. Stormy weather augmented the difficulty levels. And, just like at Birkdale, Harrington was also afflicted by a health issue which, in theory, should have made the already tough task of winning virtually impossible. But, in keeping with his unique personality, both sets of circumstances played right into his hands. He has always fared best on tough courses and when struggling against the elements, whatever those may be. "I actually struggle with things that are comfortable," he admitted. "I definitely have a little bit of, I want to be fighting it."

Play resumed early on Sunday morning with the outstanding third rounds being completed in the face of a sharp, icy breeze. Harrington teed off at 7.20am, feeling much more co-ordinated and focused, if still not swinging entirely as he wished. His assault on the title began when he reeled off four straight birdies between the 13th and 16th holes. Wielding his putter like a wand he made the ball magically disappear from 30 feet on the 14th and from 20 feet on the 15th. A third round of 66, four under par, left him one over for the tournament.

"I headed back to my house for a couple of hours' sleep while the leaders were still playing," he told fans on his website. "This way I was able to go through my normal routine again. By the time I got up again the leaders had finished their rounds and I was lying four off the lead and in the second-last group with Sergio (Garcia) and Charlie Wi. It was pretty much what I was looking for at the start of the week, to be in contention come Sunday afternoon."

For the second time in the space of just 13 months, Harrington would go head-to-head with Garcia in the final round of a major championship. Former British Open winner, Ben Curtis, was in the shake-up too, but the quality of the European duo's play, and their shared history, led to an almost match-play style shoot-out between Harrington and Garcia as the day developed.

Before Carnoustie, the Irishman and the Spaniard had enjoyed good relations. They made their Ryder Cup debuts together in 1999 and were team-mates for Europe again in 2002, 2004 and 2006. In Sam Torrance's book, 'Sam', Europe's Ryder Cup captain of 2002 says he fancied Harrington and Garcia as a fourball pairing because they were both capable of grabbing a lot of birdies. But he eventually opted against it because, "I wasn't 100 per cent on the personality side of that pairing."

Harrington instead partnered Niclas Fasth, McGinley and Colin Montgomerie at the Belfry. Perhaps Torrance had picked up on disharmony between them at that stage. Outwardly, however, there was no sign of rancour between the Irishman and the Spaniard even as they vied for position at the head of the European and world rankings. But Carnoustie was a watershed in their relationship. In the press conference after the round, Garcia lamented his terrible luck and offered little in the way of congratulation to his spirited victor. "It's funny how some guys hit the pin and it goes to a foot – mine hits the pin and goes 20 feet away," he moaned of his shot on the par 3 16th in the play-off. "You know what's the saddest thing about it? It's not the first time. It's not the first time, unfortunately. So, I don't know, I'm playing against a lot of guys out there, more than the field." He didn't elaborate on exactly who or what was conspiring against him. But the reaction was slated in the media as "graceless" and can't have endeared him to Harrington.

If a lingering resentment resided within Garcia for the manner of his defeat in 2007, he had the opportunity to exact revenge at Oakland Hills. By mastering a course with fairways that averaged around 25 yards in width and whose undulating, baked-out greens were labelled the "most difficult in the country, if not the world" by one PGA official, Garcia could make a bigger statement than any he might give in a press tent. By the same token, if Harrington hadn't flinched in the face of Norman's romantic quest for glory at Birkdale then he was hardly likely to be cowed by Garcia, a player he had genuine history with.

Garcia claimed first blood in the final round, birdieing the opening hole, which Harrington could only par after a missed eight-footer. With his svelte swing, Garcia then gunned a brilliant approach to the par 5 second and tapped in for an eagle. After another birdie on the sixth, El Nino reached the turn in four under par and looked every bit the champion-in-waiting as joint leader with Curtis on three under. Harrington, on level par, had spotted his old adversary three shots on the opening nine. "It looked like his day, especially through eight and nine when he's made two really good up and downs," said Harrington later. "This is obviously an area that he struggled with in the past and it's really looking like it's going to happen for him. And I had to try and convince myself that, you know, not to get into this sentimental thing of, maybe it's his turn. Maybe he deserves it. Maybe, you know, maybe it's his day. I had to convince myself that, no, it's going to be my day and I deserved to win three majors. You've got to be very selfish in this situation when you're on the golf course."

Back across the Atlantic, BBC Sport's website gave a blow-by-blow account of proceedings, including comments from viewers. "Garcia's cookin'! Looks determined, too," stated a contributor. "Demons? What demons? And playing alongside PH, the pressure's on Padraig," claimed another.

Paul McGinley wasn't competing but did at least have a TV to catch the coverage on. He was more upbeat about Harrington's chances. "There's no doubt that Padraig's experience of playing the Ryder Cup there helped him," says McGinley. "I think the fact that he was playing with Sergio and, effectively, against Sergio, psychologically, was good for Padraig also because he'd already beaten him in the British Open the previous year. For me, the odds were stacked ... well, personally, I thought there was only going to be one winner. Padraig had a psychological edge and I knew that if it got into a dogfight, which it did, then I really fancied Padraig to win."

Harrington had achieved his first stated aim, of getting into contention on the back nine. After that, he was confident that his competitive instincts would be enough to override any deficiencies in his health or problems with his swing, even at three shots back. "I never had any doubts about Padraig when he was under the cosh," says Torrance. "He used to say to me that what he would like to do would be tying with Tiger Woods going down the back nine in a major. He used to say, 'I would like that'. So I knew it was a position he enjoyed."

Hundreds of times throughout his career, Harrington visualised images of himself striding to victory in a major championship by coming good on the final nine holes. He made the mental projection a reality with his performance on Sunday evening at Birkdale. At Oakland Hills, he began another perfectly timed charge with a birdie on the 10th after an 8-iron to 15 feet and a successful putt. Garcia could only make a par and, when Harrington went par-birdie-birdie on the next three holes, making it three birdies in four, the grind was on.

The birdie on the Par-5 12th was significant. He'd found trouble from the tee, in the trees on the right, but squeezed a 5-wood through all the danger and left himself with a routine up and down for birdie.

"Those are the moments that change tournaments, when you take shots on like that and they come off," he recalled. "I'm a great believer in making it your own responsibility whether you win or you don't win. So that's why I took it on. I realised it was the same 5-wood that I hit to the 17th at Birkdale. It's all about that in a major, it's to get to the back nine in the last round and have the responsibility that it's on your head whether you win or you don't win. You take all the shots and you take the responsibility."

Embracing responsibility on the golf course, and accepting that some high-risk shots simply have to be taken on, was one of the first lessons Harrington learned as an amateur. "Back when we were coaching Padraig, I'd often have all the provincial coaches in together for a talk," says Howard Bennett, Harrington's first serious coach. "I'd say to the coaches, 'What we can't do is take the thinking away from the player because, once we take the thinking away from the player, then we're doing them a disservice. If they've got to have us by their side all the time then there's something wrong. They've got to be able to work it out for themselves, from the information they've got.' One of the things we ended our sessions with the players with was to say, 'There's all sorts of people trying to help you, your parents are trying to help you, the GUI is trying to help you and all the different coaches here are trying to help you. But the only one guy who can make it happen is the guy sitting in your seat'. Basically, we tried to be honest with them."

Harrington and Garcia were locked on three under as they walked off the 13th green. Curtis, in the final group behind them was two under. A fresh comment from 'Jazzy B, Scotland' flashed up on BBC's online updates, "I bet Garcia bottles it, he is good but when it comes to the majors he just doesn't have the nerve to see it through – Curtis or Harrington will take it by one stroke." Harrington moved back out of the lead after a bogey on the 14th. They both parred the 15th. With three to play the state of play was, Garcia and Curtis minus three, Harrington minus two. Curtis ultimately removed himself from the battle by bogeying the 15th and the 17th.

A year earlier, Harrington's near-perfect approach to the first play-off hole in Carnoustie was the shot that separated him from Garcia. His resulting birdie, to Garcia's bogey, left him in a strong position to close out that contest. The crucial hole at the US PGA, the game changer, was the 16th. Again, it was a loose Garcia shot that went in Harrington's favour. Both players found pole position from the tee on the par 4, leaving short irons to a green guarded by water on the front and right. Anything right was dead and, when Garcia chunked his approach short and right, he signed his own death warrant.

Harrington was surprised by the mistake. "You can't get into a match play situation," warned caddie Flood after seeing the door open. Harrington nodded silently. He was 135 yards out and decided on a wrists and arms 8-iron, under the moderate wind, with a slight draw. He overcooked it and caught a greenside bunker left, leaving 29 yards to a pin with water now at the rear. He had looked his gift horse in the mouth yet delivered in the more difficult of the two scenarios by getting up and down with a chip and 20-foot putt for par, punching the air twice to acknowledge the feat. Garcia bogeyed and they were level again with two to play. The third player in the group, Charlie Wi, shot himself out of contention with a final day 74. Walking off the 16th he turned to his caddie and said, "God, this is a lot of fun just to watch."

Earlier in the week, Harrington and Flood had agreed that the way to play the par 3 17th on Sunday was to land the ball short and let it run out on the firm green. This would probably leave a putt from the lower tier up to a raised section where the pin would be. Rain had softened up the surface though and the plan changed. Harrington took dead aim with a 5-iron, struck it superbly and watched as it touched down like a butterfly with sore feet on the softened green, close to the cup. Neck muscles tensed and showing beneath an unbuttoned shirt, he flicked a salutary hand to the crowd, his eyes out on sticks. The energy of his aura could have powered downtown Detroit for the evening. "This is it," he said to himself, thinking he'd just won the tournament. An even better shot in from Garcia, allied to the fact that Harrington was 10 feet from the pin when he thought it was only four or six, halted his gallop momentarily. But he sank the putt and Garcia, from closer, missed with a nervy pull.

With a hole to play, Harrington had reeled Garcia in and ground him down. He was reprising the Tom Watson role at Turnberry in 1977, the duel in the sun. Harrington had heard about that British Open climax when Watson came from behind to steal victory from Jack Nicklaus. Growing up, he even got his hands on a video of the epic battle and watched it over and over. What he loved about Watson was his grit. Just like Harrington at Oakland Hills, Watson had leaked a few bad shots over the week but still delivered when it went down to the wire. "It was the sheer, 'I'm going to get this job done, regardless'," recalled Harrington. "That's what made it so exciting and that's particularly what I admired about Watson. It was just sheer bravado on his part. The ability to just keep ripping it like he's never missed a shot in his life, I love that attitude."

By holing at the 16th and 17th under the most intense pressure imaginable Harrington, like Watson, had effectively wrestled major success from his great rival. But, never one to take the easy route to victory, he refused, or perhaps was unable, to coast home. And, as he watched his tee shot on the 18th land and settle in the face of a fairway bunker his eyes were back bulging again, staring manically as if awoken in his home by a violent intruder in the dead of night. Garcia was in no state of mind to steal away with the Wanamaker trophy, however, and, after taking three to reach the green, ultimately left Harrington with a 15-footer for par. Curtis was still playing behind them but, in his mind, Harrington was putting for the championship. He saw the line of the putt instantly, a doubler breaker, slightly downhill. He aimed a cup right, watched as the ball trundled down the hill and broke into a half-jig as it caught the left edge of the hole and dropped down. Two fist pumps, followed by a third for good measure, was his way of capturing the moment of a lifetime. Not that it mattered all too much now but Garcia repeated the mistake of 17 and failed to hole from the shorter range, ending a tournament he appeared destined to win with a bogey. He finished joint second with Curtis.

Almost four years on from Oakland Hills, and five from Carnoustie,

Garcia shot 75 in the third round of the 2012 US Masters. He did so after reaching the half-way point on his best number for 10 years. His slide of just 17 places from fourth in the world in August 2008 to 21th in 2012 didn't do justice to the full extent of his troubles since duelling with his Irish nemesis. Garcia's swing was still a picture of athleticism at the Masters. He was up there with third-round playing partner Rory McIlroy for sheer aesthetic beauty when swinging his woods and irons. But his putter continued to display a mind all of its own. It was a painful collapse and, at the tender age of just 32, Garcia declared at the Masters that he was incapable of ever winning a major.

It is more than just a touch ironic that this bottoming out of Garcia's career occurred at a tournament that marked the return of Harrington to the top of the major leader boards after his own lean spell. "I'm not good enough, I don't have the thing I need to have," stated Garcia. "In 13 years I have come to the conclusion that I need to play for second or third place. I had my chances and opportunities and I wasted them. I have no more options. I wasted my options." Harrington's heroics in 2007 and 2008 must have sapped the life out of Garcia. Events at Oakland Hills only added to the chasm in their relationship. "That's twice he did Garcia," says Bob Torrance, looking back. "Garcia was shattered, absolutely shattered he was." Asked if they can ever be pals, Torrance responds with a rueful shake of the head. "No, no, they'll never be pals. They'll always show each other respect. But there's always that feeling when the two of them are together. They don't sit down and talk like you and I are talking now."

Later in 2008, both players represented Europe on Nick Faldo's Ryder Cup team at Valhalla. Word reached Des Smyth via the golfing grapevine that the duo had patched up their differences that week. "I do remember a situation where they were apparently sitting together," says Smyth. "There had been the obvious build-up of tension. They happened to be sitting opposite each other and in close quarters and somebody passed a comment and there was a big giggle and a laugh. As far as I know all the tension was let go then. Personally, I have great time for Sergio. I would have said he was the player of the week for us at the 2006 Ryder Cup. Just an amazing player, an amazing talent."

If there really was a 'Valhalla Accord', it didn't last long. Harrington revealed that Garcia did indeed say 'his piece' at the tournament and let it all out. "Some of the lads eventually drew it out of him and he got to tell me that he really wanted to smash that putter over my head," said Harrington. But expanding on the situation in a separate interview, he conceded that they are just too dissimilar to ever truly get on. "We have zero in common, bar the fact that we both play golf," he told the *Guardian* newspaper. "He is the antithesis of me and I am the antithesis of him. We play the game in exactly the opposite way. He is destined to find the long game easy and the short game hard and I am the opposite." Days later again, Garcia, told the *Daily Mirror* newspaper, "He is not my best friend. It'd probably not be good for us to be paired together (in the Ryder Cup)." As 2008 rolled over into 2009, and a world of opportunity presented itself to Harrington, Garcia was the last thing or person on his mind. It was unfortunate, given the roll that he was on, that he would have to wait until the following April and the Masters tournament to tee it up again and contend for another major. But the down time did at least give him an opportunity to reflect on the incredible achievement of that 13-month spell between July 2007 and August 2008. He had overtaken Scot, Tommy Armour, as the last European to win the US PGA. He was the first man from his continent to win the British Open and the US PGA in the same year. And he was the first from his side of the pond to win consecutive majors in the same year. "I really do like the fact that no other European has won two majors consecutively," he said. "Because I obviously held a lot of those European players whom I grew up watching in high esteem. To believe that I achieved something that they hadn't is very special."

Harrington doesn't read articles about himself. But if he walked by a newsstand in late August after his third major triumph and merely glanced at the cover of 'Golf World' magazine, he couldn't but have smiled. For years, he'd been dogged by all those second-place finishes. He'd been dubbed the nearly-man of Irish golf. Many believed he'd never shake that label. Unlike Garcia, nobody was calling him the best player not to have won a major before Carnoustie. Yet there, beneath a picture of him punching the air in delight on the 18th green at Oakland Hills, fist clenched as he recoiled from delivering the knock-out blow to Garcia, were two words that summed up his journey and his new status: The Closer. Now there was a headline. One he'd waited all his golfing career to read.

PART 4 2009 - 2012

Chapter 13
2009

It felt like a meeting of Golfers Anonymous. All that was missing was the stock introductory, "Hi, my name is Padraig. I'm obsessed with my swing". It was September, 2003, and Harrington was laying bare his golfing soul to journalists at St Andrews as he set about defending the Dunhill Links Championship title he'd won 12 months earlier.

"I have been obsessive for five years," he opened up. "You know, when I came out on Tour, I kept my head down and did my own thing for a couple of years but the continual, how do you put this, the continual, sort of, knocking, 'Oh you're a great putter, you chip and putt, you scramble, you do this, you do that but it's the craziest thing that you can't swing the golf club very well' (bothered me). So I've spent five years trying to get the other part of my game up to scratch and, undoubtedly, I've become very obsessive about it. But the whole idea, and my wife will laugh at me when I say this, the whole idea is, if I do the work now, before I have a young family and things like that, when I won't have as much time, then, hopefully, in the future I won't have to work as hard. The whole intention is that, in time, I will, like Colin Montgomerie, have a low-maintenance golf swing."

Harrington's intentions in 2003 were wholesome, the reasoning sound but, truthfully, and he must have known this himself, they never stood a chance of coming to fruition. In fact, the idea of him laying off the practise and satisfying himself with a low-maintenance swing is almost absurd. His mind has always been too busy and too alive to the possibility of improvement to sit still and simply maintain a swing.

In 2006, three years after that public confession at St Andrews, he began a programme of swing improvements that would last nearly five years before he felt they were finally complete. Even in the middle of his major-winning gains of 2008, he spent 12 hours solid one particular day practising at his home in Dublin with Bob Torrance. "Just come out at 10 o'clock in the morning, look at a few things and see if we have anything to work on," he'd said to his coach when arranging the session. They didn't leave the range until half-past ten that night. "That was twelve and a half hours," recalls Torrance. Whether or not such vigorous change was necessary, is, frankly, a moot point where Harrington is concerned. Change was, and is, the only thing he has ever known so it was guaranteed to occur, for better or for worse.

"I have obsessively changed things since I was 15 years of age, obsessively changed things with my swing all the time," he said in 2011. In one rare interview he even appeared to get to the very heart of his compulsion to practise and adapt his swing, explaining that the chance to do so had been denied in his earlier years. "I was brought up on a golf course that you could never have perfection in the long game," he said. "It was a tricky golf course and you really had to have an unbelievable short game. It had a practise ground that wasn't 130 yards long. So I never got to practise as a kid, you know, working on my swing, and I think the minute I got from 16 years of age when I got exposed to practise grounds and driving ranges and things like that, I've always had a fascination for trying to get better and better and better in terms of my technique."

In Harrington's mind, becoming a triple major winner gave him particular leeway to experiment as he moved into 2009. He'd already been tweaking and changing for a couple of years, since 2006, when he'd identified that he, "tended to tilt under in my backswing and then go very lateral in my downswing ... something I've been trying to (fix) for a long time and just cannot".

Wrongly, as he would later acknowledge, he felt that he could discuss the changes he was making in public and that he would be cut some slack, in view of his tremendous recent gains. He would learn that it didn't work like that. He had thrown bread to the starving masses of golf fans and they were ravenous for more, utterly unforgiving when denied.

In late December, 2008, he gave an intriguing interview to the *Irish*

Examiner newspaper where he compared his passion for change to that of the revered musician Yehudi Menuhin. He retold the tale of a female fan who once approached the violinist after a concert and said, "I'd give my life to play the violin like that". Menuhin, according to Harrington, replied, "Madam, I already have". He identified with such application and dedication over a lifetime. "A lot of people wouldn't get involved in this discussion but I've changed everything," he said.

In the same interview, he also made the shocking admission that he had effectively won his major titles while battling the 'bunker yips', an unlikely revelation considering the many great bunker shots he'd played under pressure in those tournaments, including the up and down on the 16th in the final round of the US PGA. "I've had the yips in the bunker for about two years," he said. "Big trouble. If you asked my fellow pros, there's probably not one who wouldn't say, 'No way, I've seen you'. But it's me feeling it." He added: "Anyone looking at my game would rate my pitching as one of my stronger aspects but I think I've a terrible flaw in my pitching. I know I can putt well but I can putt better. I certainly believe I can hit the ball better, straighter, longer. I've just gone through my whole game and that gets me out to practise."

So it was that he entered 2009 with the engine of his game exposed, his overalls greasy from another winter spent beneath the bonnet. By April, he would be back on the road and ready to cruise down Magnolia Lane again at the Masters with all the efficiency of a finely tuned engine, or so the plan went.

His first taste of Augusta had come nine years earlier, in 2000. He'd just won in Brazil and was on a high, but the fabled old Georgia course still took his breath away when he arrived on its doorstep. He remembers coming up the famous driveway, reaching the clubhouse and wondering where to go next. He spotted a group of Irish and wandered over. "I went over to them looking for a bit of security and Sam Snead was with them, sitting down having a drink," he told the *Observer* in 2003. "So my first experience of Augusta was sitting around listening to Sam Snead telling all these wonderful stories. You couldn't beat it."

He performed well on his Masters' debut, recovering from an opening

76 with a 69 to make the cut and finished tied 19th. Nearly a decade on, he drove up Magnolia Lane as a veteran performer in 2009 and under the most intense pressure that he'd ever felt coming into a major championship. The media talked of the 'Paddy Slam', that Harrington might achieve four major wins in a row – like Woods did across 2000 and 2001. After his finish to 2008, he was halfway there. Since shooting back-to-back 66s at Oakland Hills the previous August, the golfing world had also been building for months towards a head-to-head between Harrington and a fit again Woods. Much like 2012's anticipated shoot-out between Woods and Rory McIlroy, the 2009 showdown never materialised, however, and, after an opening 69, Harrington shot three consecutive 73s to finish tied for 35th place on even par. He followed it up by missing the cut at the Irish Open and the US Open and, by early July, had spiralled into a tailspin with five missed cuts in a row.

It was around this time that a delivery man to his home informed him he was playing "shite". Fans felt compelled to offer advice. "I've got it all the time, advice, different suggestions, strange letters," he told the *Independent on Sunday*. "There was one telling me to bathe in salt to get rid of all that radiation." But he didn't bathe in salt. Nor did he take the delivery man's comment to heart. Instead, after that fifth missed cut in a row at the French Open – which included a triple bogey eight on the 14th hole – he retreated to the practise ground and finally solved the riddle that had plagued him for the first half of the year.

"I've been trying to find something out in my swing for a few years now but (I pursued it) wholeheartedly for the first seven months of the season," he said. "Eventually, I found out what it is. I haven't quite worked it into my game but it's given me peace of mind, clarity in my own head."

The following week he won his third straight Irish PGA title at the European Club and set off to Turnberry to challenge for a more important three-in-a-row of British Open wins. He would later observe that the third major tournament of the year came "two weeks early" in the grooving in process. He made the cut but finished tied for 65th well behind winner Stewart Cink. Still, he was as good as his word regarding the two weeks he required and the following month he finally went head-to-head with

Woods at the prestigious WGC Bridgestone Invitational.

Woods and Harrington went back nearly 15 years, to a first meeting in Rabiottis restaurant in the Welsh seaside village of Penarth. They first met there on the eve of the 1995 Walker Cup when Harrington was playing for Great Britain and Ireland and Woods was the star of the travelling USA panel at Royal Porthcawl. The young Californian already carried quite a reputation. He was soon to become the only player to win three US amateur titles in a row and, the previous April, topped the driving stats at his first Masters, averaging 311 yards around Augusta.

That season of 1995, he played in three of the four major championships before arriving in Wales. "The two teams, just the teams and the captains, went out for a meal on the Wednesday before the match," recalls GB&I's Walker Cup captain of 1995, Clive Brown. "Padraig and Jody (Fanagan) sat next to Woods. Basically, it was Padraig and Jody who carried out the conversation. Tiger was pretty quiet. It was one of the best restaurants in the area. We had it to ourselves and they had it decked out in the Irish Tricolour, the Stars and Stripes and the Union Jack. It was a really nice occasion. It would be interesting to hear what Jody and Padraig thought of that meal because I believe they came back thinking, 'You know, who is this Tiger Woods?' It was quite a good thing from our point of view."

Fanagan recalls the meal, though he doesn't buy into the suggestion that they may have been intimidated to begin with. "Maybe the fact that you meet him like that and the other American guys, maybe it does break down the barrier a bit," says Fanagan. "But I think Padraig and I were very confident anyway." The actual contest between Fanagan and Harrington and Woods and US stalwart, John Harris, has gone down in the annals of Irish amateur golf. "It was a very miserable day," remembers Fanagan. "It rained from seven in the morning until seven at night. We never really got to speak to them because we were under an umbrella, trying to stay dry. It was Padraig and his brother, myself and my caddie, and that was it. Totally focused. Knew we were in for a tough game, stuck to our own things. Never thought we were going to lose, to be honest.

"We were playing well. John Harris hit a couple of bad shots. Tiger wasn't pleased at all. It was very unusual because Harris actually topped two shots. One was on the fifth tee. He flat out topped his drive, 80 yards. Tiger said, 'That's so bad it's almost funny'. They obviously went in opposite directions (up the fairway) after that. The second one was on the 16th and, again, Tiger was not pleased. John Harris was a good player. He just had a bad day in the rain, couple of bad shots. They were actually a very strong pairing. And they put those guys against us, which said a lot. It was all square most of the way around and I think we won 16 and 17 to win 2&1. It was a great win."

Fanagan finished the Walker Cup with an enviable perfect record. He never seriously contemplated turning pro. He was in his late 20s, married and mortgaged. Though several months later, after Harrington had successfully navigated qualifying school to earn his European Tour card, Fanagan did ask his buddy if he reckoned he, too, could have made it through. "I remember we were sitting together at some sports awards, in January I think it was, and I said to him, 'Would I have had a chance out there?'" recalls Fanagan. "And he said, 'Probably not, with your current stroke play performances'. That's Padraig. That's the way he saw it. Straight and honest." Fanagan still works in the family business as a Funeral Director. He remains close with Harrington and caddied for him in the par 3 tournament before the 2005 Masters. In 2007, when he was captain of Milltown Golf Club in their centenary year, Fanagan asked Harrington to come up to the club for an hour one evening. "He came up and brought the Claret Jug with him," says Fanagan. "We had the juniors up and he did a questions and answers session with them. It was meant to be an hour, eight until nine. He left around half 11."

Harrington and Woods, of course, went on to become world golfing icons, facing off many times throughout the 2000s as both Ryder Cup and PGA Tour opponents. One of the great imponderables is whether Harrington would have won his majors in 2008 had Woods not 'shut it down' for the rest of the season and undergone knee surgery. Tiger was in the field at Carnoustie and didn't threaten but missed the events at Royal Birkdale and Oakland Hills the following year. Woods' former swing coach, Hank Haney, claims in his book, 'The Big Miss', that Woods might well have won both events had he played. He suggests that, had Woods delayed corrective surgery and battled through the pain barrier at the British Open and the US PGA, like he did at Torrey Pines, then he may have added major wins 15 and 16 to his personal haul, leaving Harrington with just one. "Based on what he accomplished at Torrey Pines with a physically compromised game, I now think there was a reasonable chance that Tiger without surgery could have won all of the last three majors of 2008," claimed Haney.

In late 2009, golfing fans finally got to see the two players clash head-on. Perhaps, they hoped, it was the beginning of one of the game's great rivalries. Harrington had finally found his touch again after the torrid start to the year. It was claimed by one media outlet that the changes, and the resulting loss of form, cost him €1.6m, a figure based on what he earned in the events he played, compared with his average earnings in the same period in the previous five years.

In reality, it was impossible to compare. He was treading new ground in 2009. He battled shingles over winter as a result of answering all the requests for his time as a triple major winner. With more cameras than ever trained upon him, he even learned, for the first time, that he has an aversion to flash photography which leaves him with headaches. But, in the second half of 2009, he finally appeared to have come to terms with his new status and, just as importantly, his new swing. If €1.6m was the price he had to pay for that, then it was a figure he could live with.

After three rounds of the Bridgestone Invitational in early August, he led the tournament by three strokes from Woods. In the final round, he played the first 15 holes just as he wanted. "I was well in the zone and felt I was buzzing along," he said, still one clear of Woods despite the world number one's Sunday charge. But a triple bogey eight from Harrington on the 667 yard par 5, against a Woods' birdie, drained all the intensity from the contest. It is possible that this meltdown affected Harrington far more than he ever admitted.

A week later, in contention once more at the US PGA championship alongside Woods, he had another meltdown and took an eight on the par 3 eighth at Hazeltine. He dropped out of contention and finished with a final round of 78. Not until the 2012 Masters would he come even close to contending again for a major title. Woods laid the blame for Harrington's collapse at the Bridgestone on John Paramor, the long-time European Tour referee who put both players 'on the clock' before their tee shots on the 16th. According to Paramor, they had fallen 17 minutes behind schedule at that stage. Harrington admitted he 'rushed' two shots on the hole, a 5-iron lay-up that left him out of position, and a bladed lob wedge from the back of the green that found the water.

Woods argued that the official's intervention "got in the way of such a great battle". He claimed that, "if he was able to take his time, look at it and analyse it", Harrington wouldn't have boned his chip into the water. "I should have been able to control that situation," said Harrington with typical magnanimity. "I failed miserably that day."

The thing was, Harrington was the one player who should have been capable of coping with the situation. He has never been a fast player and, as a result, has had to learn to take the interventions of rules officials in his stride. "I'm never going to be the quickest player, I think too much," he said in 2003. A year later he confided to Bob Rotella that being a slow player had cost him the Buick Classic title.

"He lost that tournament in a play-off with Sergio Garcia and Rory Sabbatini," wrote Rotella in 'Your 15th Club, The Inner Secret to Great Golf'. "He told me he lost it because, just before a crucial shot, he was distracted by some noise or movement in the gallery. He knew instantly that he needed to step away from the ball, clear his mind and begin his routine again but he didn't because he was concerned with his reputation as a slow player. So he hit the shot without a clear mind and a focus on his target. It did not go well and he lost the play-off to Sergio Garcia. 'I knew I should have walked away', he said later."

Retief Goosen famously called Harrington on his slow play as they battled for the European Order of Merit title in late 2002. "I'm really happy he's playing behind me – so I can finish," said Goosen on the eve of the Madrid Open. "He's definitely the slowest player on Tour. He's not getting fined so, clearly, he operates just inside the rules. Harrington's on the limit. If he's got 40 seconds to play a shot, he plays it in 39. I know other players who used to be slow but they have learned to play quicker. I don't know how he'd last in America. They are stricter on slow times over there. In America, they'll just come up and say, 'You've got a fine', no warnings or anything. I don't really get annoyed with slow play, I just like to get into some sort of rhythm. That's why I struggled at the Dunhill [a slow-placed tournament that includes amateurs]. I'm not one of those players who can hit a shot and then wait 20 minutes to hit another, though that suits Harrington."

Colin Byrne, who began working as Goosen's caddie the following year, until 2008, shares his former boss's opinion on the pace of Harrington's play. "I don't think it's a secret to anyone, even now, that Harrington is a particularly slow player, and there's no doubt that he does put pressure on the people he plays with," says Byrne. "I suspect, in his own head, he can't play quickly. If he plays quickly he plays badly, in his own head. It doesn't benefit him. He is trying to squeeze the round dry, which is what he's done best all his life. For him to squeeze the round dry, unfortunately, seems to take an awful long time." Byrne argues that, "A referee timing him is so part of his routine … just another thing that he accounts for in the whole process. It's not a surprise. It's not a shock."

Yet it obviously came as a shock at the Bridgestone tournament. Exactly how much Paramor's action affected Harrington and precipitated the subsequent collapse at Hazeltine a week later is the great unknown. What's definite is that he wouldn't know form like those two weeks for nearly three more years.

Chapter 14
2010

By winning three majors, Harrington empowered those around him. He broke the door down for his European Tour colleagues and, in 2010, they began to follow him through. First to step over the major threshold was Graeme McDowell at the US Open, followed by Louis Oosthuizen at the British Open, and Germany's Martin Kaymer at the US PGA. Darren Clarke and Rory McIlroy have since joined the club.

"He definitely broke down that door for the whole of Europe and I think he deserves a lot of credit for that," says Des Smyth. "Because there was a period there where no one here could win a major. It was all Tiger. Monty didn't do it, he should have done it. Sergio was moving up, he should have been doing it but never did it. So, when Padraig did it, and did it again, he gave all the other guys belief. That's the way it works. If we're out there competing every day, you and I, on Tour, and I know I can beat you if my game is right and then you step onto the big stage in a major and win it, well, I'm thinking, 'Fuck, if he can do it, I can do it'. That's the effect it has on players. And it goes wider than just Ireland. The other European guys are seeing this and going, 'Those Irish, I can beat them. Even though they're my buddies, I should be doing that'. He gave them all that belief."

Jean Van de Velde concurs. "Look at Darren Clarke winning the British Open in 2011," says the French man. "I think when someone (like Harrington) comes from where you come from and was bred the way you were bred and has the same way of thinking, it gives you the confidence and the trust and the belief to say, 'He's like me. Why not me?' It is a great inspiration. Without a doubt."

Pat Ruddy, the European Club owner who saw Harrington off to Carnoustie and Royal Birkdale in 2007 and 2008, perhaps sums it up best.

"In the world of man, getting him to believe in himself is the battle," says Ruddy. "But if he can do that, then he can get others around him to think differently as well. It's like the four-minute mile, and Ronnie Delaney coming back from Melbourne and the Olympics in 1956. Before then, the four-minute mile was the goal, a distant target, but run a four-minute mile now and you won't even get to the grocery shop first for your loaf of bread. The shelves will be cleared when you get there in four minutes. So, these thresholds are hugely important, that you take them down. Padraig Harrington took down that barrier for the Irish. There's no question about that. He took down the barriers and history has to be recorded in that way. Not that anyone would ever want to, but no one should ever forget that he was the man who tore that barrier down."

Harrington helped his rivals in other ways over the years, too. He would regularly pass on Rotella's books, for instance, to anyone who was interested in learning more about the inner psychology of golf. He felt comfortable doing so because he was sure that none of them would invest themselves in the concept, or essentially live it, like he would. But, as 2010 also came and went for him and he missed cuts in three of the four majors, earning a best finish of 22nd in the US Open, it was clear he was being passed by. The world of golf stands still for no man, not even a triple major winner.

The Irish golfer of 2010 was, unquestionably, McDowell, who capped his major-winning year by securing the winning point in the Ryder Cup at Celtic Manor and then beating Woods in a straight head-to-head at his own tournament. With McIlroy emerging as a giant of world golf and Shane Lowry, in 2009, taking Harrington's title as the last Irishman to win the Irish Open, he had noticeably slipped back. His excellent form of late 2009 had petered out and though he put together a brief charge in Killarney to take second place behind Ross Fisher in the Irish Open of 2010, he would finish the year in 23rd position in the world rankings. It was the first time in a decade that he had ended a calendar year outside of the top 20. As one commentator put it, he had morphed from European golf's evangelist to its great enigma, still trying to perfect his swing.

He offered a bullish defence of his position to 'Golf' magazine, in April

2010, disregarding various statistics that appeared to confirm his diminishing returns. For instance, he torpedoed the stat that suggested he was driving the ball 10 yards shorter. "On the hole, where driving distance is measured at Torrey Pines, I hit 5-wood," responded Harrington. "It's suicide to hit driver on that hole. So I wouldn't believe stats. There's no good player out there who has a driving distance advantage over me. Length is not an issue." He also explained in detail the exact changes he had made to his swing early in 2009 and again across the winter of 2009 and into 2010, which he insisted made him a 'better' player. "It was a number of things," he said. "The sequence of my downswing was out, which basically meant that my hips were late, causing my torso to be late. So I was trying to establish the timing of my downswing. I changed the impact position of my wrists so I'm more pronated than ever. I changed the coil in my backswing – I used to come out of my coil. But, ultimately, it came down to needing to stabilise my hips more so that my upper body is being forced to catch up, to keep accelerating." And though he accepted that he was still a 'work in progress', he was confident that he would score well in 2010.

That it didn't happen, and that he finished the year outside the top echelon of world golfers may, in his defence, have been down to more than just swing issues. For, in mid-2008, the R&A and USGA confirmed new rules regarding the volume and sharpness of grooves on irons which affected him deeply. The changes kicked into place on January 1, 2010. They were spurred on by the rise of so called 'bomb and gouge' golf. The game's governors watched with horror as big hitters opened their shoulders from the tee, safe in the knowledge that wherever they landed, even in thick rough, high spin 'box grooves' would allow them to gouge it out and still control the ball on the greens. These deeper, sharper grooves reduced the chances of a 'flier' – where grass and moisture is caught between the club face and the ball, adding unwanted yardage – and allowed players to spin the ball even from poor lies. But, under the new rule, manufacturers were forced to round out, or dull, the edges of their grooves, producing less bite on the ball and making it more difficult to impart spin and control the ball.

The change divided players. Some weren't concerned. Others claimed it was a huge adjustment. Harrington fell into the latter category. He is a player who has always known his clubs intimately and has always set them up to perform the most specific of functions for his unique swing.

As a kid, he'd shared a set of fake Ping irons with one of his brothers. When he was 15, he finally got a set to himself. He wanted flashy blades, like all the good players used at the time. But even at that young age he bowed to pragmatism and settled on a set of more forgiving, perimeter weighted Maxfli clubs. "I wanted to use the blades but I also wanted as much help as I could get," he explained. "I wasn't good enough for blades." In more recent years, he's been teased for carrying a forgiving hybrid club instead of a 4-iron. "It gets the job done," he shrugged. Performance, in his eyes, has always been paramount and, until 2010, he had been extracting peak performance from his irons by taking full advantage of the old rules regarding grooves.

Up to 2010, both box grooves and traditional 'V' grooves were legal and conforming. He would take a set of each with him to every tournament he played in, two sets of irons. It was the appliance of intricate golfing science as he found that each set possessed differing and contrasting qualities that could be exploited on different courses. Out of the rough, for example, his 7-iron with the V grooves flew 170 yards. The 7-iron with box grooves flew 130. "I explained this to two pros last week," he told 'Golf World' magazine in mid-2010. "They looked at me like I had two heads. But from two-inch rough there's 40 yards difference between the 7-iron in each set."

Sometimes he would use one set, sometimes the other. Often he would mix them up and choose a composite set, like he did at the Dunhill Links championship. "So I might have a V groove 7-iron, knowing it goes 170 yards, but out of the rough I'd hit the box groove 6-iron," he continued. "I may get a flier with the 7, so I could hit the 6 safe in the knowledge that I won't get a flier."

Harrington may have been one of the 'bomb and gouge' players in the minds of officials when they introduced the groove rule. In his major winning years he drove the ball far but not always straight – he was 139th in driving accuracy on the European Tour in 2008 – yet continually escaped with expert short iron and wedge play. Unsurprisingly, there was an instant and quantifiable effect on his game playing under the new rules. He'd been first in 'scrambling' – getting up and down for par after missing a green in regulation – on the European Tour in 2009 yet, for 2010, after the new rule, he wasn't even ranked in the top 180.

Initially, he put on a brave face and predicted he would cope. He said one of his great skills was course management and argued that this would be rewarded more now with a premium placed on better strategising and navigation. But, reflecting several months later on how the changes actually impacted on him, he admitted it had hurt him badly. "I would say to you that the groove change has made a massive change to my game," he revealed. "Like, an incredibly big change. Like, a massive change. The game is a lot easier with the other grooves for me. So they have gone back on the rules and made the game tougher for certain people."

Another issue that emerged for Harrington in 2010 related to a reported €4m hole in his finances due to a failed investment. To what extent it impacted on his game only he knows. But to a level-headed man who grew up in modest surroundings as the son of a policeman, the loss surely stung. The *Sunday Independent* newspaper reported in August, 2010, that Harrington lost a little over €4m after a technology firm that he had invested money in, U4EA Technologies, went into administration. He refused to confirm the exact amount, only confirming that, "a company in which I'm a minority shareholder in went into administration".

When probed about the loss, he said, "I'll tell you that it made no material difference to my life. I'm quite happy to say that. A UK company manages my finances and does safe, secure stuff. I then take some money and invest it myself in private equity things." With estimated gross career earnings of around €70m in 2010, even allowing for Bank of Ireland's decision not to renew their sponsorship deal with him that May, Harrington was financially healthy enough to write it off, on paper at least. His mind was a different matter. In 2012, a *Sunday Times* rich list tagged Harrington's net worth at Stg£33m. As the global recession took its grip, Harrington noted that 'birdies are recession proof'. He claimed that he was one of the lucky ones with a strong income source still at his disposal. Yet that income source and the extent of his earnings depended to a great extent on how well he was playing.

A third and more intangible issue that may have played on Harrington's mind was exactly where to go next. It may not have been noticed by most but his professional career had now played out to exactly the same point as his amateur career.

Consider the following: After a period of finding his feet as an amateur, that included several years of frustrating runner-up finishes, he finally won his first major amateur title in 1994, the West of Ireland title. The following year, 1995, he won two more, the Irish Open and Close amateur championships. Then he turned pro. Once in the paid ranks, another period of finding his feet took place, followed by an uncannily similar run of second-place finishes. Eventually, just like his amateur career, he made his breakthrough with one major title in 2007, the British Open. Then, just like his early amateur days, he followed it up with two more major title wins the next year, 2008, at Birkdale and Oakland Hills. His three major titles as a professional came in a 13-month spell. It had taken almost exactly the same, 16 months, as an amateur. But where to now, in 2010?

His apparent answer was to return to the dirt, Hogan style, and dig out a new, improved swing. The public and media openly questioned the sanity of a triple major winner continuing down a road of apparent self-destruction, though his peers were more sympathetic. They realised that by leaving no stone unturned to find some morsel of improvement, Harrington was merely sticking by the habit of a lifetime. Anyone that doubted his commitment to cracking the code that had so far eluded him need only have followed him around his practise round at the 2010 Masters.

A golfweek.com reporter did just that and was stunned by the lengths that he witnessed Harrington and caddie, Flood, go to as they prepared for the first major of the season. "At each green, Harrington would remove a small levelling tool (a block layer's spirit level), then nudge it here, tweak it there, all to determine, well, one can't be exactly sure what the Irishman was factoring in," he reported. "As he moved it fractions of inches here and there, Harrington rolled golf balls towards it, then golf balls away from it. And with every couple of balls, Harrington would remove a yardage book from his back right pocket and make notations. All the while, mind you, Flood was at another portion of the green making notations in his book. This started at the 10th, then through Amen Corner and onward through 14, 15 and even to the majestic par 3 16th. This was truly a study in meticulous preparation and, as Harrington moved from 16 to 17 and up 18, several patrons hung around to watch, as did the litter crew, the men working the mowers and even the security officials. Fascinating stuff."

More recently, at this year's British Open at Royal Lytham and St Anne's, Harrington and Flood performed their spirit level tests again on the greens. "It was really more an exercise in, 'This is what I see and this is what the spirit level says I see', and just calibrating my eyesight more than anything else," he explained.

The sort of excellence that Harrington was now chasing as he attempted to rival Seve Ballesteros and Nick Faldo as European's most successful player ever, was, arguably, lost on amateur players and non-golfers who were perplexed by his antics. "Well, I don't think people understand him, and that's the truth," says Des Smyth. "They don't understand the mind-set of a pro. I mean Tiger Woods never stops trying to improve, and he's the best player that ever played in my opinion. I know Gary Player quite well and every day Gary went out to practise, he had something on his mind, to try and improve. I just think that's the way the game is set up – if you're not out there trying to get better, you're going to go backwards. Padraig realised that and that's the way he's been all his career."

Woods' former swing coach, Butch Harmon, who went on to work with Phil Mickelson, says improvement, or the constant pursuit of it at least, is the natural state for top players, particularly those who have been hugely successful. "I think great players get bored," said Harmon, discussing in early 2011 why Harrington went to such great lengths to improve a major-winning technique. "I think they're bored because everything comes so easy to them. I think they love a challenge, whether it's a challenge of changing or trying to get better. I don't think Padraig is any different. It's one of the things that make them the great players they are – they're never satisfied with who they are and where they are. They're always trying to get better. We can sit back and say, 'What is wrong with this guy, why would he change when he's had so much success?' But we're not living in his shoes. We don't know what motivates them and drives them. Padraig Harrington is a perfect example. Here's a guy who won three majors very quickly, was a very consistent winner around the world for many years. All of a sudden he goes in and revamps his game. He hasn't won as consistently. But I gotta give him the benefit of the doubt. I think change is difficult and when he gets comfortable with what he's doing I think he'll win majors again. He's that good. That's for sure."

Another former Woods coach, Hank Haney, suggests in his book, that Woods overplayed the extent of his own swing changes at various points in his career, to take pressure off himself. There is no suggestion that Harrington has been anything less than honest about his overhaul though some believe it is not as dramatic as has been publicly portrayed. "It's really just tinkering," claims Jody Fanagan, who has remained close with Harrington since their amateur days. "It's not picking it all apart and reassembling everything. It's minor things. I think people are probably a bit harsh on him in that respect. A swing is a swing."

Ex-amateur colleague and ex-European Tour member, Gary Murphy, says he could see method in what most were describing as madness throughout 2009 and 2010 as Harrington continued to change and refine. "The thing a lot of people don't understand is that his knowledge of himself, and his knowledge of his golf game, are second to none," says Murphy. "That's why he's able to change things so often. He's a highly intelligent guy who's motivated by change and trying to get better. It's a process but it's not a life-changing experience, because it's the way he lives his life. He's in constant pursuit of perfection. I think there's a lot of guys who don't understand what they're doing. When they try to understand they actually can't do it. Others are almost afraid to try and find out and are happy to plod along and do their own thing whereas he's the complete opposite of that. He's not afraid to change. He thinks that'll make him better. That's why he's in constant pursuit."

Beacons of hope popped up for Harrington in late 2010. The first was a controversial wild-card selection by European captain Colin Montgomerie to be part of his side for the Ryder Cup at Celtic Manor. The inclusion of Harrington, Monty's partner at Oakland Hills in 2004, effectively came at the expense of world number nine Paul Casey. But, as ever with the Ryder Cup, the selection was justified by the team's subsequent victory, to which Harrington contributed two points. When the celebrations died down, Harrington returned to playing for himself alone. The Ryder Cup has always provided a good boost to his game, with wins at the Dunhill Links championship in 2002 and 2004 after successful European missions. He came good again with a tournament win shortly after the Celtic Manor victory also. It was in far-off Malaysia where he ended a 26-month trophy drought since the 2008 US PGA by winning the Iskandar Johor Open. He led by five after three rounds and closed out a three-shot win from Korean teenager Seung-Yul Noh with a final round of 69.

"As I like to point out, I won in 2008 and I've won in 2010 so I've only missed one year as it turns out," said Harrington, an accountancy graduate, arranging 26 months into more palatable figures.

Torrance, rarely one to indulge in hyperbole, or empty backslapping, claimed that Harrington was swinging 'as well as ever'. But the player himself still wasn't happy and would reflect on 2010 as the "most frustrating" season of his professional career. That winter, he went into golfing hibernation again, walking down the steps into his personal golfing laboratory at home in Dublin and spending an entire month in the basement practise area. Under the watchful eye of biomechanics expert Paul Hurrion – an area of swing science he had increasingly turned to – and Torrance, he pressed the reset button.

Chapter 15
2011

Harrington shot 65 in his opening round of 2011 at the HSBC Championship in Abu Dhabi. The round contained five birdies, an eagle and not a single bogey. Yet he still felt he was only swinging okay. The desire to take up a position on the range for the rest of the day and seek out perfection was strong. "I spent probably the last hour of my round trying to convince myself, and I'm still trying to convince myself, not to go near the range to try improving things," he told a group of reporters by the 18th green, intrigued at his solid start to the year. It had been a long winter and, despite the promising beginning, which left him just one off the lead, he accepted he was still putting it all together. Inevitably, the question arose as to what exactly he had been working on. As usual, it wasn't a straightforward answer. But, even by his standards, the list of alterations that he reeled off was staggering.

"I changed the actual grips on my golf clubs," he explained. "Most people would think, 'Well, what's that?' I have a reminder in my grip – I've taken it out. I've gone to round grips. That's a big, big change. I've knocked all the clubs a degree flat, that's a little change. I have weakened my grip, lowered my hands a bit and pushed them a bit further forward, small things. Probably the biggest one, and this is partly why I've changed other things, I've changed my trigger to take the club away in my routine. I used to take the club away from a moving position. I now take the club away from a static position. Part of that, I used to have a big squat to take the club away, so that's gone. There's a little (squat). I'd love to get it all gone but it's hard to change your trigger, full stop. I'm taking the club away without my hips so there's a much smaller hip turn.

"Obviously, that changes my plane in the back swing. I've changed my chin position at the top of my backswing. I used to try and swing my shoulder under my chin, so I'd poke my head out to do it, which we think has contributed to my neck issues. So now I'm tucking my head in at the top of my backswing. Through impact I'm going back to squatting a bit at the start of my downswing, as I used to. So I'm going back to that. I'm going back to trying to get my chest more down through impact, to get my hands lower through impact and reduce the lateral through impact.

"From seven feet out I probably was 150th in every putting stat, so I've changed my putting routine as well. I'm not standing off the ball when I'm taking my practise putts. I'm practise-putting over the ball. When you see a raw beginner, they often do that. When they take a practise putt, they lift up and do it over the top of the ball. I'm doing that so when I put the putter back down, I'm not adjusting anything. I used to line up and get a feel for the putt, which you see a lot of guys do, then I'd take the putter inside and try a practise putt. But when I take the putter inside, I move my eye line, so the practise putts I'm getting a feel for are not the same as the putts I actually have. So I'm not changing my eye line."

Just listening to the list of changes was exhausting. And it begged an obvious question – how did he win three majors with the old swing? "At the end of the day," replied Harrington, "if I focus, I hit a good shot. If I don't focus, I hit a bad shot. All of these changes are to help me hit a decent shot when I don't focus." Distilled even further, he revealed a basic, underlying reason for change. "I was world number three when I won three majors and I didn't think I would get to world number one," he said. "I wanted to improve and try and get there. I felt I had plateaued at that stage."

Howard Bennett wasn't as surprised as everyone else to hear that Harrington was as committed to improvement as ever in 2011 despite the lows of 2009 and 2010. "The big thing about Padraig is that, if he gets into something that he thinks will be an improvement, he will give it a fair chance to see if it works," says Bennett. "It won't be a sticking plaster that might work for a week or two. He wants something that's going to be long-term."

Martin Kaymer – the eventual winner – and Louis Oosthuizen were

Harrington's partners on that first day in Abu Dhabi, both long hitters. But the eldest of the three-ball was consistently longest. He put it down to his 'tighter coil', the spring-like effect that is generated from rotating the upper half of the body and working it against the rooted legs. It resulted in shortening his swing slightly. As far back as 2009, no less a golfing icon than Tom Watson had noticed this aspect of Harrington's swing and openly questioned it. "I look at Padraig Harrington right now, he shortened his swing and I think he's having troubles because of it," said Watson. "I liked the length of the swing last year and now he's shortened the swing and he's having a hard time with it. You lose your rhythm when you shorten the swing."

In early 2011, Harrington was too far down the road to turn back. And anyway, he didn't want to. In fact, once he bedded in the latest crop of changes, a process that took just a matter of weeks, he finally began to maintain his new swing. The process of overhaul that first began five years earlier in 2006 was now virtually complete. Unfortunately, an early season victory, or even a high finish at the HSBC tournament, which would have served as a bright green light for the rest of the 2011 season, and endorsed much of his winter's work, was cruelly denied of him.

A couple of armchair fans who'd been watching live coverage of the event on TV tipped rules officials off, via email, about an infringement involving Harrington that was so trifling it was actually invisible to the naked eye. Thanks to the wonders of high definition TV and the pause and rewind function, they identified that Harrington's finger brushed off his ball as he replaced it on the seventh green. He'd felt the contact but satisfied himself that the ball didn't move as the Titleist logo was still in the same position. Only it wasn't. And modern technology proved it. Extensive pausing, rewinding and reviewing proved that the ball had actually moved three dimples forward before regressing about one and a half dimples back.

"There was no physical way I could tell at the time," said Harrington, who had reason to be believed. During the second round of the US Open at Pebble Beach in 2000, in fading light, he had sensed the ball move slightly after addressing it with his putter on the ninth green. Or was his mind playing tricks in the dimming light? His partners weren't watching and he couldn't be sure so, just to be safe, he called a penalty on himself. It meant that he finished tied fifth instead of tied fourth, costing him tens of thousands of dollars in prize money. Character, as they say, is how a man conducts himself when no one is looking.

That US Open incident came just weeks after he was involved in one of the most unfortunate rules cock-ups in golfing history. Leading the Benson and Hedges International Open by five shots going into the final round at the Belfry, victory and a cheque for Stg£166,600 was all but his. Saturday had just been one of those sunshine days; eight birdies, no bogeys and a course record 64. "I remember his caddie at the time told me, 'The guy could have broke 60 if he'd putted, I never saw anyone hit the ball as good as that'," recalls Bob Torrance. The biggest title of his career was close at hand. Back in Dublin, nobody was happier than Stackstown professional Michael Kavanagh. A few weeks earlier he'd been out watching Harrington practise on one of the spare holes at the club. "Jesus, you're hitting the ball fantastic," he'd said. "Yeah, I've been working hard with Bob," replied Harrington. Strolling through Dun Laoghaire the next day, Kavanagh called into his local bookie and asked what price Harrington was for victory at the Benson and Hedges? He was given odds of 33/1. "I don't gamble but I put 100 on each way," he says.

It was all looking good for player and punter when, on Sunday morning, after just two practise shots on the range, Tour referee Andy McFee came wandering over to Harrington. "Padraig, we've got a problem," he said, and a sorrowful story unfolded. Harrington hadn't signed properly for the 71 on Thursday that he shot in the company of Jamie Spence and Michael Campbell. Spence had signed his name correctly in the marker's area. But in the space left for 'signature of competitor', the name Michael Campbell was written by mistake. It should have been Harrington's name and so, under Rule 6-6b, he was disqualified. In a game built on trust, he had unwittingly broken the most symbolic rule – failing to attest to one's own score.

The trio had been sitting in a line, marking their cards, when Spence passed the card down to Harrington. But it only got as far as Campbell and he signed it by accident. "He did a brilliant interview after it happened," recalls Kavanagh. "There were nearly tears in my eyes watching it. Then he went to the putting green. I think he was to play with Olazabal and Thomas Bjorn and he shook both of their hands and wished them luck. It was brilliant. I couldn't get over that part. The President of the United States wouldn't have given the interview he gave. And it wasn't scripted or anything, it was just off the cuff."

Harrington was distraught. "That was the most upset I've seen Padraig," says Torrance. "The most upset for sure. I went up to his room and he never came out of it. And do you know how they found out about the card? Padraig had broken the course record and they wanted to put the card up on the wall. So they went back looking for his three cards and found the wrong signature for Thursday."

The following week at Wentworth, Caroline watched from behind the ropes as her husband trudged through the opening round at the Volvo PGA championship, arms folded, head down, a man at unrest. "I'm jaded," he confessed to her afterwards. He lost half a stone in body weight because of the stress. He was happy to do so, though, as he figured it meant he wasn't bottling it all up. And when he won the Turespana Masters in October he finally began to move on. There was a bright outcome for Kavanagh, too. His bookmaker agreed to pay out on a Harrington win at the Belfry, a marketing ploy that left him quids in. "It was something like 3,000 pounds he was giving me, when there was no need to," recalls Kavanagh. "I looked on it as free money. So I put 250 of it on Tiger Woods for the British Open. I got him at 7/2 and they paid out on the Saturday because he was so far ahead."

Back in Abu Dhabi, Harrington felt the numbing pain of disqualification when in a good position again, this time for touching and moving his ball – even though he didn't know he'd done it. If he'd noticed it at the time, he could have called a penalty on himself and moved on. Because he didn't, he signed for the wrong score at the end of the day. It was McFee that broke the bad news again. "You know what?" said Harrington with remarkable diplomacy, "A lot worse things could happen – I could have been five ahead going into the last round!"

The reaction was typical of a man who'd just been selected as an ambassador for the R&A. But the incident was to prove a terrible omen for the year ahead which, in scoring terms, was even worse than 2010. He would later identify that he was swinging well but without being able to transfer it to the course. And his short game wasn't up to his old standards either, particularly his putting. The very best putters will average out at around 28 putts per round. Harrington led the European Tour's 'putts per round' stat in 2003 with 28.2. In fact, in the seven seasons between 2003 and 2009 he was never outside the top 12 in this vital league and never once strayed into the 29s for his season average. For 2011, his average was 29.5 putts per round, a full shot per round on the greens more than he used to take. It was a considerable handicap and one largely to blame for pushing him out to 31st place in the 'stroke average' table. Twice, in 2001 and 2002, he had held the lowest stroke average for the season but now, clearly, he was struggling.

"I walk away from a lot of tournaments thinking I could have been two shots better," he said, blaming his putting. After the Dunhill Links Championship in October, he told the Press, "The last tournament I played, I finished eighth and I missed 21 putts from about 12 to 15 feet, and that's a lot of putts. You need a few putts to drop. It's the difference between winning and doing okay."

There were some positives in 2011. For the first time in his career, he finished a season on the European Tour with an average of over 300 yards off the tee. He smashed it, on average, 300.7 yards, just 12 yards less than Alvaro Quiros. That, and decent ball-striking on the range, was held up as evidence that he wasn't far away. "I'm losing correctly at the moment," he stated. But all the public could see were the missed cuts, the slide down the world rankings and his failure to record a tournament win all year.

Harrington missed the cut at the 2011 Masters, finished 45th at the US Open but travelled to Royal St George's for the British Open in July convinced that big things could still happen for him at a tournament he adored. "I actually think every part of my game is better now than it was in 2008," he declared with confidence before play began on the south eastern coast of England. But his dodgy driver cost him dearly on Thursday and he admitted that he turned a possible 70 into a poor 73. When he did manage to split a fairway, on the 17th, he pulled off a fantastic birdie. But too much had gone on before – four bogeys and a double bogey – for him to be redeemed.

Afterwards, at the official press conference, there were five questions. Four of them related to the curious looking flat cap he was wearing. He explained that he wanted to wear a badge to acknowledge one of his friends at Wilson who'd got cancer. "The cap helps the badge stand out," he said. "Is this what you expected from your first-round interview?" asked one journalist, miffed by the lack of golf talk. "No, I thought I'd be talking about my birdies," admitted Harrington. But there was little to report on that front and after a second round 71 he departed early on four over par.

"If I'm looking for reasons why I didn't perform to my own standards over the last period of time, it would be much more to do with the mental side of the game than the physical side," he would reflect. "I know I need to get to grips with that and I have been trying to get to grips with it and, probably, at the end of the day, if I am going to pinpoint one thing, it's over-trying."

For the first time, he admitted that the pressure of trying to live up to the apparent 'perfection' that he had delivered during his major wins was getting him down.

"Like, I don't remember hitting a bad shot at Carnoustie or Birkdale or, well, I did hit lots of bad shots at Oakland Hills, but oftentimes you think you never missed a shot or hit a bad shot," he said. "Sometimes that expectation makes it tough on yourself. Certainly, I would have gone down the road of wanting to recreate the feelings and the game that I had those weeks. But trying to recreate something even I can't … like, I was there and I still misjudge (how well I played)."

Describing how far away from perfection his weekend at Oakland Hills actually was when he shot a pair of 66s, he revealed that he played with 'fear' throughout Saturday and Sunday because he was so far outside his comfort zone. "I was a damaged man going into that weekend," he said, referring to his dehydrated state. "I didn't have any expectations and I shot two 66s. And the people that have come up to me since that have said, 'Wow, you shot two 66s', I'm going, 'I didn't feel like that'. I would say I never played with more fear than those two rounds of golf."

A fortnight after his early exit at Royal St George's, Harrington headed for his national open in Killarney. He had slipped to 64th in the world and though he still maintained he was playing well, on the range at least, it wasn't transferring to tournament play on Thursdays and Fridays. By the end of July, he'd already failed to make it to the weekend at five tournaments. He achieved his sixth missed cut of the season at his home tournament, the Irish Open. It was a point of no return. After rounds of 73 and 72 that prolonged the agony of a terrible season, he was convinced that he needed to get rid of Torrance. "I will be wheeling him out in a wheelchair if I have to," he'd said five years earlier, vowing never to leave his guru.

The mind was similarly drawn back to an interview Harrington had given to 'Golf' magazine in August of 2009. He was finding form after a poor first half of the season at the time and he heaped praised on Torrance for his part in the recovery. "He doesn't need a video to tell him what's happening," said Harrington. "You know these biomechanical analysis machines? I've been on those. He teaches exactly what the computer would say. Exactly. It's 100 per cent."

In light of those comments, it is ironic that Torrance points to an incident just a couple of months later, in December, 2009 at Titleist's biomechanics institute in San Diego as the start of the breakdown in their relationship. He recounts how he openly disagreed with what Harrington was being told about his swing by biomechanists there. "That upset Padraig because I was telling this guy that he was telling Padraig the wrong things," says Torrance.

Bombing out in front of his biggest fans in County Kerry was the end of the line for the Harrington/Torrance working relationship. Just hours before confirming the split with his long-time coach, Harrington admitted that he needed to change something urgently. Not for any particular reason. Just because what he was currently doing wasn't working. "Unfortunately, a change is required for the sake of it, rather than anything else," he said. "Because I'm doing everything that I would have done that won me three majors." For a player who has always been so in control of every facet of his game, from his preparation to his play, it was a startling admission – he was changing for no reason that he could immediately quantify. Torrance reckoned the biggest problem of all wasn't physical, but mental and told reporters so at the time, "His game is in bad shape because of his mind, not because of his golf. I've told him that and he agrees."

Torrance once described Harrington as a 'perfect student', willing to listen. "He lets me make my case," said Torrance. "When I taught Seve, he would argue. Seve learned very little. Padraig has learned a lot." The Scottish swing maestro was to Harrington what David Leadbetter had been to Nick Faldo. He had harnessed the drive and energy of his workmanlike Irish student and turned him into a triple major champion, something many believed was impossible from an apparently limited player. As he walked up the 72nd hole during his win at Birkdale, Harrington scanned the crowd for Torrance's face. He spotted him next to the green and when the deed was done and the final putt sunk to clinch victory, he embraced his mentor. No words were spoken. None were needed. It is why, sitting in the modest kitchen of his golf school in Largs with just days left in 2011, chugging on a cigarette, Torrance says he will always 'love' Harrington, 'like a son'. But it was a laboured love in the last few months. They disagreed more and more and their relationship was stretched.

"For long enough now," wrote golf journalist John Huggan in his 'Golf World' magazine column, "Bob, a regular visitor to media centres where he avails himself of a cup of coffee and an in-depth perusal of the scoreboard, has answered Harrington related questions with only a brief shake of the head. The spark was gone, as was the enthusiasm this 79-year old man always had for the golfer he was born to teach. He never said anything negative – he has too much class for that – but there wasn't much positive to listen to either. For even a kindergarten level reader of body language, the signs were far from good."

Asked if they'd begun to bicker, Torrance says, "Well, he was doing something that I disagreed with," referring to an issue with the positioning of his elbow that Harrington was unhappy with at the time.

"I've been working with Padraig for the best part of 15 years. He was

24 then, 25. So they're fine at that age. But when you get a bit older, up to the 40 mark, it is difficult to do it (keep changing). You get a young person whose bones are supple and his muscles are strong, you can do a lot with him. But once you get to 40 …" Torrance's voice trails off. He doesn't finish the sentence. His point is clear. He feels Harrington is too old for any more tinkering. "Bobby Locke, he had a huge draw, he never changed that," says Torrance. "He won four Opens playing that draw. Sam Snead used to straighten his right leg quite a bit at impact. He used to separate his legs to start the downswing. He worked on trying to stop that and he couldn't. But if he had stopped that you may nae'r of heard of him. You've got to be very careful. I think Padraig, he's gone 40 years of age, it's a bit late in life to strip your swing down. Okay, he's not exactly stripping it down. But I've looked at his swing. His swing is not as good as it was when we were working because his swing when we were working together was nearly perfect. But he believes it's right. So he'll probably win again."

Harrington turned 40 on August 31, 2011, a few weeks after the Torrance split. The anniversary barely registered. He got a retro Coca-Cola fridge as a present, hardly an extravagance on such a landmark birthday considering his wife had bought him an Aston Martin sports car a few years earlier. But he was more than happy. "That was exactly what I wanted," he smiled. In reality, 40 was just another number to him, could just as easily have been 30. "I think I'm in the prime of my sport whereas if I played soccer I'd be retired," he claimed on The Late, Late Show on RTE, in April 2012.

Torrance's replacement as swing coach turned out to be the man of the moment, Pete Cowen. The Englishman built his reputation as Lee Westwood's long-time coach, coaxing the Worksop man from 266th in the world rankings in 2003, to top spot seven years later. At one point in 2010, Cowen was coach to the world's number one player, Westwood, as well as two of the four major winners, Louis Oosthuizen and Graeme McDowell. In 2011, a few months before Harrington enlisted his services, Cowen helped Darren Clarke become British Open champion, at 43. He also coaches rising English sensation Tom Lewis, who led that Open championship as an amateur after day one.

Colin Byrne is currently caddying for Lewis and has observed Cowen's methods up close. "He's not such a self-promoter as many of them," says Byrne. "I think what's happened now in modern coaching is that it's all about 'be seen, be associated with certain players' and even if you're only seen with the players for a while you can still make a name for yourself. I'm not saying they're bad coaches but they're very much business minded. Self-promotion is a big priority for a lot of them. I don't think that's the case with Pete Cowen. His actions do the promotion, how he teaches, who he is. That's what promotes him."

One of Harrington's closest friends in golf, Paul McGinley, also made the same move from Torrance to Cowen, years earlier. "Pete is a very skilful coach in a lot of ways," says McGinley. "He's had an unbelievable amount of success with so many different varieties of players. He certainly won't make things complicated for Padraig. I'd expect Padraig to have success with him, the same way Peter has had success with every other player he's worked with."

Cowen's initial analysis of his new client, given at the Portugal Masters in Vilamoura, wasn't sugar-coated. He reckoned Harrington spent too much time practising and said he didn't need to punish himself on the range so much. One of his first changes was to add stability to the right side of Harrington's back-swing. "If you load the swing right, you unload it correctly," he explained. But by far his most penetrating observation was that Harrington's short game was in near tatters. He'd always been regarded as one of the best chippers and putters on tour. But Cowen took a look at the stats for 2011 and reckoned he had become, "almost non-competitive" in the vital short game area. Harrington finished a creditable 16th in Portugal. One of Cowen's other students, Lewis, won the tournament. In November, Harrington put up a spirited defence of his Iskandar Johor Open title, finishing third in what is now a European Tour sanctioned event. The early signs were good.

The second big change that Harrington made, and the more interesting one, was the recruitment of Dave Alred. Loosely described as a 'Performance Coach', he sought him out amid the maelstrom of his meltdown in Killarney. Harrington met him twice that weekend, the second of which was on the Sunday, when Alred was working with Irish rugby kicker, Jonathan Sexton.

Alred's background is as a rugby player with Bristol and Bath. He then joined the England national team as an assistant coach in 1995 and stayed with the management team until 2006. He earned the reputation as the world's leading kicking coach, a man who possessed the secret of how to perform under extreme pressure. He is also a low, single-figure handicap golfer and, much like his one-to-one, kicking-under-pressure work with rugby players like Jonny Wilkinson, he began to help out golfer Luke Donald in January 2010. Donald was ranked 32nd in the world at the time. Just 15 months later he was number one. Few made the link between Alred and Donald's incredible improvement, aside from Harrington.

"I'm looking at this and saying, 'This guy must be the man who has made the difference'," said Harrington. "I was just fascinated that more people didn't pick up on, I mean, everybody was saying, 'Why has Luke Donald gone from maybe a nice top 10 player in the world to world number one and is consistently delivering at world number one?' To me, he (Alred) was the one that made the difference. So, as I do with everything, I want to have that guy in my camp."

Harrington believed Alred could help him convert his practise ground form to tournament form. He had his homework done in this regard, for Alred's modus operandi is to make practise more engaging and, ultimately, more profitable for his players. In April 2012, he spent a couple of days at Harrington's home and devised a series of co-ordinated practise sessions. "My wife was going out during the day, she wanted to talk to me and she said she'd never seen me as grumpy because I was in the middle of a practise session and Dave is always trying to create angst, as he calls it, a bit of competition, a bit of pressure," said Harrington. "I'd just been on a bad run. I said, 'You might come home and find Dave buried in the garden'. He gives you these runs of tests to do and sometimes in them might be an easy one, and, of course, you've got to complete the easy one to get onto the harder one. It's amazing, I should be able to do this! And if you fail on the easy one it just drives you up the wall because you want to get onto the harder one, the more exciting one, let's say. It's about making your practise as competitive and real as can be."

Whether he's coaching golfers, rugby players, Australian Rules footballers or even Gaelic footballers, a technique of Alred's is to identify an 'ugly zone' within his pupils. It is the area they feel most uncomfortable in, most under pressure in. Once identified, he tries to recreate this feeling during specific drills. With time and practise, the idea is that the pupil will achieve a level of competence and even comfort under this extreme pressure.

"During a short-game session I might suddenly throw in one 3-wood high fade," explained Alred. "Perhaps the player will ask for a couple of warm-up shots but this will be denied. 'No, you have one shot'. It's quite disconcerting. Or we might halve the diameter of the hole. Generally, we do things to make it frustrating. I think everyone, as long as they are clear mentally with what they are trying to achieve, should work in that area. I see it as my job to get a player to go where he's never been before, in terms of the level of performance."

One of the drills that Alred devised for Donald is called 'Fuck, I'm Good' or FIG. "Any golfer at any level can do this," Alred told Golf World magazine. "It works almost a little like a one-man Texas Scramble. When the course is quiet you play nine holes, allowing yourself up to five attempts per shot. As soon as you hit a shot you're happy with – it doesn't have to be perfect, just acceptable to you – you give it a tick and move on. If it's not good enough, give it a cross and replay it. Repeat this process over the nine holes. By the end you will have a score that shows what you could potentially shoot based on your ability right now."

Playing by these rules, and giving himself three attempts at each shot, Donald would 'routinely' shoot seven under for nine holes. "I remember the 2011 Barclays Scottish Open when he twice shot minus five for the front nine and it was no big deal to him," said Alred. "We commented after they were just like FIG rounds with no crosses. So he was starting to be matter of fact about great performance." The coaching style is not for everyone and Harrington reckons that, "Dave would struggle to work with certain personality traits". Demanding 100 per cent application, it's hardly coincidence that his golfing clients are Donald and Harrington, two players renowned for their gargantuan spirit.

Caddie Ronan Flood has remained a constant throughout all the change, a loyal confidant. He was there before the good times, experienced the peak of the major wins and has soldiered through the lean spell since. What initially began as a six-month career break from his employer has turned into a job that has placed him at the forefront of Irish sport for almost a decade. It surely crossed his mind that he, too, could be part of the cull approaching this year.

Caddies are often first in the firing line when a player wants to freshen up his game. "I have to say that there's way less loyalty to caddies here in Europe than there is in America," says Colin Byrne. "They're just firing caddies left, right and centre in Europe."

With his boss plummeting from third in the world to almost outside the top 100, Flood must have considered how the loss of form might affect him. He was thankful then that Harrington didn't follow Donald when it came to caddying issues.

It is notable that, aside from Alred's influence, the Englishman also enjoyed his best years as a professional after releasing his long-time caddie, in 2009. And, just like Harrington, Donald's caddie was a family member, his brother, Christian, who'd been on his bag for eight years. "It was a tough conversation to have with your brother but things worked out great," reflected Donald. Christian was immediately picked up by Paul Casey and Byrne reckons that, should the worst ever come to the worst for Flood, his reputation as a triple-major-winning caddie will stand him in good stead.

Harrington has never once talked about going down that road though. "It would probably make it more difficult (to sack a family member) but Padraig Harrington is a professional," says Byrne, a fellow major-winning caddie. "If he needs to do something, he'll do it to promote his career, to promote his play, whatever he needs to do he'll do it. It may make it more difficult that he's family, and I'm sure it does. But I think, ultimately, he would be honest and say that if there is a problem, I don't know, that sometimes a fresh voice is necessary at some stage when you're struggling. Like, as we saw there for a while, he was struggling. He changed his coach.

We've all been through it, as caddies, we've all been sidelined for the sake of a change of voice or a change of opinion. Whether it's right or wrong is irrelevant, the player has to do what's best for him, in terms of deciding to change caddies or not."

For now, Harrington's entourage appears complete. Perhaps he took note of the criticism of Rory McIlroy's caddie, his old amateur colleague, JP Fitzgerald, before eventually helping the youngster capture the US Open and the 2011 US PGA crown. Ultimately, it all comes down to the individual player himself and Harrington hasn't avoided that essential truth of the game as he tries to get back to the top.

"I'll tell you what it really comes down to – how committed you are," he maintained in early 2011. "After about 20 years for a golfer you get burnt out. As long as you can get up in the morning and have the enthusiasm, the nerves, the butterflies, then you can still compete."

The butterflies, he assures, are still there.

Chapter 16
2012

Harrington was playing the ninth hole at Muthaiga Golf Club in Kenya when he was interrupted by an official with an urgent message. It was late February, 1996, a Tuesday afternoon. He was only there because he'd missed out on a spot at the more prestigious FNB Players Championship in South Africa. So, when he was informed that several places had suddenly become available in South Africa, he didn't waste any time.

A number of Europeans hadn't fancied the long-haul trek for a single tournament but he was already on the continent, albeit 2,000 miles away, so he downed tools and joined David Higgins and Francis Howley on the bus to Nairobi where they caught the next plane to South Africa.

Planes, trains and automobiles took the trio to Johannesburg and on to Durban for the tournament. Somehow, Harrington made his tee time on the Thursday. It was his first European Tour event of the year, just the second of his career. He was badly dehydrated after the desperate dash and, looking back, reckons he probably needed medical attention. But the adrenaline that coursed through his veins got him through the first day. With golf clubs that were four degrees too upright, and a caddie that snarled at him when he hit a bogey, he battled bravely and made the cut at the event. And when he finished in a tie for 49th position with Des Smyth, he thought he had made it as a pro. He picked up a cheque for IR£1,865 and wore the look of a contented man as he and Higgins caught a courtesy bus back to Johannesburg.

"I remember coming back on the bus and he couldn't believe that they were giving him that much money," says Higgins. "I remember his exact comment, 'Jaysus, they're giving me this amount of money and I didn't even play that well'. It was just being calculated in his head, not that this was easy but that this was great. It was fantastic. Padraig's family weren't wealthy by any means. And at that time it was quite a lot of money to get and he felt, 'Jeez, I didn't even play that well. Wait until I do play well'. I'll always remember that comment."

It wasn't long before Harrington found out exactly what his best play really was worth. That May, on just his tenth start on the European Tour, he won the Spanish Open. Immediately, he left behind any money worries he may have had. Aside from receiving a cheque to the value of over IR£100,000, a whole new world of endorsement deals and lucrative sponsorship arrangements opened up. Clean living, charming and utterly dedicated to improvement, he was well placed to take advantage of the deals his manager, Adrian Mitchell, was able to broker. Stuart Cage, a Walker Cup partner of Harrington's at Interlachen in 1993, and later a Tour colleague, is currently an agent with Chubby Chandler's ISM group. Cage admits that ISM tried to sign up Harrington early on though he went with Mitchell's International Management Group, IMG.

"Chubby and ISM were really keen on him but I think he obviously made the right choice," says Cage, Rory McIlroy's personal handler when the Northern Irishman won the 2011 US Open. "From what I observe, the way Padraig deals with people, the way he deals with sponsors, his whole view on his role in the game is unbelievable. There's nobody will stand and sign autographs like Padraig will or converse with people like he will. It seems from the outside looking in that he is always happy to be doing anything he can to help anyone involved in the game. So, from that side of it, he would be fantastic to work for. On the other hand, I would imagine he would be quite demanding in what he wants also, not in a bad way. When I say demanding, I mean he would know what he wanted, and he would stay on your case regarding what he wanted doing. There would be no kind of quick jobs and just getting away with it."

In May 2012, Harrington was rated as the second richest golfer in Britain and Ireland behind Nick Faldo. It was Faldo who'd predicted after Harrington's Carnoustie breakthrough that, "the way they support him in Ireland, he'll get commercial deals coming out of his ears. In the next ten years he will make an absolute fortune". The Englishman was proved correct. Despite enduring the worst season of his career in 2011 – he dropped 60 places in the world rankings from 25th to 85th – Harrington still made a reported Stg£5.3m before tax and expenses from various sponsorship deals. In February of 2011, he purchased a private jet for a reputed €2m. He's had the Aston Martin and the high-end Audi jeep parked outside his stunning home in another testament to his earning power. But, behind it all, those who know him say he is still the same man who almost hospitalised himself to play in that tournament in South Africa with a set of clubs that felt as alien to him as a bag of shovels. They say he is still the same Padraig who gave up all the other sports to focus on golf alone, purely for his love of the game. If the money truly hasn't changed the man then it is one of Harrington's greatest achievements of all.

"He hasn't changed one bit from his amateur days when I first knew him, and that's 15, 17 years ago now," insists Higgins, tenth at this year's BMW PGA Championship, in which Harrington played. "I think that's a credit to him given how much of a profile he has."

Jody Fanagan first began playing with Harrington in 1988 when they were members of the Leinster squad. "He's got a great life out of it, golf's been very good to him," says Fanagan. "But he's earned everything he's got, every last cent of it."

Conor O'Shea, the Irish rugby legend, goes back even further as a teenage pal of Harrington's at Stackstown. The prize they used to play for was a pint of 'dogwash', a cheap concoction of cordial drinks that the barman would throw together for the local kids. If they had pocket money to spare, they might even play for a plate of chips. "For me, he's the perfect example for how you should prepare yourself for sport, in terms of qualifying first as an accountant at night school, not rushing into the professional game and giving himself a solid base if golf didn't work," says O'Shea. "And that all comes from the family. He just had an incredibly solid family base. And, you know what, I contacted him many years later, we probably hadn't spoken for a good few years but a friend of mine had got terminally ill. I contacted Padraig and told him it was this friend of mine's dream to go to the US Masters. He was a young fella, terminally ill. Padraig, straightaway, not a problem, handed over his Masters tickets to allow this chap go over. In the end, he wasn't well enough to take up the offer. But that's just the type of person Padraig is. He's incredibly selfless and has never forgotten his roots."

Des Smyth isn't about to challenge any of the assertions about Harrington's nature. But, for him, it's the sports story that captures his imagination most. It is the tale of a young player completely lacking in any sort of ego or conceit, perhaps even short on self-confidence at the start, eventually bringing the world to his feet.

Sitting in the clubhouse at County Louth Golf Club, an old amateur haunt of Harrington's, and where he played in the 2009 Irish Open, Smyth smiles at the memory of the youngster he encountered in South Africa 16 years ago. He says he was drawn to Harrington straightaway, by both the strength and warmth of his character.

"The Padraig story, it's a great one," says Smyth. "He broke the ice for a lot of people in all kinds of ways. And the fact that he wasn't the most talented, that just gave the guys coming behind him even greater belief. He just had that desire and that ambition, that, you know, nobody is going to stop me when I'm on the golf course. He mightn't have it off the course, not in the early years anyway, but he just transformed when he went on it. In the pressure, he stood up. Other guys were backing off. That's what I always admired about him. He had less talent than some of them but he got a lot more from it. I don't know how you can explain that but you could see it. Like, with Seve, for example, with all his talent he never quite controlled it. He couldn't quite control that talent. He was left, right, everywhere, but nothing stopped him winning either. He had it. Tiger Woods the same, didn't matter how he played, if he got it on the green, he got it in the hole. He had it. It's that mystical thing. Some people have it. Some people don't. Padraig had it in spades."

Has he still got it, even after all the difficulties? Undoubtedly. There is nothing to suggest the competitive edge has been rounded off by the millions he's earned. And for all that he has tinkered and changed, on and off the course, the raw ability to do great things is still there. Proof of this was fleeting in 2010 and 2011, admittedly. But by roaring back into contention at the first two majors of 2012 and making the cut in all four –

for only the fourth time in his career – he proved that he still has it. More than that, he is still capable of delivering it. The first green shoot of recovery popped up in March 2012 and making the cut in all four - for only the fourth time in his career - he proved that when he opened the Transitions Championship with a course record and career best 61. Then, at the Masters, that April, he rolled the clocks back three years by contesting in a major championship for the first time since the 2009 US PGA.

"I was nowhere near as nervous as I thought I would be getting back into contention," he said. "I found myself very, very balanced. Off the golf course I was just completely relaxed. I'd prepared properly, I'd accepted it, it was a lovely place to be. The interesting thing about it was, the best golf I've ever played was the 2002 British Open when I missed the play-off by a shot. Then I needed three pars to win the US Open in 2006 at Winged Foot. I was in the zone (both times) and it was an unbelievable experience. So, you're always trying to recreate getting back in the zone. It was interesting, I think I found something at the Masters that really helped, in much more of a conscious way than necessarily getting everything right. I was still definitely in the zone, without necessarily, like, if you watch when I'm in the zone before, my eyes were bulging out of my head and there's a massive amount of energy in it. There was nowhere near the (same) energy in the Masters. I was just very, very comfortable in what I was doing."

Harrington believed he had a chance all the way until the last hole on that Sunday evening at Augusta. He took a double bogey on the 72nd, dropping him into a tie for eighth.

It wasn't the poor finish that ruined his chances though. It was his errant putting. From tee to green, he played some of the best golf of the week, a tribute to his work with Cowen. But his hopes of claiming one of the two majors that have eluded him were undone by a putting stroke that has been at the root of his troubles. Off the course, in testing, it appeared fine. He declared his technique 'perfect' a couple of months into 2012. But the proof of the pudding was in the eating. And, after that opening 61 at the Transitions, for example, he followed up with rounds of 73-72-71 to finish in a tie for 20th.

Short, jabbed putts that missed the cup from only a matter of feet were uncharacteristic and eroded his confidence in a tournament where his unease on the greens was apparent. What was once a great strength of Harrington's game had become his greatest weakness. For much of 2012, he propped up the vital 'putts made between three and five feet' stats chart. He tried everything, even moving to a revolutionary new P2 grip on his putter at one stage that put the club in a more upright position. It worked for a while, early in the year, but he discarded it within months.

Then, through the cloud of confusion and uncertainty, came a surge of illuminating light. Early on Masters week, he sought out Bernhard Langer. It was actually Caroline who had demanded he do so. She realised that, in golf, it often takes one to know one, and nobody could identify with her husband more than the German. Apart from being so closely aligned to Harrington in temperament and style, Langer had also overcome the putting yips. Harrington wasn't too big to admit that he, too, had contracted the affliction, labelling it in more colourful terms as the 'heebie jeebies'.

"Maybe just because I was looking for him, the first person I met was Bernhard Langer, so I stopped and had a chat with him about putting," recalled Harrington. "So, Bernhard got into the fact that, for him, it came down to, 'you've got to have the attitude that you can hole it or you can miss the putt. There's nothing more to it'. So it was a level of acceptance – it goes in or it doesn't go in. After that, I found myself in a very nice place mentally for the rest of the week on the greens."

On Saturday and Sunday, he extended the principle to his long game – the ball either flies down the centre of the fairway or it crashes into the trees. Either way, it's no big deal. It was another way of applying the Rotella principle of acceptance, and it worked. The more he accepted that he may miss the fairway, the more he calmly stroked it into the correct position, allowing him to routinely traverse a course that demands expert management. When it came down to it on Sunday, however, when the tournament was there to be won and lost, his putting let him down. It wasn't the nervous, flicked efforts that haunted him throughout the season but he was still unable to convert several gilt-edged opportunities that came his way, particularly on the front nine.

Four years earlier at Birkdale or Oakland Hills, you felt those putts would have dropped. By missing them, he lost vital ground and watched as Louis Oosthuizen – at the top of the putting stats all year – went on to contest a play-off with the eventual winner, Bubba Watson.

The worst of Harrington's missed putts came on the seventh after a brilliant approach. It was at a point in the tournament when he needed to be applying pressure, to be making the leaders aware of his intimidating, major-winning presence. "I had missed two short putts for birdie before that, on the fifth and on the third," he reflected. "I continued to miss a few putts. Afterwards, I looked at it and I realised I did the classic thing. It's what happens when you're leading tournaments, when you're under pressure and things are more important. In some ways, if you extrapolate this, you might call it a bit of a choke. But I tried harder on reading those putts. Instead of standing there and going, 'I see this putt breaking from outside the right of the hole', I was looking at it going, 'Is it a ball outside? Maybe it's a ball and a half outside. Maybe it's only half a ball. Okay, I'll hit a ball (outside) and I must hit it there'. Whereas if you read it generally, you say, 'It's down the right'. If you hit it two balls out, well, the hole is wide enough, two balls or no ball out, it's still going in. You just need a general acceptance of that line and I just got a little bit cautious on the lines."

A month or so after the Masters, in mid-May, former PGA Tour player, Howard Twitty, used a computer programme to analyse Harrington's stroke. It showed that he was decelerating on his putts, the opposite of the acceleration he favoured through impact. "It made perfect sense as to how I had been putting," said Harrington, hailing his eureka moment and casting his mind back across 18 months of torment.

Identifying the problem and applying the cure, however, proved two different things. He concentrated on taking a shorter back swing, forcing him to accelerate through the ball. But, when he lapsed back into autopilot and hit 'no thinkers' he found himself decelerating again on his downswing. A week after Twitty's intervention, he travelled to the European Tour's flagship BMW PGA Championship event but shot 76-79 and missed the cut. It had been that sort of season, one step forward, two steps back. Hours after departing Wentworth, the world rankings for week 21 of 2012 were released. He'd fallen another four places to 94th position. He would slide to 96th shortly before the US Open in June.

There have been many points of fortitude throughout Harrington's career, little signposts that directed him to the successes ahead. His decision to study accountancy at Dublin Business School in his late teens and early 20s was significant early on. His father insisted upon the course and though Padraig never actually put the qualification he received to any professional use, the process of attaining it gave him great discipline. He felt this complemented his game. He was reassured at the time that, when competing in tournaments, a missed putt, or worse still, a missed cut, wasn't the end of the world. He would soon possess a coveted qualification that would secure him a good job. (He believed he would end up working somewhere in the game, perhaps managing golfers). So doubling his work load by attending evening classes actually eased the stress on his golf game and, by extension, helped him to reach the professional ranks. Once there, his solid start to life on Tour and victory in just his tenth event at the Spanish Open in May of 1996 convinced him that he had a decent future. Two years later, in the summer of 1998, his experience at the Olympic Club in San Francisco was another landmark moment. The USGA set up a course that asked the most extreme questions of its players. Big-hitting John Daly, nicknamed 'Wild Thing', left his driver in the bag for the first two days to make sure he hit the devilishly thin fairways. The penalty for wild play was ankle-deep rough, something that frustrated him greatly. "If the USGA want to set up a course like this let's all go to Disneyland," complained Daly, echoing apparent locker-room disapproval.

Harrington, typically, stood apart from the gang. He viewed things differently and, instead of complaining, wondered how he might possibly gain from the experience. He finished 32nd and, in so doing, felt he'd maxed out his short game. Reflecting on the event, he pinpointed his long game as the area most in need of improvement. The course may have beaten him this time. But it was the radical changes he would make, largely as a result of this tournament, that turned him into a triple major champion. Shortly after, he informed his coach of ten years, Howard Bennett, that he was switching to Bob Torrance. It was the beginning of one of the most successful player/coach relationships the game has known.

These days, San Francisco has a warm glow of familiarity about it whenever Harrington returns. He has embraced its large Irish community over the years and treated Johnny Foley's Irish Bar and Restaurant as his unofficial clubhouse when he returned to the Olympic Club for June 2012's US Open. Evidently, it is a course that continues to inspire him as his tied fourth place finish trumped even his Masters achievement. Like the Masters, however, he endured difficulties on the 72nd hole, going birdie hunting to chase down winner Webb Simpson and finding the sand. His subsequent bogey left him in a finishing position that barely reflected his efforts. Had he wedged and putted for a birdie, he would have taken Simpson to a play-off. "I don't feel like the course beat me up this week," he said poignantly, contrasting with the dark disillusion of '98 and throwing rays of splendid sunlight on the remainder of his career.

Time will tell, but his second experience of the Olympic Club had all the feeling of another watershed moment. After nearly three years of inglorious isolation in major tournaments, he proved that the Masters wasn't a one-off spike in form. And, in an otherwise average first six months, top-eight finishes at both majors was irrefutable evidence that he now peaks solely for these competitions. "If you can't win all year, then play well five months of the year," his father used to tell him, eyeing the majors between April and August. Happily, he finds that they now offer him his best chance of tournament success. Jack Nicklaus often made the same curious observation. The 18-time major winner claimed that these competitions are so difficult that they give the experienced and the battle-hardened all kinds of advantages, reducing much of the field to crumbling rubble.

It is a touch ironic that, 14 years on from the humbling experience of his first Olympic Club outing, Harrington this time left cursing his putter. It had been his saviour in '98, rescuing mediocrity from the jaws of disaster. But two four-putts in his opening round upon his return in June 2012 was where his mind wandered to when considering how he might have recouped the two shots between he and Simpson. It had been a fine showing all week from the tees and fairways. Equally intriguing was the fact that the competition validated his long game work with Cowen, the man who now guides him in place of Torrance.

After two strong major performances, and a good showing at Royal Portush where he finished tied seventh in the Irish Open, Harrington was among many bookies' top three tips for the British Open. But his failure to break 70 on any of the days left him well out of the running, eventually finishing tied for 39th.

A decent US PGA championship better reflected his overall performances in the season's marquee events. Entering the final round at Kiawah Island he was only five off leader, and eventual winner, McIlroy, and got to four under with just nine holes to play. If he'd held his ground there, he'd have finished joint third. But a couple of poor strikes on the way home knocked him down to tied 18th. Once again, his short game let him down. Commentators despaired of his putting stroke at times during the week, claiming that his posture looked less stable than before. Old ally, Colin Montgomerie, suggested he wasn't aggressive enough with his putts. Harrington himself blamed his chipping.

Once feted for his short game skills, it was the area that ultimately cost him most in 2012, despite his overall return to form. Renowned short game coach, Dave Pelz, who works with Phil Mickelson, claimed Harrington has been spending too much time on his long game. Pelz compared him to Tom Kite who 'lost his short game' while trying, similarly, to improve his overall game. "Back in 2007, 2008 and 2009, everywhere I went with Phil I would see Paddy working on his short game," said Pelz. "He'd say, 'Watch this, David,' when we'd meet at Augusta and, boy, he'd hit shots that were really good. But I haven't seen him working on his short game for three years. Not a single time. I think what he needs to do now is stop working on his long game, maintain it and get his short game sharp. He is not putting as well as he used to. And he is not chipping as well he used to, which makes his putting worse."

Distilled right down, poor putting cost Harrington his place on Europe's Ryder Cup team at Medinah. He failed, firstly, to qualify automatically for Jose Maria Olazabal's team and was then overlooked for a wild card, leaving him outside the ropes of the event for the first time since 1997. A suspect putter will rarely thrive in the intense heat of Ryder Cup battle. It is the area of his game he must principally improve upon if he is to be a Ryder Cup player again, and indeed, a major winner.

All season long he languished at the very bottom of the 'putts inside five feet' league on the PGA Tour. A veteran player now, it is tempting to suggest his difficulties from close in reflect shredded nerves. Harrington insists there is a more straightforward explanation though and, having pinpointed it, is optimistic about shooting up the putting charts in 2013.

"If you looked at my stats, I'm not a lover of stats, but looking at it over, say, 2009, 2010, I would be excellent from short range and not great from medium range," he said. "I'm particularly trying to improve my ability to hole 15 footers and I did a lot of practise on them. But I ended up with a 15 foot putting stroke for a four foot putt and I didn't realise that. But I was just classic decelerating on those putts. I had no idea that's what I was doing. But that's what it turned out."

Harrington turned 41 in August 2012 and remains as inscrutable a figure as ever, his golf as joyously unpredictable as the winds that gust around his home course of Stackstown. The only certainty is that he will keep building for the majors and that he won't sweat the small stuff. And he will continue to find salvation on the range, through the hard graft that he lives for. He found a kindred spirit in the German, Martin Kaymer, who had a telling conversation with him during a tournament last year. "He was saying that it's nice to find something to work on with your swing that you never actually get," said Harrington. "Because that means you can keep working on it. So you always have something to go back to on the range to keep working on, to keep going forward."

The past has been good to Harrington and, even if the present tests him at times, he has every reason to believe the future is bright after his 2012 revival. On the very day he was overlooked by Olazabal for a Ryder

Cup wild card at Medinah, he returned to 59th in the world rankings, his highest position in over a year.

Based on his assumption that elite golfers have about 20 years of serious competition in them, he has a few years yet until 2016, his 20th anniversary of joining the Tour. As it happens, that's the year that golf will be included in the Olympics. A proud Irishman, Harrington was a leading figure in the drive to have it included on the programme and, naturally, wants to represent the Tricolour on one of the great sporting stages. There is an obvious fear that, having spent so long flogging himself on driving ranges around the world, his body might give in sooner than then, or sooner than he'd like at least. But Liam Hennessy sees no reason for this to occur. "You're not dealing with the standard here," argues Hennessy. "You're dealing with someone who is an outlier. All those at the top of the game are outliers. They are not normal standard people. We can debate it and it's an interesting point to say, 'Look, he's overdoing it'. He's certainly not underdoing it. But, at the end of the day, Padraig's longevity would be a key goal in what we do. It always has been. In other words, what we're doing is, hopefully, going to improve his longevity in the game and limit the risk of serious injury. Because the game, the golf swing, it's one of the most powerful, athletic things that you can engage in. We'd be very conscious that the stuff we did with him ten years ago isn't necessarily going to be what he needs now. Building huge levels of strength, which was a requirement early on, has now changed to maintaining the strength at that level."

Harrington is fully committed to the longevity that Hennessy espouses. Reports surfaced in 2010 that he uses a refractometer while away at tournaments. It is a device that determines if he's properly hydrated through an analysis of his urine. This year, he also confirmed that he has teamed up with medical experts to monitor his blood. "What the system does is measure the responsiveness of white blood cells to light," he explained. "They've taken thousands of blood tests from athletes and established markers that show what a normal curve is like. I can read the curve myself at this stage and see when I am completely fatigued. It would show up if you had a cold coming on or a viral infection." With himself in mind, he added: "The big problem successful people have is that what got them successful is doing more than anybody else. But that's what breaks them down later." He also spoke of a new exercise that has 'basically cured' his long-term neck problem. The injury, he says, used to keep him out of up to half a dozen tournaments a year.

The body then remains willing. As ever, it would appear that the mind holds the key to unlocking Harrington's best form and the victories he still craves. At this stage of his career, he is pursuing major titles with a tunnel vision approach. He remains smitten with the sheer simplicity of the game, stating, 'I just love playing, it's fascinating, I'll be playing when I'm 70 years of age'. But it is hard not to imagine that someone so inherently ambitious is not entirely focused now on catching Phil Mickelson and Ernie Els ahead of him. Aside from Tiger Woods, Mickelson and reigning British Open champion, Els, are the only current players with more major wins than Harrington.

If he does remain competitive until the end of 2016, he could have as many as 16 more attempts to add to his three major wins and catch the duo on four. If he can do it, and win just one more, which he came so close to doing twice in 2012, it may be his greatest achievement yet, given the demons he's encountered since 2008. "I believe I have more than one (more) major in me," he insists. "There was definitely a time when I'd never say that. I'd just be afraid that I was tempting fate and silly things like that. Now I know that if I don't believe it, nobody else is going to believe it. I'm happy to say it."

For a while there, Harrington lost the belief of the public at large. Until 2012 he only featured strongly in one major championship since his victory at Oakland Hills. But his performance at the Masters, and his ability to exact his own personal revenge on the Olympic Club at the testing US Open, has won over the doubters. The backing of his peers, for what it's worth, never wavered. They'd seen too much, first-hand, to lose faith. "I think he might win one more major," says Gary Murphy, who has turned to broadcasting and conducted a fascinating feature interview with Harrington for Setanta TV. "I think he'll certainly win another five to ten more tournaments. I'd say he'll play in at least another Ryder Cup, so there's a lot left for him to achieve."

"He had a tough couple of years there," reflects Jody Fanagan. "But any time I see him he's so positive about what's coming down the line, where he sees himself going. He sees that he's got another five, six, seven years of being competitive. He's very positive about Pete Cowen and where they're going. To be honest, it's the same old Padraig in many ways. Every winter I'd meet him at the Links Golf Society and I'd say, 'How's it going?' He'd say, 'Great, I've got five things to work on, I'm doing this, this and this.' He doesn't want to believe that when he retires he might say, 'Maybe I could have been even better'. He doesn't want to feel he left anything behind. He'd regret that. In fairness to him, all he ever says is that he wants to be good enough to be in the hunt coming down the back nine of a major. That's what he does it all for."

Jean Van de Velde has known that feeling. He memorably chased success on the Sunday evening of a major championship himself but without the joyous outcome that Harrington has experienced three times. "I'm quite sure that's why we all play the game, Padraig included, to go down that stretch once in a while and get that excitement, when it absolutely kills your stomach or maybe it makes you feel like you could walk on air," says Van de Velde. "How many people going through their lives feel these kinds of things? That's what golf gives us."

Bob Torrance has seen what great men with strong minds can achieve and, more importantly, what they can bounce back from. Like his idol, Ben Hogan who, four years after crashing his Cadillac head on into a Greyhound bus and suffering life-threatening injuries, won the British Open at Carnoustie in 1953. Torrance was there for that victory, just like he was in 2007 when Harrington won the same tournament at the same venue. He has seen it all and believes that, like Hogan, Harrington can rise again and win a fourth major title. "He's a bit like Woods," says Torrance. "I wouldn't put anything past Padraig. He could win anything. He could win in another eight years' time. His mind is strong enough for him to do that. And he's fit enough. Padraig takes care of his body. I never even saw him drink, bar the Ryder Cup after Europe won it. He's got as strong a mind as anyone in golf."

Hogan once appeared on the front of 'Time' magazine under the phrase, "If you can't outplay them, outwork them." It could easily be Harrington's motto. "It's silly to pay attention to someone so gifted and expect to learn from him," said Rotella during a discussion about Tiger Woods. "You can learn a lot more from someone like Harrington who had to make himself great."

Yet, we may never truly know what makes Harrington tick, what those tiny subtleties, strengths and insecurities are that combine to make up his immense character. Indeed, those same complexities of mind that helped him pulverise the golfing world for 13 months between 2007 and 2008 may very well be what have held him back for so long since then.

"Complicated, but not eccentric," is how he recently described himself. As a golfer, he remains capable of greatness but, equally, of random tragedy, throwing in twos and threes beside sixes and sevens. He is a bucking bronco of thoughts and ideas that even the world-wizened Torrance couldn't hold on to. Shortly after their split, during a six-week winter break, Harrington drove himself to distraction as he fixated on his game at home in Dublin. "I'm trying to perfect every little nuance," he revealed in his interview with Gary Murphy. "I'll tell you how bad it is – I've changed the position of my tongue in my mouth. To relax my jaw I put my tongue in the top of my mouth."

Ahead of his time or hopelessly obsessed? Good luck figuring that one out.

As for his future, who can truly say what it holds for a player who has rarely profited from self-confidence? And how does one predict what lies in store for a golfer who has produced his very best form when railing against swing problems, low expectations, terrible weather, poor form and, most notably, injury?

To drill inside the head of Harrington and shine a torch into the deepest recesses therein would be a fascinating experiment. "My putter doesn't suit my stroke, yet I'm still using it," he admitted in 2009, three major wins later. The journalist he was speaking to at the time concluded that, "One can't help feeling that the Harrington thought process requires equal amounts of logic and wisdom, plus an all-important, undefined ingredient that is familiar only to Mary Poppins." That is not to poke fun at his detailed mind, merely to acknowledge that it is powerful and, at times, unfathomable.

"Harrington's biggest problem remains Padraig Harrington," wrote experienced golf reporter and Harrington follower, Bernie McGuire, during the nadir of his poor form in late 2011. He proceeded to recount a story that Colin Montgomerie had told about Harrington at the Ryder Cup in Celtic Manor: "'Padraig was just driving the ball so well in practise that he was winning all the money, so when the Ryder Cup got underway what does he do off the first tee? He virtually snap-hooks it,' said Monty. 'I walked up to his caddy and wondered whether Harrington had a new driver in his bag because he was driving the ball magnificently just a day before. His caddy said, "Yeah, it's a new driver". Why's he got a new driver in the bag? I asked. "Because Padraig wanted to see if he could hit this one as good as the one he'd been using in practise". I can't repeat the words I said to his caddy.'"

The enigma continues to confound. As Torrance puts it, "He's got a funny mind, Padraig. But it's a good mind, capable of anything."